KU-443-127

30126 01654459 2

FOR SALE FROM

Spanish
VENTURE

Spanish
VENTURE

BOB GOULD, LILIANA NOGUEIRA PACHE
& KEVIN BRUTON

BBC
Milton Keynes

dti
the department for Enterprise

EURO
TUNNEL

National Westminster Bank

British Library Cataloguing-in-Publication Data.
A catalogue record for this book is available from the British Library.

ISBN 1 874434 00 X

Other elements of this course:

complete pack: 1 874434 01 8
cassette set: 1 874434 02 6

WITHDRAWN FROM ENFIELD LIBRARIES

London Borough of Enfield Arts And Libraries

7/08

First published 1992

Published by The Language Consortium: BBC Milton Keynes, Eurotunnel and National Westminster Bank, supported by the Department of Trade and Industry
c/o BBC Milton Keynes
     Walton Hall
     Milton Keynes MK7 6BH

This book © Bob Gould, Liliana Nogueira Pache and Kevin Bruton.
Video and audiocassettes © BBC Milton Keynes
Complete pack © BBC Milton Keynes, Department of Trade and Industry,
Eurotunnel and National Westminster Bank.

Project Manager: Roger Penfound
Project Assistant: Rosemary Morton
Editor: Catriona Dawson
Design and production: Liz Rowe
Illustration: Hardlines and Ian Heard
Film origination: Wearset
Printed by Butler &Tanner Ltd, Frome and London

All rights reserved. No part of this publication may be reproduced or transmitted in any form or by any means, electronic or mechanical, including photocopy, recording, or any information storage and retrieval system, without permission in writing from the publisher or under licence from the Copyright Licensing Agency Limited. Further details of such licences (for reprographic reproduction) may be obtained from the Copyright Licensing Agency Limited, 90 Tottenham Court Road, London W1P 9HE.

Contents

This course has been written by a highly experienced team of authors:

Bob Gould is Lecturer in Business Spanish at Portsmouth Polytechnic and has already co-authored a successful Business Spanish coursebook with Liliana Nogueira Pache;
Liliana Nogueira Pache is a native speaker and has taught Spanish for the last fifteen years. At present she is a writer/editor in a leading Spanish language magazine for language learners;
Kevin Bruton is Professor of Spanish at Stirling University and has spent many years living, working and teaching in Spain.

Marianne Howarth, Principal Lecturer in Modern Languages at Brighton Polytechnic, and *Professor Nigel Reeves*, Head of Modern Languages at Aston University, have acted as course consultants throughout. Both contributed to the earlier courses in the series, **Making your Mark** and **Franc Exchange**, and bring a combined wealth of experience in the field of language learning teaching for business.

The course has been produced by a consortium of organisations which are dedicated to supporting and promoting the activities of British business people in overseas markets.

BBC Milton Keynes has over twenty years of experience in multi-media distance teaching in partnership with the Open University;
Department of Trade and Industry, together with the Foreign and Commonwealth Office, provide, through Overseas Trade Services, a wide range of services to UK exporters;
Eurotunnel, as a international transport company, has a strong interest in encouraging European language learning;
NatWest is a leading British bank with many years' experience in helping UK businesses trade successfully in Spain through the 200-branch network of Banco NatWest España.

Acknowledgements

The authors and publishers would like to thank the following individuals and companies for their help and cooperation in the production of this course:

Action Computer Supplies, Addison España SA, Banco NatWest España, Curzon Direct, La Cruz del Campo, Expo '92 Sevilla, Marks and Spencer (España) SA, RENFE, Trafalgar House Construction Management Ltd, Ana Valle, David Staward and all the staff at Wearset.

The authors and publishers would also like to acknowledge the following for the use of materials reproduced in this book:

Actualidad Económica, Alianza Editorial SA, Cajas de Ahorros Confederadas, Edita Comunicar SA, La Gaceta, Grupo Hispano-Suiza SA, Junta de Andalucía, El País and Telefónica.

Every effort has been made to trace and acknowledge ownership of copyright. The publishers will be glad to make suitable arrangements with any copyright holders whom it has not been possible to contact.

INTRODUCTION

Spanish Venture is an integrated, multimedia business language training pack, designed to develop communication skills in business Spanish at beginners' level.

The pack consists of:
- an 80-minute video
- a 192-page coursebook and separate video transcripts
- three C90 audiocassettes

LEARNING OBJECTIVES

The principal objectives of **Spanish Venture** are to help learners to:
- understand authentic business Spanish with reasonable accuracy and confidence;
- develop an ability to communicate in simple Spanish in typical business situations;
- gain an insight into the Spanish business environment via the experience of others;
- appreciate the business opportunities afforded by the Spanish market.

On completion of **Spanish Venture**, you should be able to get your message across in simple terms in standard business situations, such as:
- meeting and greeting your Spanish business contacts;
- introducing yourself and your colleagues;
- showing someone round your company premises;
- making telephone calls and leaving messages;
- talking about your company, its products and services;
- taking part in meetings.

You will be able to order some food and drink and socialise with your Spanish business associates. You will also have a good idea of what to expect and the pitfalls to avoid in your business dealings with Spanish companies. In short, though you will not be fluent in Spanish, you will not go hungry and you will not be at a loss when conducting business in Spain.

AUTHENTIC VIDEO MATERIALS

The video represents a key feature of the Spanish Venture pack. It consists of seven authentic case studies, each featuring a company already active in the Spanish market. Some of these companies are household names, like National Westminster Bank, Marks and Spencer and Guinness. Others are relative newcomers, like Addison, Curzon Direct and Action Computers. All of them share the same experience of doing business in Spain in two key areas:
- their personnel have had to acquire sufficient Spanish for business communication purposes;
- the company has had to adapt aspects of its business approach to fit in with Spanish business culture.

The varied experiences of these companies are of great benefit to other businesses wishing to tackle the Spanish market. Between them, they offer an unparalleled breadth of insight, at first hand, into Spanish business language and practice.

At the same time, authentic video poses a special challenge to the language learner. The video sequences have not been scripted or rehearsed. The business people you will see are real British and Spanish business people going about their business in what is, for them, the normal way. They concentrate on the matter in hand, rather than the camera following them; as such, the video represents a genuine slice of business life and makes few concessions to those with little or no experience of handling the language. Although this may seem daunting, the support provided by the other elements in the pack makes this valuable resource accessible for even the complete beginner.

For those with no prior knowledge, the video seeks to represent a logical language progression, as well as a logical business progression; in other words, it starts with a relatively simple business situation – a reception – and builds up to a more complicated scenario – a series of meetings. For learners who already know some Spanish but who wish to improve their language skills specifically for business purposes, the video represents a wealth of information on business Spanish and Spanish business culture.

How the components relate

The video, book and the cassettes represent an integrated learning resource. By watching each video sequence several times, you will build up your confidence in understanding spoken business Spanish.

The book combines information and advice on the business environment in Spain with language exercises carefully designed to develop listening, reading and writing skills, along with business vocabulary and grammar explanations.

The video and coursebook are accompanied by three audiocassettes as follows:
The Tutor cassette is an indispensable learning tool for the beginner. This cassette provides a step-by-step guide on how to tackle the exercises in the book and will help you to make the most of the video sequences.
The Travel cassette presents extracts from the video soundtrack plus further listening material. This cassette provides a flexible learning resource for you to listen to in the car, while travelling, taking exercise or just relaxing.
The Business cassette contains interviews and comments from business people and other experts with first-hand experience of doing business in Spain. This cassette is mostly in English.

A learning strategy

Spanish Venture offers a wealth of material to help you access the Spanish market and develop your business in Spain while communicating in simple but acceptable business Spanish. As a learner, you will eventually find your own way of working though the pack to develop your confidence and skills.
Meanwhile, to help you get started, we suggest the following approach.

1 Refer to the three **Business Files** at the beginning of the book. They contain useful information and advice on the general business context. Return to them to consolidate your own experience.

2 Familiarise yourself with the **Study plan** for each unit. It summarises the main language points featured in the individual sections of the video sequence and the main sections of the accompanying **Business Notes**.

3 Study the key words and phrases (**Palabras y frases útiles**) listed in your coursebook and watch the video sequence as often as you like. To begin with, concentrate on understanding the gist of what is being said – the **Comprensión** questions will help you here. As you become more confident, you will find you understand more and more each time you watch the video. Remember that if you really get stuck, you can refer to the **Video Transcripts** booklet for help.

4 Use the **Tutor cassette** to help you work your way through the language exercises in each unit of the coursebook, section by section. It will offer you prompts, explanations, examples and practice to help you develop your skills in understanding and speaking Spanish.

5 Look out for the Ⓖ symbol. Grammar explanations have been kept to a minimum in the main body of the book, so refer to the appropriate part of the **Grammar** section for explanations of individual grammar points.

6 Use the **Wordlist** at the back of the book to check the English equivalents of the Spanish vocabulary. Many learners find it valuable to build up their own vocabulary note book, not only for isolated words, but also for phrases to place things in context.

7 Use the **Recuerda** box at the end of each unit to check that you have covered all the major language points and that you understand and know how to use them.

8 Read the **Business Notes** at the end of each unit for specific information about individual industrial sectors.

9 Watch the video sequence again, picking out the most important details for you and your business.

SYMBOLS

00.00 This refers to the counter on the screen, indicating where this section of the video sequence starts. This will help you to find the section you are working on quickly and easily. Note that only the last four digits of the time code are given; the first two digits are 10 for units 1 to 6 and 11 for units 7 and 8.

Ⓖ This refers to the **Grammar** section at the back of the book. The number refers you to the part of the Grammar section where this particular point is explained in detail. This will help you to understand individual grammar points more easily.

TUTOR SUPPORT

Spanish Venture is a course designed primarily for an individual learner working on his or her own. As a learner, you can decide when and where you will study and how much time and effort you will put in. Remember, your learning will be more effective and your confidence more readily boosted if you spend, say, half an hour each day over a period of time, rather than an hour every now and again.

Many people using **Spanish Venture** on their own will also find it helpful to practise with a tutor and other users of the pack. Contact BLISS (Business Language Information Services) on 0908 607739 for information and advice connected with **Spanish Venture** and the other packs in the series, **Making your Mark** and **Franc Exchange**, whether for learning or teaching purposes.

Marianne Howarth, Series Consultant

Useful Addresses

- Department of Trade and Industry
Overseas Trade Division (Spain desk)
Kingsgate House
66-74 Victoria Street
London SW1E 6SW
Tel: 071-215 4284 (capital goods)
    071-215 5624/5307
    (consumer goods)

British Embassy and Consulates

- British Embassy
Calle de Fernando el Santo 16
28010 Madrid
Tel: 010 34 1 319-0200
    010 34 1 319-1528
Fax:010 34 1 319-0423

- British Consulate-General
Avenida Diagonal 477, 13º
08036 Barcelona
Tel: 010 34 3 419-9044
Fax: 010 34 3 405-2411

- British Consulate-General
Alameda Uriquijo 2, 8º
48008 Bilbao
Tel: 010 34 4 415-7600
    010 34 4 415-7711
    010 34 4 415-7722
Fax:010 34 4 416-7632

- British Consulate
Plaza Nueva 8, Dpdo
41001 Sevilla
Tel: 010 34 54 228875
Fax:010 34 54 210323

Spanish Embassy and Consulates

- Spanish Embassy
24 Belgrave Square
London SW1X 8QA
Tel: 071-235 5555

- Commercial Department of the Spanish Embassy
66 Chiltern Street
London W1M 1PR
Tel: 071-486 0101

- Spanish Consulate – London
30 Draycott Place
London SW3
Tel: 071-581 5921

- Spanish Consulate – Manchester
Suite 1A
Brook House
70 Spring Gardens
Manchester M2 2BQ
Tel: 061-236 1233

- Spanish Consulate – Edinburgh
63 North Castle Street
Edinburgh EH2 3LJ
Tel: 031-220 1843

Spanish Chambers of Commerce

- Spanish Chamber of Commerce in London
5 Cavendish Square
London W1M 0DP
Tel: 071-637 9061

- Plaza Santa Bárbara 10
28010 Madrid
Tel: 010 34 1 308-3081/4
Fax:010 34 1 410-4605

- Paseo de Gracia 11
Barcelona 08007
Tel: 010 34 3 317-3220

- Alameda de Mazarredo 5, 3º
48001 Bilbao
Tel: 010 34 4 423-8605
Fax: 010 34 4 424 9389

- Plaza Mariano Benllure 5
46002 Valencia
Tel: 010 34 6 351-7612

Financial advice

- Banco NatWest España
Level 25
National Westminster Tower
25 Old Broad Street
London EC2N 1HQ
Tel: 071-920 1290

Business File 1

THE BUSINESS ENVIRONMENT IN SPAIN

Introduction

Since the mid-1980s, Spain has experienced a boom unprecedented in its history, as the tremendous socio-economic and political changes of the past thirty years have come to fruition under a stable democracy, proud to be member of the EC. Indeed, Spain has led the EC in rapid growth, with a average annual GDP growth rate of 4.5%. Rising domestic demand has been accompanied by real increases in incomes, greater employment, and growth in company investment, industrial production and corporate profits. What strikes the foreign observer above all else, however, is the genuine enthusiasm and outward-looking philosophy of Spanish business people and their companies. The introduction of the Single Market was viewed by most Spaniards not just as the real start of fuller integration with Europe but as the opportunity for Spaniards to parade their country's many virtues to the outside world. The Olympic Games in Barcelona, Expo '92 in Seville and the choice of Madrid as cultural capital of Europe in 1992 were obviously important events in themselves, but, more crucially, symbolised the further aspirations of Spaniards to cast off the final shackles of an isolationist past and become important players in the Europe and world of the future.

Opportunities for foreign investment in the Spanish success story have been, and are still, increasing, as the customs barriers and taxes which made it difficult for foreign firms to compete previously have gradually been removed since EC entry in 1986. The Spanish government has actively promoted such investment from abroad, and the different regions have followed suit, encouraging joint ventures or acquisitions of Spanish firms.

A new breed of entrepreneurs is emerging in Spain, as a business career becomes the fashionable thing to do for many from the wealthy classes. The new business executives will have an MBA from a US university or from one of the flourishing Spanish business schools, which have barely been able to cope with the avalanche of prospective students. Management training is expanding at a phenomenal rate, and the ambitious aim is to turn out 'Euro-managers' able to operate with equal facility in a variety of business environments.

Language training, mainly in English, is finally being taken seriously, although it will be decades before Spain produces, if it ever does, sufficient numbers of linguistically competent business people to obviate the need for British companies to have staff who speak Spanish.

Spain's infrastructure and public services have also improved dramatically in recent years, and especially since the government's unprecedented 40% increase in public works investment in 1989. Trunk roads and motorways have been expanded. Business communication has been made much easier by the upgrading of domestic airports and a subsequent upsurge in business travel. A high-speed rail link between Madrid and Seville has recently been constructed. This will eventually allow high-speed trains to run from northern Europe to southern Spain and across to the Portuguese capital, Lisbon.

Spanish consumers have seen the arrival of hypermarkets and out-of-town shopping centres and have eagerly purchased products from all over the world. At the same time, Spanish designers have forged a world-wide reputation, which in turn has attracted foreign companies to Spain. With over fifty million foreign visitors in 1991, the Spanish tourist industry continues to be a dynamic force in the economy, generating growth, providing employment and stimulating investment and development. Industry is booming, as Spain sets out to be the high-tech capital of southern Europe. British companies have barely begun to discover a country which does not just have tremendous potential in itself but which also provides a walkway to the Spanish-speaking countries of Latin America and to the historically linked countries of the Arab world.

Facts and figures

LAND AREA

Spain covers an area of 504,750 km², slightly smaller the area covered by France.

POPULATION

In mid-1990, the population was 38.87 million. This is one of the lowest population densities in Western Europe, although the fifty million annual foreign visitors have to be taken into account. Distribution is uneven, with major concentrations on the coast and in several clusters in the interior. Forty per cent live in towns of over 10,000 inhabitants, while there are fifty municipalities with populations over 100,000. The annual birth-rate has been in decline since 1964, when it was 21.9 per 1,000, to 11.2 per 1,000 in 1991. One quarter of all Spaniards are under the age of sixteen.

MAIN CITIES

The major urban centres of population are:

Madrid	3.1 million
Barcelona	1.7 million
Valencia	0.7 million
Seville	0.7 million
Zaragoza	0.6 million
Malaga	0.6 million
Bilbao	0.4 million
Las Palmas (Canaries)	0.4 million
Valladolid	0.3 million
Murcia	0.3 million
Palma (Balearics)	0.3 million
Cordoba	0.3 million

(Source: *Avance del Anuario Estadístico de España, 1989*)

Population by region is approximately:

Andalusia	7.1 million
Catalonia	6.1 million
Madrid	5.0 million
Valencia	3.9 million
Galicia	2.9 million
Castile-Leon	2.6 million
Basque country	2.1 million
Castile-La Mancha	1.7 million
Canaries	1.6 million
Aragon	1.2 million
Asturias	1.1 million
Extremadura	1.1 million
Murcia	1.1 million
Balearics	0.8 million
Cantabria	0.5 million
Navarre	0.5 million
La Rioja	0.3 million

(Source: *municipal register 1989*)

CLIMATE

Despite common preconceptions, Spain has three different climates. The Atlantic climate is most like our own, so the climate of San Sebastian or Santander in the north would be much like an English south-coast resort. The Mediterranean climate enjoyed by much of Spain is characterised by dry, warm weather, with mild winters, which can become almost subtropical in parts of the south. Finally, the Continental climate which affects much of the interior means extremes of temperature and often shortages of water.

WEIGHTS AND MEASURES

Spain follows the metric system for all weights and measures.

BANK HOLIDAYS

The statutory holidays generally observed in Spain are as follows:

1 January (*Día del Año Nuevo*)

6 January (*Epifanía/Día de los Reyes Magos*)

19 March (*Día de San José*)

Good Friday (*Viernes Santo*)

1 May (Labour Day – *Fiesta del Trabajo*)

15 August (Assumption – *Asunción de la Virgén*)

12 October (National Day – *Día de la Hispanidad/día de la Raza*)

1 November (All Saints' Day – *Todos los Santos*)

6 December (Constitution Day – *Día de la Constitución*)

8 December (Immaculate Conception – *Día de la Inmaculada Concepción*)

25 December (*Día de Navidad*)

Other holidays vary according to the province, but the legal number of holidays allowed in a year is fourteen. When a bank holiday falls on a Thursday or Tuesday, Spaniards usually take the intervening Friday or Monday off (known as *hacer puente*). The proximity of the holidays on 6 December and 8 December means that a week or more's holiday may be taken at this time, making it difficult for businesses to be contacted.

Most business people take their summer holidays in August (for the whole month) or in July, with occasionally an overlap between the two. July–August is therefore a period when little business is done. Also, from June to September, many business people spend weekends in a second or holiday home, and this affects business on Friday afternoons.

School and university holidays vary somewhat according to region, but the long summer vacation usually lasts from the end of June to mid-September (schools) and from the end of June to mid-October (higher education).

CURRENCY

The Spanish peseta (pta/s) is divided into 100 *céntimos*. There is a tendency to substitute coins for notes of 100 and 200 pesetas, and for other new coins to replace old currency. Note also that the term *duro* is often used to refer to 5 pesetas.

BUSINESS HOURS

The hours of foreign companies in Spain are usually from 8.30am or 9am to 5.30pm or 6pm, with an hour for lunch. Many Spanish companies have a longer lunch period, often two hours, and a later closing, between 7pm and 8pm. Between June and September, most companies follow an *horario intensivo* (intensive timetable) of seven continuous hours' work from 8am to 3pm.

Working breakfasts are not yet common in Spain. Business is often conducted over lengthy lunches at restaurants or, in the evening, over drinks and *tapas*, followed by a late evening meal starting after 9.30pm.

Banks are open to the public from 9am to 2pm on weekdays and from 9am to 1pm on Saturdays. Government offices vary, but are generally open to the public from 9am to 2pm.

POLITICAL ENVIRONMENT

Spain is a parliamentary democracy, with a constitutional monarch, Juan Carlos I. Parliament comprises two elected chambers, with the Congress as the lower chamber, with supreme legislative power, comparable to the House of Commons, and the Senate as the upper or revising chamber, carrying out similar functions to the House of Lords. The rights of Spaniards are enshrined in Spain's Democratic Constitution of 1978, which paved the way for a Regional Government system.

Spain now has seventeen regional governments, or *autonomías*, with elected parliaments, which represent a totally new framework in Spanish history within which businesses must operate. While central government decides overall policy for taxation and income, social security contributions, defence, foreign affairs, internal security and justice, the seventeen regions have considerable independent powers, which vary from one region to another. Crucially, regions have enjoyed wide discretionary powers over expenditure and have been employing these to attract inward investment. Businesses therefore need to recognise the devolutionary dimension.

Local authorities, i.e. town and provincial councils, also exist, with considerable freedom over expenditure but not over the raising of revenue. The regions and local authorities' expenditure has grown rapidly since 1978 and accounts, for instance, for half of spending on state education, a fifth on health care, and two-thirds of total fixed investment. The trend throughout the 1980s has been toward greater regional expenditure rather than local decentralisation, as many regions press for greater responsibilities in the 1990s.

POLITICAL PARTIES

The major parties in Spain are the Socialist Party (PSOE – *Partido socialista obrero español*) and the Popular Party (PP – *Partido popular*), which is of centre-right disposition. There are also two very small groupings in the National Parliament: the Democratic and Social Centre Party (CDS – *Centro democrático y social*) and the United Left (IU – *Izquierda unida*) including the Communist Party. Regional parties also fill thirty-seven seats out of 350 in Parliament, with eighteen seats for the main regional party of Catalonia, Convergence and Union (CIU – *Convergència i Unió*), and five seats for the Basque National Party (PNV – *Partido Nacional Vasco*).

CENTRAL GOVERNMENT

Modern Spain has experienced a remarkable and peaceful transformation from centralised authoritarian rule under Franco, who died in 1975, to a healthy and stable democratic government, which has been in the hands of the Socialist Party of Felipe González, Prime Minister since 1982 and victor in two further General Elections in 1986 and 1989. The transitional period in this process ran from 1975 until 1982, when the Union of the Democratic Centre, a centre-right grouping no longer in existence, was in government led by Adolfo Suárez, King Juan Carlos's nominee as the man who could help him steer Spain towards democracy. The transition could truly be said to be over when Spaniards elected González with an overwhelming majority in 1982. Since then, González's government has followed a social-democratic path of moderation, combining centre-left social policies with centre-right economic and fiscal policies. The result has been, following years of crisis up to the mid-1980s, a buoyant economy with dynamic growth which actively encourages British companies and others to invest. The bench-mark of Spain's progress was undoubtedly 1 January 1986, when Spain entered the EC, an event almost unanimously acclaimed by Spaniards, who see their future in ever closer liaison with their European neighbours.

Economic environment

MACRO-ECONOMIC SCENE

It is important to understand that Spain's socio-economic revolution was already underway in the 1960s and 1970s, even as the Franco dictatorship was struggling to stay in power. After decades of isolation, Spain then began to open up to international trade, assisted by the vast revenues from mass tourism. Migration from the countryside to the towns accelerated in response to rapid industrialisation and the service needs of growing urban centres. If not overnight, certainly over decades, the Franco regime became an anachronism in a country desperate for closer economic and political ties with the democracies in the rest of Europe.

Following Franco's death in 1975, the first centre-right governments of the democratic transition were left to inherit a number of major economic deficiencies. Among these were technological backwardness, an inefficient agricultural system, a relatively low level of education and training in the population and the Francoist legacy of corporatism, i.e. the large role within the overall economy occupied by a massive infrastructure of over-manned, loss-making state-owned industries. Additionally, there was, and is, a unique company profile, since Spain has a multiplicity of small firms (employing less than fifty people), estimated to constitute some 90% of all companies.

The incoming Socialist government of 1982 also faced a decade of rapidly deteriorating macro-economic indicators, following the first oil price shock. Spain's performance in this period was substantially worse than other European economies, especially in employment. Spain's unemployment rate in 1982 was 16.2% compared with an EC average of 9.3%, while inflation at 13.8% was also higher than the EC average of 9.3%.

Since 1982, González's government, with three General Election victories, has pursued a tight monetarist policy based upon containing inflation, promoting greater freedom and flexibility in business, and carrying through a policy of industrial 'reconversion', i.e. a rationalisation and modernisation of Spain's heavy industry. EC accession in 1986 has assisted the government in its objective of opening Spanish businesses up to European competition and has helped to propel the economy – and much of business with it – into the forefront of world economies, with booming growth in the late 1980s which has outstripped that of most other countries (e.g. GDP growth in 1988 at 5% was one and a half points above the EC average).

The Socialist government has implemented a stabilisation programme featuring monetary and budgetary policies which converge on the policies of EC member states. This programme, including membership of the European Monetary System and action to moderate wage rises, has helped to reduce inflation to a fairly constant 5–6% between 1988 and 1991. Unemployment has proved more intractable, with González's first period in office seeing unemployment rise to 21% in 1986, the highest in the OECD. Since 1987, however, unemployment has moved downwards on a month-by-month basis to stand at 15.9% at the end of 1991. This improvement reflects the government's promotion of special employment programmes and tax incentives to industry to create new jobs, as well as growth in real domestic demand (up by 30% between 1983 and 1989 compared with an EC average of 18%), and a general moderation in wage settlements. The unemployment level is, however, still too high, especially for the sixteen to twenty-five age group, and further employment and training initiatives are being taken by the government.

EC membership has meant a 'cold shower' of competition for Spanish industry after years of protection through tariff barriers. In the first two years of EC membership, an estimated 150,000 small firms went to the wall as imports flooded into Spain. While the initial reaction of some sections of the Spanish business community was to 'cry foul', most enlightened employers, along with the government, have taken the view that a significant proportion of the increase in imports has been due to plant and machinery urgently needed to modernise and revitalise industry into more dynamic competitive attitudes.

Certainly, there is no question that constant increases in Spanish exports to the EC since 1986, as well as annual increases of 15% upwards in both fixed investment and investment in plant and machinery, support the majority pro-EC view.

STRUCTURE

In 1960, 39% of the Spanish working population were employed in agriculture. By 1991, this figure had dropped to 14%, a level equivalent to Spain's Mediterranean EC partners, but still significantly higher than France (7%), Germany (5%) or the UK (2%). Spain's manufacturing workforce changed very little in this period, from a much lower base, with 23% employed in manufacturing in 1991. Employment in services, however, saw an even more rapid expansion in Spain than elsewhere in Western Europe, with the percentage increasing from 31% in 1960 to 53% in 1991. Agriculture now accounts for 5.2% of GDP. Manufacturing, mining and the utilities account for 28.8%, while construction accounts for 8.9% and services for 57.1%.

The state-owned firms of the public holding company, the *Instituto Nacional de Industria* (National Institute for Industry, or INI), have long set the business agenda in Spain, even, arguably, in the post-1992 era, where the principal challenge for much of Spanish business is to throw off the shackles of recent decades by major capital investment, so as to compete successfully with established Western rivals. Thus the advent of a marketing-orientated philosophy has come later to Spanish companies, but the performance of many of these companies, for instance in the new sectors of electronics and telecommunications, shows that the new

lessons are being applied. INI is one of the fifty biggest trading groups in the world, and in Spain accounts for more than 30% of all production in a wide range of industries – coal, iron and steel, shipyards, electricity, aluminium, air and rail transport, etc. Successfully rationalised during the 1980s, many profitable companies, including the airline IBERIA, are now, under 1991 government plans, destined for part or full privatisation.

Spain's largest employer is the tourist industry, which provides work, directly or indirectly, for one million families and approximately 10% of the active population. Spectacular growth since the 1960s shows little sign of plateauing out, as the number of foreign visitors now exceeds fifty million annually. The industry, however, provides abundant opportunities for foreign intervention, both in construction and in hotel and catering services, as new tourist resorts continue to spring up, and diversification of supply attracts more tourists out of high season and to the cultural hinterland.

The construction industry in Spain is very powerful, after a property boom in the late 1980s and increased public spending on infrastructure (for more information see the Business Notes in unit 2 **Laying Foundations**). The electronics and telecommunications sectors have mushroomed from a virtually zero base in 1985 to make their presence felt internationally. A recent overhaul of high-tech industry has made this possible, and government strategy to build up Spain's IT base has been vital in wooing foreign investors to Spain. The 1986 agreement between ATT and the Spanish telecommunications company, Telefónica, led to the construction outside Madrid of Western Europe's biggest microchip factory. Government investment in the industry continues to increase, to between 1.1% and 1.5% in 1992.

Spain is the fourth largest car manufacturer in the EC (after Germany, France and Italy) but has perhaps the greatest potential for continued growth, due to levels of car ownership 20% lower than the EC average. In terms of exports, though, Spain leads the field in Europe, with over 60% of its total production of one and a half million cars destined for the export market.

The proliferation of small and medium-sized firms, known as the PYMES (*Pequeñas y Medianas Empresas*) has determined major shifts in business planning in the last few years. In 1989, a new programme was launched geared to helping the PYMES in post-1992 Europe. The programme aimed to boost R&D, to involve the PYMES in greater European communication via such schemes as Sprint, BC-Net and Europartenariat, and to streamline management structures. Also, in the late 1980s, a movement toward new (for Spain) types of financial corporations, holding companies and consortia became evident, as the PYMES, supported by the government, sought wider markets in Europe. Thus, Spanish firms, both large and small, have begun to diversify horizontally, i.e. into areas unconnected with the business of the original firms, and vertically, i.e. in the same sector. Current and real-estate firms are the leaders in this diversification drive, which has attracted private and state-owned concerns. Indeed, the state tobacco company, Tabacalera, has pioneered the trend.

Regional inequalities, which have always existed, have become exacerbated in recent years, as Spain's growth has generally benefited already prosperous areas, notably the areas around the two major cities of Madrid and Barcelona, the Valencia region and the Balearics and Canaries, at the cost of the traditionally poorer, agricultural areas of Extremadura, Castile, Andalusia and Galicia. Business File 2 deals with the regions in more detail.

FOREIGN TRADE

Spain has been running a trade balance deficit since the mid-1980s, as its export drive, while successful, has failed to match the flood of imports. There has, though, been a major shift in trade toward EC countries since the early 1980s. In 1982, only 32% of the value of all imports came from the EC, compared with 57% in 1991. Exports to the EC also increased, from 49% of total revenue in 1982 to over 67% in 1991. Spain's leading trade partners in 1991 were, in this order, France, Germany, Italy, USA and the UK.

The sectors showing the biggest increases in imports in 1991 were food and drink, furs and textiles, and optical, photographic and musical instruments, although it must be remembered that almost every sector showed a considerable rise. In exports, Spain was most successful in raising exports of cars and tractors, fuels and mineral oils, machinery and electrical appliances, and vegetable produce.

ANGLO-SPANISH TRADE

Spain is the UK's eighth largest export market, while the UK is Spain's fourth largest. UK exporters have begun to make steady inroads into Spanish markets but start from a very low base. Most British firms established in Spain in the 1930s pulled out in the early years of Franco's rule, unlike French, German and US companies which kept a large Spanish presence.

The Department of Trade and Industry has drawn up the following list of priority sectors in recent years:

machine tools

telecommunications and broadcasting equipment

scientific instruments and laboratory equipment

building materials

computer software and informatics

airport and related equipment

food and drink

pollution control and environmental technology

automotive components, garage and forecourt equipment

There are numerous stories of successful export trade with Spain by British companies since Spain joined the EC. For instance, before 1986, imported breakfast cereals were virtually unknown in Spain, and yet, by 1988, with little or no publicity, Weetabix was turning over £1 million. Amstrad only began selling to Spain in 1987, and within two years were billing over £100 million in personal computers and hi-fi equipment. Chloride Batteries set themselves a £$^1/_2$ million sales target over a four-year period and achieved the target in half the time. Further success stories abound

and pay witness to the tremendous potential of the Spanish market.

Social environment

THE LAW

Businesses in Spain, although operating openly in a democratic environment, are still largely bound by a legalistic framework established during the Franco era when the business community was given a free rein. Although changes are being introduced, most existing legislation dates back to before 1975. The most glaring anomaly has been the failure in the past to compel firms to carry out independent audits, and the consequence has been wide popular mistrust of published accounts. Only in recent years have the majority of firms been persuaded that external auditing is in their own interests, as they learn to take the views of shareholders and employees seriously. The laws relating to employment, on the other hand, have been extremely rigid and have made it very difficult for businesses to dismiss employees, although, as is explained later in the book (see the Business Notes in unit 4 **Starting up in Spain**), the government has promoted flexibility in recent years.

Spaniards have been noted throughout history for a healthy disrespect for authority, or for a feeling that laws passed by the State can either be flouted or used to one's own private ends. Widespread tax evasion has been endemic in Spain for decades, and businesses are not immune from colluding with the banks in dreaming up ingenious schemes to escape paying taxes. Similarly, the Spanish tradition of *enchufe*, an almost untranslatable term which means 'maximising connections, whether family and friends and whether above or below board, to make progress', is deeply ingrained. The absence of guilt makes Spaniards self-confident and great fun to be around. However, the Spanish have a deep sense of personal pride, or *honor*, and an ill-considered personal insult may have disastrous results on one's business.

BUSINESS EDUCATION

Business executives in Spain are very well paid in comparison with their EC counterparts and generally more so the higher up they go. The business revolution of the 1980s has been accomplished by an explosion of interest among young people in pursuing a business career. As a result, many thousands of bright young executives are streaming out of the business schools and the universities to become sharp managers.

Spanish business schools have been proliferating since the late 1980s in an attempt to meet spiralling demand. The Ministry of Labour estimates, however, that Spanish firms require a minimum of 30,000 executives per year trained in business and management studies and that less than half of this requirement is being met. Nevertheless, the top business schools in Spain, of a standard comparable with other EC countries, are producing high-quality students, often with MBA degrees. By general consent, the top business schools are IESI (*Instituto de Estudios Superiores de*

Empresa) in Navarre, recently ranked fifth best in Europe, ESADE (*Escuela Superior de Administración y Dirección de Empresas*) in Barcelona, and the Instituto de Empresas in Madrid.

The urgent need for Spain to produce more managers with business qualifications and/or with expertise in the new technologies has also led to a general overhaul of the education system. School-leaving age has been raised to fifteen, a greater priority is being given to technical and practical skills, and university degree courses are being updated to incorporate the knowledge and expertise needed by Europe's fastest-growing economy. New private universities have opened since 1990 in Barcelona, Madrid and Valencia with the active participation of Spanish companies, notably Repsol, the petrol giant, El Aguila, the brewing company and Petromed, the oil firm. More are expected to open in the next decade, as public and private enterprise work together to provide the managers of the future.

AFFLUENCE AND LEISURE

1992 heralded a period in which earnings, employment and consumption are expected to continue to rise in Spain, although more moderately perhaps than in the preceding years of spectacular growth. Spaniards have seen their standard of living improve quite considerably in the 1980s, although a continuing high level of unemployment is an uncomfortable statistic. In a 1991 comparative survey of employment provision in the EC member states, the *European* ranked Spain in eighth place in terms of overall employee conditions (with Germany first, France third and the UK in ninth position). Employees in Spain do, however, have a government guaranteed and inflation-linked 'minimum interprofessional salary', as well as thirty days' minimum paid holiday per year and fifteen days off for marriage! Rising standards in health care and education since the democratic transition have been the result of government measures to establish a social welfare state on a par with EC partners. Spain has the second highest ratio (after Italy) of doctors per head of population, and life expectancy has risen from the 1950 level of fifty-nine for men and sixty-four for women to the 1984 level of seventy-four for men and eighty for women. Ownership of cars, telephones, computers, etc. is rapidly growing but is still some way short of the northern EC countries. Interest rates are among the highest in the EC, although reductions are planned, and indirect taxation is set to increase as the Spanish VAT rate of 12% is forced up to conform with EC directives. New lower rates of personal income tax are being introduced in stages, however, with the top rate of 56% planned to go down to 50% and the minimum rate of 25% set to reduce to 18%.

Spaniards are among the most consumerist of peoples. They enjoy spending money and have one of the lowest savings ratings of any country in Europe. The average Spaniard expects to eat out at a restaurant with family or friends several times a week and does not regard this as an extravagance. The Spanish business executive, along with many blue-collar workers, will expect to own, or aspire to own, a holiday or second home, which may be modest, close to the sea or in the mountains and which will be used regularly at weekends and during the summer holidays, when at least a month's break is taken. It would not be a truism to say that the Spanish 'work hard and play hard'. They socialise until the early hours of the morning quite regularly and often in the company of their family, including children. Although comparisons are difficult, they probably sleep less than most of their European neighbours and, apart from holiday periods, the siesta is no longer observed. Above all, Spaniards are usually generous hosts, both with their time and with their pockets.

Business File 2

THE REGIONAL ENVIRONMENT

Writers on Spain have often claimed that a more accurate name of the country would be 'the Spains', since within its frontiers, the differences of landscape, climate, peoples, languages and cultures are probably greater than in any other country in Western Europe. Granting a measure of autonomy to the repressed regions was one of the first priorities of post-Franco democratic governments, and there are now seventeen regions of widely differing sizes, responsibilities and resources, with four of

them – linguistically distinct Catalonia, the Basque Country, Galicia and later Andalusia – clearly more autonomous than the others. Financial assistance from the EC has increased dramatically to assist massive investment in infrastructure, and since 1989 Spain has overtaken Italy as the EC's biggest recipient of regional development funds. The regions themselves are resurgent and expansionist, a reaction against the centralised authoritarianism of the Franco era, and a reflection of enthusiasm for being part of a thriving democracy now integrated into Europe. As people have become disenchanted with central government, regional parties have gained strength and now rule three regions (the Basque Country, Catalonia and Galicia) as well as holding thirty-seven seats out of 350 in the national parliament. Virulent forms of regionalism, as in the case of the Basque terrorist group ETA, have been on the wane, however, as the vast majority of the population demonstrate their rejection of violence and extremism.

Madrid, although an important industrial region, has never enjoyed the automatic supremacy over the rest of Spain as, for instance, Paris over France or London over the UK. The region of Catalonia, based around Barcelona, has traditionally led the way in industrial and commercial endeavour, and has vied both with Madrid and with the heartland of Spanish heavy industry in the Basque Country. Other regions have sprung to prominence in recent years, notably the Valencia area, Asturias in the north (and especially the Gijón–Oviedo–Avilés triangle) and Andalusia in the south (with Seville as its capital). Mass tourism has boosted many regions, including of course the Canaries and the Balearics. The end result is a regional framework which encourages new initiatives, such as regional universities and science parks, and which actively welcomes and supports inward business investment. The regions' ability to do this stems from an explosion in their public expenditure during the 1980s, as additional resources have been decentralised from central government. According to the Bank of Spain, public expenditure in the regions has risen from 1.8% of total public expenditure in 1981 to 16% in 1990, and from 0.9% of GDP in 1981

to 9.4% in 1990. The bulk of this expenditure derives from central government transfers, since the regions only raise 1% of their own revenue and have inevitably encountered charges of wasting money. An Interterritorial Compensation Fund (*Fondo de Compensación Interterritorial*, or FCI), designed to transfer money to the poorer rather than the richer regions, has failed dismally and is under review in 1992. Demonstrably, the big three regions of Madrid, Catalonia and the Basque Country have benefited most from central grants, while some of the smaller regions, such as Extremadura and Castile–La Mancha, remain rooted in agricultural deprivation. The table on the next page provides some idea of the economic importance of the different regions in relation to their size and their level of development.

Spain is, of course, a major agricultural as well as industrial nation, and a rapid review of the traditional regional strengths in agriculture and industry provides an essential background for the more detailed regional profiles which highlight more recent developments and business opportunities. Spain's main crop is the olive, mostly grown in Andalusia, with 40% of the world total coming from Spain. In wine production, Spain rates third in the world league after France and Italy. Wheat is the most common cereal and, with maize and rice, is grown in the north and along the Valencian coast. Fruit is Spain's main agricultural export, with oranges and lemons grown in Valencia and Murcia, and bananas in the Canaries. Cotton and tobacco support the economy in Andalusia, while potatoes and vegetables sustain the Galician economy. Asturias is the prime dairy farming region of Spain. Despite export success, Spain still imports agricultural produce. The fishing industry is the fifth largest in the world in tonnage of catch,

Spain – the regional picture (1987)

Region	% ALL GDP	% TOTAL POPULATION	INDEX OF LEVEL OF DEVELOPMENT (NATIONAL AVERAGE = 100)
Catalonia	19.5	15.4	108.7
Madrid	16.5	12.5	115.5
Andalusia	12.5	18.1	95.6
Valencia	10.4	9.8	105.8
Basque Country	6.0	5.5	103.9
Castile Leon	5.9	6.6	92.0
Galicia	5.8	7.4	80.8
Canaries	3.7	3.9	100.3
Aragon	3.5	3.0	97.9
Castile–La Mancha	3.3	4.3	89.2
Balearics	2.7	2.8	110.3
Asturias	2.7	2.8	90.9
Murcia	2.2	2.7	98.7
Extremadura	1.8	2.8	79.0
Navarre	1.5	1.3	101.1
Cantabria	1.3	1.4	92.5
La Rioja	0.7	0.7	99.4

(Source: *Banesto and Economist*)

with over half of this accounted for by the Basque Country and Galicia. Very little fish is exported, and indeed Spain is a net importer of fish and seafood. In the first two years of EC membership, Britain's export of agricultural produce to Spain increased 1,000%, with seafood exports improving 1,500%.

In industry, Spain's traditional strengths have been in heavy industry. In shipbuilding, Spain is sixth in the world league, with El Ferrol in Galicia, Cadiz in Andalusia and Cartagena in Murcia the leading centres. Spain's mineral resources have long been a pillar of the economy. Asturias is renowned for coal and mercury; Andalusia for lead, uranium and copper (particularly the Río Tinto mines near Huelva, built by British engineers in the last

century); and Catalonia for potash. These industries supply the iron and steel industries around Bilbao in the Basque Country, and also in Catalonia and Asturias, which in turn supply the motor, aircraft and shipbuilding industries. Textile factories (cotton, silk and wool) have been a mainstay of the Catalonian economy since the eighteenth century. The Valencia region is responsible for major export markets in the footwear industry.

In general terms, most of the regions have invested in infrastructure and are modernising capital equipment and production processes while attempting to support new high-tech industries and the improved banking and financial institutions which underpin all such endeavours. It is already true to say that a UK business interested in investing in a particular region must deal directly with that region and not just with Madrid. Increasingly, the trend will be for all significant business and financial decisions to be made in the appropriate region. The regional profiles that follow concentrate on the nine most promising regions for potential trade and investment.

Regional profiles

CATALONIA (CATALUÑA)

POPULATION

6.17 million

REGIONAL CAPITAL

Barcelona

DATE STATUTE OF AUTONOMY APPROVED

December 1979

Catalonia, situated in the north-east of Spain, bordering the south of France, is the Spanish region most likely to reap great benefits from a more united Europe. It is one of the largest and most industrially developed regions in all Spain, and within the EC only four regions have greater weight in the industrial sector: Lombardy, Stuttgart, Hamburg and Oberfranken. The corner-stone of the Catalan economy is a well-developed industry, since Catalonia, unlike other Spanish regions, experienced its industrial revolution at the same time as other industrialised regions of Europe. Catalonia accounts for 22% of Spanish exports, the highest volume per region, and 28% of imports. Linked closer to Europe culturally,

psychologically and economically, Catalonia absorbs about one third of all foreign investment in Spain and is responsible for more than 40% of all Spanish investment abroad. The EC accounts for 60% of Catalonia's foreign trade.

Major international companies such as Volkswagen, Hewlett-Packard and Dow Chemicals are already established in Catalonia. The food industry has been thriving, based upon a prosperous agriculture and production of *cava*, a sparkling champagne-like drink. Massive high-tech investment has been led by the Japanese buying stakes in Catalan firms. The textile industry, which led the region's development in the last century, is ripe for foreign intervention and rationalisation. The region's car industry has been very successful since Spain's indigenous SEAT models were incorporated into the Volkswagen group in 1982.

Catalonia also makes a significant contribution to the tourist industry, with 160 miles of Mediterranean beaches and a dozen top ski resorts in the Pyrenees. A major attraction is the excellent co-ordination between private industry and research work at Barcelona's three state universities. The regional government (the Generalitat) has also been cooperating with the town council in Barcelona and with the state

holding corporation, the INI, to establish a technopolis near the three universities. The aim is to attract advanced technology projects specialising in robotics, biotechnology, new materials and electronics. A wide range of facilities and grants are given to firms which set up in the area, including free provision of premises. The 1992 Olympic Games in Barcelona and the high-speed rail link south to Madrid and north to France have inevitably generated further business activity in this, the most dynamic of Spain's regions.

MADRID

POPULATION

5.03 million

REGIONAL CAPITAL

Madrid

DATE STATUTE OF AUTONOMY APPROVED

February 1983

Madrid's importance as an industrial centre dates from the 1960s, as a result of development plans carried out by the Franco regime. The population swelled as Spaniards flooded in from depressed rural areas. Today, the population growth is close to zero in Madrid, but economic analysts are predicting a new upsurge in industrial activity and population after the arrival of the single European market.

Madrid has experienced growth pains in the 1980s, attracting the highest level of direct foreign investment, much of it in technological and industrial areas. Sharply rising real estate prices, reflecting a demand from businesses with an eye on the European market, have seen a population move to the suburbs and a tremendous shortage of housing for young people. While Madrid has become one of Europe's top cities of investment, it still faces major transportation and communications problems, being perhaps the most isolated of all EC capital cities, with the highest altitude and surrounded by mountains. The high-speed rail track to the south and to the north hasn't come a day too soon for Madrid, which also needs a much more extensive radial motorway network to other parts of the country.

Madrid-based enterprises are leading the way in joint ventures with other countries. The telecommunications giant, Telefónica, a combined private and state-owned monopoly, is spearheading a drastic revamping of the country's tele-communications network and is currently developing a joint European venture to produce a mobile telephone system which will be internationally compatible. Another major company set to benefit from this internationalisation process is Tabacalera, originally a tobacco firm, but whose diverse products are now marketed throughout the world via joint ventures. In the UK, for instance, the company holds a

49.5% stake in Eagle Star insurance and is a major partner in food production and tourist chains throughout the European community. Tabacalera is to join forces with Nabisco in the new European market after 1993.

Madrid is, of course, also the hub of the country's financial network. Caja de Madrid is the most profitable of Spain's seventy-seven savings banks and is also Spain's leading savings bank in terms of credit granted and customers' deposits. The bank's positive attitude toward European financial integration at the end of 1992 is perhaps typical of Madrid's self-confidence as a whole. Anticipating more competition, shrinking profits and a demand for greater productivity, Spanish bankers nevertheless look forward to establishing cooperation agreements with foreign banks and the opportunity to distribute their products in other markets.

ANDALUSIA (ANDALUCIA)

POPULATION

7.10 million

REGIONAL CAPITAL

Seville

DATE STATUTE OF AUTONOMY APPROVED

December 1981

Andalusia has traditionally relied on agriculture as its main source of employment and principal earner. Much of the agricultural system has, however, been slow to invest in new farming methods. Migration to other parts of Spain or abroad has often been the chosen escape route for thousands of

Andalusians, and unemployment, currently standing at 24%, has always been high. There has been little industrial tradition in the region, despite massive development around Seville in the past twenty years, with 60% working in the services sector, mostly in tourism. An estimated three million people depend indirectly on EC subsidies, and per capita GDP, at 54.4% of the EC average, compares with a national average of 76.7% and 99.1% in the Madrid region.

The hope of the regional government is that Expo '92 in Seville will catapult the region into the twenty-first century. An enormous infrastructural build-up has already taken place, with thousands of kilometres of new roads, a new airport, railway station and opera house, in addition to the high-speed rail link with Madrid. The region's future is dependent upon a 1991–1994 Economic Development Plan, which only started in October 1991 and which aims to modernise the production system; it sets aside 80 billion pesetas over four years to assist the creation of new companies and the technological overhaul of existing ones. The Plan also allocates funds for the training of future managers. Despite the Plan, problems remain for the region, especially the road communications network, which provides good links between Seville and Madrid, and other important regional centres such as Cordoba and Huelva, but which is appalling in the Malaga and Almeria area.

A number of multinationals have already pledged to stay on the Expo site after 1992, and there are encouraging signs of new technological developments being sited in the region. The state-owned aerospace firm, CASA, is developing carbon fibre avionics at its plant outside Seville. Malaga has induced Hughes Microelectronics from the UK to produce sophisticated components in its Science Park (see the Business Notes in unit 3, **Tapas and Technology**). With a Prime Minister in Madrid representing Seville in parliament and with the undoubted impetus of Expo, Andalusia is set to cast off its 'poor neighbour' image.

VALENCIA

POPULATION

3.9 million

REGIONAL CAPITAL

Valencia

DATE STATUTE OF AUTONOMY APPROVED

July 1982

Visitors to Benidorm and beaches around Alicante may not realise that tourism is only one of three main sectors of this region's economy. The other two are industry and agriculture. Half of Europe's oranges and lemons come from this region. In addition, Spain's biggest automobile factory, near the city of Valencia, distributes Fords all over Europe. The highly successful Lladró ceramic firm is also in Valencia. Tourists, farmers and industrialists have all benefited from great improvements in the road network, which now includes bypasses around Valencia and Alicante to allow a continuous motorway route from Alicante to Perpignan in France. More upgrading of roads to dual carriageway and the prospect of a new high-speed rail link down the coast to Alicante will assist the regional growth rate, which has been well above the national average since 1987.

Several factors have contributed to Valencia's recent industrial growth, notably a boost in local investment and reinvestment, substantial expansion in the construction sector and the development of new, non-traditional industries. Industry, often with foreign investment and technological updating, has begun a massive transformation. Traditional Valencian industry consists of areas such as textiles, shoes, toys and furniture. New industries are emerging, especially industrial machinery and high-tech, to change the region's profile. Traditional sectors now represent 47% of the overall industrial sector, a drop of five points in five years, while new sectors account for approximately 52%. The majority of new investment has, however, come from within the region. The Valencian banking sector, too, is undergoing transformation, especially the Bank of Valencia. After suffering serious economic problems involving the real estate industry, the Bank of Valencia now has multiple investments in different sectors of the region's economy and itself has hundreds of foreign investors.

Although it accounts for 16% of Spain's industrial exports, Valencia still lags behind Catalonia to the north, although Valencia's trade balance is better. Attempts to improve export performance characterise many Valencian firms. One of the oldest companies, Monerris Planellis SA, maker of *turrón*, a nougat-style confectionery popular at Christmas, has always been strong in exports to South and North America, but has recently been in talks with UK and German firms to broaden its network. Such readiness to internationalise on the part of many Valencian companies, allied with good regional infrastructure and a healthy overall economy, gives this region a head start over most others in Spain.

THE BASQUE COUNTRY (EL PAIS VASCO)

The Basques have always preserved their distinctive character, founded upon a fierce pride in their own mysterious language and a tradition of separate development from the rest of Spain throughout most of their history. The heartland of Spanish heavy industry, with iron and steelworks and shipyards, the Basque Country has had to contend with political extremism from the die-hard terrorist group ETA, while at the same time trying to rebuild the Basque economy and foreign investment, at an all-time low after the 1973 oil crisis. Today, the region has a steadily improving modern economy with growth rates well above the European average.

Under a plan called the Special Europe '93 Plan, the Basques are currently updating their telecommunications industry. To do so, they need industrial investment,

POPULATION

2.16 million

REGIONAL CAPITAL

Vitoria

**DATE STATUTE OF
AUTONOMY APPROVED**

December 1979

and the Basque regional government is offering generous financial inducements and credit terms to foreign investors, with the greatest levels of support destined for high-tech projects. The UK and the Basque Country have a long history of economic and industrial relations, but, by 1975, British investment in the Basque Country was virtually zero. Since 1984, however, when the British Chamber of Commerce began to have some influence, a number of British companies have become involved in joint ventures in the region. The Bilbao superport is one of the most important in Europe, and the anticipated creation of a central bank in the Basque Country would provide futher credit for interested investors.

A new, younger generation of Basque business people, who have travelled abroad and know English, is leading local and foreign-financed firms. Alongside the newcomers, long-standing industries, such as the iron and steel giant, Altos Honos de Vizcaya, will continue to play a major role. After a rationalisation and economic recovery programme in the 1980s, Altos Hornos, as Spain's leading private steel company, is well able to compete internationally. Similarly with Babcock and Wilson Española, a well-established manufacturer of metal pipe, iron castings, machine tools and gas cylinders.

The Basque Country is also home to the giant cooperative group, Mondragón, which has attracted world-wide attention since its foundation in 1956, and still welcomes foreign delegations of interested business people and politicians anxious to discover the secret of the world's most successful cooperative. Over 100 enterprises, employing almost 20,000 people in a variety of industries, constitutes a cooperative whose international fame undoubtedly derives from its unique supporting organisations: its own bank, social security system, medical and hospital care and a technical college.

The activities of ETA have undoubtedly damaged the region's image and its industries. However, the Basque people have demonstrated their rejection of the terrorists, and the region's combination of traditional and new industries suggests a brighter future.

CASTILE–LEON
(CASTILLA–LEON)

POPULATION

2.61 million

REGIONAL CAPITAL

Valladolid

DATE STATUTE OF AUTONOMY APPROVED

February 1983

Castile–Leon is Spain's largest region, accounting for 18% of national territory, and one of the richest in natural resources. The region has large resources of uranium in Salamanca, iron in Leon and is a leading mining region, with 25% of national mineral production and 35% of total mineral reserves. Food production is important, with emphasis on livestock, wheat, barley and vegatables. Tobacco and wood products are also major contributors to the economy of a region which still relies on agriculture for the bulk of its wealth. Following Spain's entry into the EC, the region's sales to other countries have increased by more than 25%, although Castile–Leon accounts for less than 3% of the national export total and buys less than 2% of the country's imports. The region's many exports include machinery and electrical equipment, metals, leather, and animal and vegetable fats and oils.

The great challenge for this region is industrial development, since much of industry is backward. To attract new investment, the regional government has provided public land for factories and warehouses, and has at its disposal a whole host of incentives to promote technological investment and job creation. The private investor is the stated priority of the region's centrist coalition government, which is committed to a policy of improving the regional infrastructure to create the right climate for investors. The region wants to improve the road and motorway links to Portugal and the Atlantic seaboard in Galicia and Asturias. There is also the possibility of a high-speed rail link through Castile–Leon which, if it became a reality, would run from the French border to either Lisbon or Oporto in Portugal.

Currently, the region's industrial sector comprises various subsectors such as coal mining, hydraulic and thermal energy and uranium production. Tourism is relatively underdeveloped, although it has considerable potential, since Castile–Leon is rich in cultural and historical artefacts, along with its lakes, mountains and varied countryside.

GALICIA

POPULATION

2.91 million

REGIONAL CAPITAL

Santiago de Compostela

DATE STATUTE OF AUTONOMY APPROVED

April 1981

Fishing, coupled with agriculture and livestock production, has always been the economic lifeline of Galicia. The region is strategically situated on the Atlantic, with two major port cities, Vigo and La Coruña. Galicia, with only 7% of Spain's population, produces half of the fish products consumed in Spain, as well as 25% of the country's agriculture, 30% of its forestry resources and 20% of its livestock. Although firmly anchored in traditional sectors, industry is sprouting under the regional government's new industrialisation and modernisation plan, which aims to bring the region in line with highly industrialised regions such a Catalonia and the Basque Country. Industry has begun to take off, especially around La Coruña, but much remains to be done.

The fishing industry will inevitably continue to play a major role in the Galician economy. Vigo, one of the most important ports in Europe and top of the European league for the movement of fresh fish, plays the double role of fuelling the fish industry and stimulating commerce. Among the most important fishing companies is Pescanova, established in 1960 as a distant-water trawling company. It has pioneered various techniques in the highly competitive fishing industry, being the first European fleet to incorporate an on-board refrigeration system. It also pioneered the setting up in Spain of the first organised distribution network of deep-frozen foods covering the entire country. Investment in research, both in fishing and food technology, has paid off, giving Pescanova the leading position it occupies today as a fishing company and a frozen food producer and distributor.

The Galician government is conscious of the region's backward image and wants to give tourism a greater role in the regional economy. Current projects and objectives include improving the quality of beaches, ocean-related sports, and hotel expansion and promotion. The Department of Industry and Trade in the region has also embarked upon a massive plan to attract investment and update the region. Stimulation of technological institutes and areas set aside for technological development, the renovation of industrial infrastructure and the encouragement of small and medium-sized companies represent some of the initiatives being taken to ensure that Galicia is fully integrated into post-1992 Europe.

ASTURIAS

POPULATION

1.13 million

REGIONAL CAPITAL

Oviedo

DATE STATUTE OF AUTONOMY APPROVED

December 1981

Asturias has been the coal-mining centre of Spain since the eighteenth century and is blessed with large deposits of zinc, iron and other mineral resources. It is a mountainous and forested region which sustains remote farming communities alongside traditional and newly established industries. In the past fifteen years, significant industrial progess has been made in all areas, including agriculture, farming and mining. But the regional government is anxious to attract more foreign investment by advertising the availability of land for further development and by improving the generally good communications and transport networks.

In the run-up to 1993, the regional government has been offering grants of up to 45% on approved investment in the region, grants which consist of soft loans, guarantees for loans, privileged credit and other incentives. The attempt to boost foreign investment has been successful, with important foreign companies now located in Asturias. These include Alcan, the Canadian aluminium processing company; Agar de Asturias SA, a United States–Mexico chemical firm; Bel Asturias, a UK milk company; and Celulosas de Asturias SA, a paper paste industry supported by British capital. The US company, Dupont, has invested over one billion dollars in an industrial chemical complex, and Siemens and Corning Glass are combining to set up Spain's first optical fibre plant.

The Asturian government has created the Regional Development Institute, an independent agency designed to support balanced industrial development in the region while at the same time preserving the region's picturesque features, such as its mountains and beaches. Quality tourism is on the increase in a region which has provided evidence of its ability to develop new industries in the built-up triangle between the regional capital, Oviedo, and two coastal towns, Gijón and Avilés, both important ports and shipyards. Fifteen years ago, this triangle enclosed a landscape dotted with farms and villages. Now there is a patchwork of roads, industrial estates and dozens of new companies.

NAVARRE (NAVARRA)

POPULATION

0.53 million

REGIONAL CAPITAL

Pamplona

DATE STATUTE OF AUTONOMY APPROVED

August 1982

Navarre is the home of the city of Pamplona, known worldwide for its annual bull-running festival. Less well known is the remarkable transformation of the region from a predominantly rural economy to a highly industrialised one, all in one generation. Navarre has a per capita income above the Spanish average, while its middle class comprises an estimated 80% of the population. Some eighty multinational companies, including General Electric and Volkswagen, have a base in the region which, situated on the French border, is strategically well located for business, with the added inducement of generous government investment. Major infra-structural projects are underway, including the construction of highways to lure European travellers into Spain via Navarre and to create smoother links to other Spanish regions. Communications and educational facilities are also being upgraded to include a new state university.

Crucial to the economic upturn of the region was the creation in the mid-1980s of SODENA, or Society for the Development of Navarre, which has acted as a conduit between local firms and prospective foreign partners. Although the region's agricultural sector is important, the industrial sector is even more powerful and is dominated by the automobile and car parts industry. Several automobile giants are based in Navarre, notably SEAT, Volkswagen, Nissan and Motor Ibérica. Regional companies have also stepped up investment in recent years in a bid to become more competitive and to extend international markets. The food producer Viscofan, by dint of substantial investment in research and development, has become a leader in technology applied to the food processing and packaging industry. It has also captured new markets in Australia, Canada and Japan.

Tourism is not a major earner for Navarre, but a recent survey, showing that Navarre has been second only to Catalonia in its success at wooing foreign investment, indicates that Navarre can more than compensate industrially.

Business File 3

SPAIN AS A MARKET FOR THE FUTURE

The impact of EC integration

It is important to remember that there is near-unanimous enthusiasm for the benefits of EC membership among ordinary Spaniards. Indeed, the Socialist government won their second General Election in 1986 largely upon their success in achieving EC membership for Spain some months earlier. Thus Spaniards have borne with remarkable equanimity the painful adjustments necessary to move from a protected to a competitive economy, and have quickly acquired, within the institutions of the EC, a reputation as whole-hearted Europeans.

The terms of Spain's EC entry meant a variety of transitional arrangements for full economic integration. In agriculture, the transitional period was seven years, except for fruit and vegetables (ten years), with special conditions for wine and olive oil. The banks and financial services also faced a seven-year transition, in which European banks were limited to a maximum of three branches in the first four years, rising gradually to eight branches in the seventh year, with no restrictions in place after this period. The terms for industry and commerce union provided for a gradual dismantling of tariff barriers over seven years. Thus, the first tariff cut was 100% in March 1986, followed by 12.5% in January 1987, 15% in 1988 and 1989, 12.5% in 1990, 1991 and 1992, and a final 10% in 1993. In the first year of EC membership alone, imports to Spain from the EC went up by 32% as a result of the first tariff reduction, and trade between Spain and the EC moved from a surplus position of 268,000 million pesetas in 1985 to a deficit for Spain of 139,000 million pesetas in 1986. Further tariff cuts have meant a multi-million peseta boom in Spain for other EC countries and the demise of many thousands of Spanish companies, especially in vulnerable sectors such as light engineering (including manufacturers of bicycles, motorcycles, electrical appliances and machinery), clothing and some food industries. At the same time as some Spanish companies were going out of business, a more streamlined industry began to channel major investment toward modernising production equipment and increasing production capacity. This process of technological innovation, still underway, hit of necessity at the competitiveness of Spanish products while presenting opportunities for foreign companies.

While companies like the Valencia-based Tycesa group, which manufactures Western Europe's best-selling Lois jeans, demonstrate that Spanish business can be as efficient as any in the world, there is evidence that many Spanish industries still fear competition. The main employers' confederation, the *Confederación Española de Organisaciones Empresariales* (CEOE), which is the equivalent of the British CBI, has carried out studies which reveal the extent to which the legacy of corporatism persists in Spain and claims that at no point in their government's EC entry negotiations was there any discussion of the private sector's role in the economy. Instead, the question was debated in terms of what the government was or was not doing to help business.

Since EC entry, the government and the business community have made tremendous efforts to overcome a legacy of under-investment, over-manning and poor training. Infrastructural weakness – the roads, railways, etc. – is also being addressed. As a result, the Spanish market is becoming increasingly more attractive to EC competitors. At the start of the 1990s, Spain's manufacturing costs were just 54% of Germany's, and Spanish wage levels are still (after Greece and Portugal) the lowest in the EC. Recent legislation on active business practices has enhanced competition, already galvanised by the lifting of import quotas and the reduction of tariffs since EC accession. Finally, Spain's historical links with Latin America and friendly relations with the Arab world are other factors which gave Spanish business a distinct trading advantage over EC partners, a fact acknowledged by those foreign companies which have bought into Spain precisely to gain a foothold in markets notoriously difficult to penetrate.

Foreign investment opportunities in Spain

Inward foreign investment was almost non-existent in the Spain of the 1950s, was still small in the 1960s, began to grow in the 1970s and the first half of the 1980s, but only rose sharply after 1986. Net foreign investment grew from 199 billion pesetas in 1982 to 1,830 billion pesetas in 1990, a ninefold increase explained by Spain's low labour costs, national and regional fiscal and financial incentives, a growing domestic market, political stability, EC membership, Latin American and Arab links, and a strong peseta. Liberalisation of foreign investment in the 1970s and especially since 1986, which allows the transfer abroad of unlimited capital, profits and dividends, has placed Spain in fourth position world-wide in respect of volume of investment, after the US, the UK and France. The only formal restrictions on investment relate to the defence industry, telecommunications, radio and television, and the gambling industry.

Since Spain entered the EC, there has been a move by investors from industrial sectors toward financial institutions, insurance companies, real estate activities and services rendered to companies. The trend is clearly seen in the following table.

Direct foreign investment by sector (% of total)

	1984	1990
Financial institutions, insurance, etc.	17.5%	46.5%
Mineral and by-product extraction	14.8%	12.7%

	1984	1990
Miscellaneous manufacturing	11.6%	12.1%
Business, hotels and restaurants	16.9%	9.5%
Energy and water	0.6%	3.5%
Construction	1.3%	2.2%
Transport and communications	0.5%	1.5%

EC countries are the main investors, especially Germany, the Netherlands, France and the UK, followed by the US and Japan. In 1989, the UK became the largest single source of direct foreign investment, a position maintained since then. A major part of Spain's inward investment has been in the Madrid and Catalonia regions (with Japanese investment by Nissan, Suzuki and Sanyo particularly strong in the latter), which together have accounted for between 40% and 60% of total foreign investment since 1986. As a footnote, outward foreign investment has also grown very rapidly from a very low base and again has been directed mostly to the EC and the US and especially in financial services, commerce and the hotel and restaurant trade.

Although global foreign investment is growing yearly, Spain still wants more, to compensate for limited sources of indigenous capital and the historic tendency of Spanish banks (though this is changing) to prefer to invest in real estate rather than in industry. In 1990, foreigners in effect owned 10% of Spain, accounting for 9.3% of GDP, as more foreign firms bought into or bought out Spanish firms. Many small and medium-sized Spanish companies, especially family firms, are ripe for purchase: they are relatively cheap and do not have the finance necessary for technological updating. Opportunities abound in every sector, as can be seen from a sample selection of foreign investment initiatives in recent years. State-owned car manufacturers SEAT and ENASA have passed into German hands. Banks have changed ownership, with, for example, a 75% stake in Banco Atlántico taken by the Arab Aresbank. In construction, the Arabs and Italians have been to the fore, with Gianni Agnelli now owning one third of HUARTE. In food and drink, the brewers El Aguila now have Heineken as major shareholder, while Benedetti from Italy own 27% of the food manufacturer Pascual Hermanos. Household names in Spain, therefore, have gone 'foreign', and the trend is accelerating. Spain's traditionally strong electrical sector, comprising 1,000 companies, is vulnerable to rationalisation and foreign intervention, with the German company RWE leading the way. British companies, such as Wiggins Teape, have shown how to invest successfully in Spain. The British firm was eager to purchase CEASA, a wood pulp manufacturer owned by the Banco Español de Crédito. The route chosen was to form a new Spanish company in order to make a 100% investment through the acquisition of shares. Wiggins Teape report that three essential steps were crucial to their success. Firstly, they employed a first-class Spanish lawyer who understood Britain, not a British lawyer who claimed to understand Spain or Spanish. Then they found a first-class accountant and thirdly, obtained the backing of a bank.

There are, of course, a number of important considerations that a potential British investor should bear in mind before investing in Spain. The main ones are detailed on the next page.

• With very few exceptions, prior administrative verification is no longer needed for direct investments, regardless of the percentage of shareholding in the Spanish company.

• The trade unions in Spain are not against foreign investment, and the labour movement welcomes it to the extent that it relieves unemployment.

• Tax concessions are available to the foreign investor, under the same terms as for Spanish companies. There are eight main kinds of concession:

1 tax credits for investment and as employment incentives;
2 promotion of new technology;
3 tax reduction for investment in specific industries and in designated promotional areas (*zonas promocionables*);
4 tax reductions for investment in enterprises under productivity agreements;
5 tax benefits on mergers and spin-offs;
6 local tax concessions;
7 tax benefits for joint ventures and regional industrial development corporations;
8 tax benefits granted to certain industries.

• Regional incentives are available through central government, regional governments and local government, especially in regions of the country which have not benefited from industrial expansion or which are experiencing economic difficulties. There are two main groups of incentives:

1 tax incentives, comprising a reduction of local taxes, relating to the establishment or expansion of industrial plants, based on location, and a reduction of the business licence tax during the construction and start-up period;

2 non-tax incentives (by far the larger), comprising subsidies, varying between 20% and 50% of total investment, subsidies of interest on loans, and reductions of up to 50% of employer social security contributions.

• Special-use company incentives are also available for: investments in mining, gas and oil exploration; investments in research and development programmes; investments by publishing houses, exporting companies, individual business people and industrial banks and entities engaged in promoting companies.

Finding out more about the Spanish market

Despite numerous individual cases of British companies successfully entering the Spanish market, in general terms there has been little awareness of the available opportunities. A 1989 CBI conference entitled 'Spain – Europe's new economic miracle' reported the reluctance of the British business community to participate in Trade Fairs to Spain, despite the boom. In the intervening years, the British Embassy, the Department of Trade and Industry and the British Chamber of Commerce have all worked hard to rectify the situation, and, in the words of a DTI video, to put the 'Spotlight on Spain'.

A good way to research the Spanish market is to make use of the government's export services. The Department of Trade and Industry together with the Foreign and Commonwealth Office (FCO) provide, through Overseas Trade Services, a wide range of services for UK exporters. The obvious starting point is to identify the best person or people in the company qualified or able to spend time, effort and resources in researching the market. The DTI is able to provide names, addresses, contact points, lists of agents and distributors in Spain, and also publishes regular reports on Spain and on a variety of market sectors. Two specific services provided have already assisted many UK firms and are worth outlining. The first is the Market Information Enquiry Service, in which research on a requested area of the Spanish market is carried out by FCO commercial staff. The second service is called the Export Representatives' Service. Appointing an overseas representative is a key decision; this service provides a comprehensive package of information and specific recommendations of potential agents and distributors. A firm using this service will need to provide full information about itself and its requirements or aspirations so that the information can be passed on to the British Embassy in Madrid, where potential agents and/or distributors will be interviewed on the company's behalf. The two services mentioned above attract a charge, while a number of others are provided free to exporters.

The next crucial stage is to visit Spain for oneself to pursue contacts. It is important to maintain direct contact with the market yourself. You will need to gauge at first hand the potential for the market and assess methods of entry and prospective partners/agents/customers, etc. One of the best ways of doing this is to join a trade mission to Spain, organised by the DTI, Chambers of Commerce or other organisations. Trade missions are perhaps especially suitable for small to medium-sized companies because of clear financial and administrative advantages. Savings on group travel and accommodation can be made, while trade missions can also facilitate introductions to the right contacts in local government and the media. Trade missions may assist with the language barrier by furnishing interpreters and arranging translation of trade literature into Spanish. In addition, a follow-up report is usually written. Examples of the success of trade missions to Spain are the missions which were organised by Scottish Council Development and Industry (SCDI) in June 1988, June 1990 and June 1991. Fifty-one companies participated in the last mission, with twenty-four visiting Spain for the first time. The value of immediate business arising from the missions is put at £472,000, while the value of continuing business generated is estimated at £3,798,000.

As well as the British Chamber of Commerce in Spain, which has excellent up-to-date information, its counterpart, the Spanish Chamber of Commerce in the UK also produces very useful booklets. The national Chambers of Commerce work in concert to publish a bi-monthly booklet in Britain listing companies interested in the Spanish market, information on potential partners and on trade fairs. The British Embassy and British Council Offices in Spain are also helpful, while the Economist Intelligence Unit (EIU) publishes a variety of journals and reports which give information on overall business trends and on specific sectors. Euromonitor also publishes reports and produced a hefty volume, *Consumer Spain '91*, which is essential reading for any business contemplating the Spanish market and contains a lengthy section entitled 'Sources of Information in Spain'. The *Financial Times*, the *Guardian* and *The Economist* have all produced regular surveys on Spain in recent years, which are a useful source for private (and free!) research.

Finally, the EC can provide practical advice and assistance in a number of areas. Currently Spain and the UK collaborate in more than twenty projects under the EUREKA programme and a whole host of other EC collaborative schemes such as BRITE, ESPRIT, etc. The British Embassy has identified areas in which research and development is taking place in Spain and the UK and in which industrial technological collaboration might be useful, particularly in sharing often enormous costs, and which might lead to participation in EUREKA and other industrially-led European projects. The main areas identified include microelectronics, new materials, information technology and engineering, advanced manufacturing systems and biotechnology. Clearly the EC has prioritised high-tech, precisely the area where Spain is most interested and needs help. The EC COMET scheme, which promotes cooperation between enterprises and higher education institutions in the different member states, would allow, for instance, a Spanish MBA student to work in a British company on a six-month or one-year placement. The British Council, in conjunction with the Spanish Ministry of Education and Science, also administers an *Acciones Integradas* (or 'integrated actions') scheme which supports collaborative research at universities and public research bodies.

Direct exporting

Although Spain's import regulations have been relaxed significantly since EC entry, a small number of restrictions still exist. Exchange controls were abolished in February 1992. Spain's import duties are gradually being eliminated on imports from other EC countries and will disappear completely on all manufactured goods by 1 January 1993. It is necessary to present a prior notification (*notificación previa*) for certain imports and also, in some cases, an import authorisation (*autorización previa*). All imports over 500,000 pesetas (in 1991) and those being financed for a period of more than one year must be registered with a Spanish bank and the related documentation dealt with by that bank (*domiciliación bancaria*). Imports are subject to VAT at rates of 6%, 13% (the most common rate) or 28%, depending on their classification.

There are a number of factors exporters to Spain should bear in mind.

• **Documentation procedures.**
Documentation requirements have eased considerably since Spain's accession to the EC. Advice on documentation can be obtained through banks, Chambers of Commerce and freight forwarders. Basically, all exports to Spain should be accompanied by the Single Administrative Document (SAD) and two sets of commercial invoices. Many products will need to meet Spanish technical standards and many food products will require special certification.

• **Customs and storage facilities.** The norm in Spain is to have rigid control of such facilities, which will be quite secure. Under certain conditions, an exporter may be able to store goods on Spanish soil for a limited period of time without incurring cutoms duties and may be allowed to fulfil cutoms clearance requirements on his own storage premises.

• **Port of entry and domestic transport.** Inland transport within Spain is unlikely to pose any problems except in peripheral regions, since Madrid is the focal point of the road and rail network. However, it is worth verifying domestic routes before choosing the port of entry.

• **Local representation.** Although not actually required, local agents are invaluable in arranging the documentation procedures, customs clearance and storage, and the domestic transport arrangements for imported goods. The Customs Department of the Ministry of Economy and Finance keeps a list, although it is wise to follow recommendations of the DTI or other agencies (see **Finding out more about the Spanish market** above). Similarly, the engagement of an independent sales agent should follow reliable independent advice.

Forming a Spanish company

Foreign companies setting up in Spain have to register their existence in the Mercantile Registry of the provincial capital in which the company's head office is located, a requirement which also extends to Spanish companies. The details are open to public inspection. Listed below are the principal vehicles used to conduct business in Spain, with the SA and the branch being the forms most commonly used.

1 Sociedad Anónima (SA)

This is the most prestigious type of company in Spain, similar in all major respects to a UK public limited corporation (plc) or limited liability company. It can be in the public or private sector and may be a larger company quoted on the stock exchange or a smaller family business. An SA requires a minimum capital of ten million pesetas, although no minimum size is stipulated.

2 Sociedad de responsabilidad limitada (SRL/SL)

This type of company is similar in many ways to an SA but is limited to fifty stockholders and has a minimum capital requirement of 500,000 pesetas. There is no maximum capital requirement. An SL does not have shares, and the capital is divided among the shareholders. They are often found in the retail and service sectors. There are legal restrictions on the transfer of stock holdings but few other legal requirements on this type of company, for example to provide audits or reliable financial information.

3 Sociedades colectivas

Partnerships are not widely found in Spain, although two types exist in law: the *sociedad colectiva*, or general partnership, with unlimited liability; and the *sociedad en comandita*, or limited partnership, with a minimum of one general unlimited partner and one limited partner.

4 Cooperativas

A separate Cooperative Register exists, and the Spanish government has encouraged the development of cooperatives in recent years, especially in the agriculture sector. The huge Cooperative of Mondragón (in the Basque Country) is arguably the most successful in the world.

5 Comerciante

Extremely numerous in Spain, *comerciantes*, or sole traders, are found in many sectors, especially food and drink, retail, and crafts and services. They are automatically members of the local Chamber of Commerce. Any individual may, subject to regulations, establish his own business, with unlimited liability.

6 Sucursal

A sucursal, or branch of a foreign company operating in Spain, is not a legal entity in Spain, as SAs or SLs are. A branch must also be registered at the Mercantile Registry, along with duly notarised documents.

Joint ventures/networks

J oint ventures are proving increasingly attractive to UK companies as a means of penetrating the Spanish market using existing know-how and resources. Joint ventures appeal especially to large UK companies confident of making a significant financial commitment to the success of the venture. Sequences 1 and 7 of the video, which look at the experiences of NatWest Bank and Marks and Spencer respectively, provide excellent illustrations of this. Many other British companies have followed suit. Among them are Boots (linking with Liade), Abbey National (Grupo Cor), De La Rue (Lerchundi), BP (Petromed), Barclays (Banco de Valladolid), Mountleigh (Galerías Preciados), etc. Numerous opportunities still exist, especially in the high-tech industry, and the textile industry, which urgently needs rationalisation and the application of marketing techniques from abroad.

T here are four main types of joint venture permissable under Spanish law, and all of them enjoy excellent tax benefits.

1 Sociedad de empresa

T his is a joint venture corporation of at least three participants, who may themselves be SAs, SLs or individuals and constitute a separate legal entity. Venturers may contribute capital in cash and/or other assets, but their holding in the joint venture corporation is limited to 30% of their own paid-up capital. The object of this corporation is normally the expansion or modernisation of manufacturing facilities, sales promotion, or the requisition of machinery or other assets for exploitation.

2 Agrupación de empresa

T his is a grouping of firms who agree, without creating a separate legal entity, to combine to progress the common business interests of their members.

3 Unión temporal de empresa

T his is business agreement, concluded for a fixed or indeterminate time, for the purpose of carrying out a construction, service or supply contract.

4 Cesión de unidades de obra

T his provides for a subcontracting arrangement whereby a subcontract can be passed in part or in full to third parties.

O pportunities may also be found by British companies in forging networking arrangements across Europe which include Spanish firms. In the past two years, a fee-sharing network of banks has been formed, which combines the Hambros group in the UK with Banco Bilbao Vizcaya (BBV) in Spain and with banks in Germany and Italy. Similarly, a supermarket network has been set up, under the name Associated Marketing Services, by Argyll Foods from the UK, which owns Safeway, Presto and Lo Cost, and includes the Mercadona group in Spain. The network controls sales of £27 billion a year in 11,500 stores spread across seven countries. Inevitably, the Single Market is bound to generate further network prospects.

Acquisitions

A prospective UK investor should obviously ascertain at the outset as much information as possible about the business in which he is interested and should therefore employ legal and tax advisers from the beginning. Important considerations for the potential acquirer of a Spanish firm would include all the usual factors relating to the company's history, trading results and markets, but might perhaps pay special attention to an evaluation of the current management, in terms of training and linguistic ability in the investor's language, and also to a workforce evaluation, with particular attention paid to terms of employment, often more inflexible in Spain than in the UK. The location and premises of the Spanish firm will also be a crucial element, given the regional basis of much of Spanish industry and commerce, a factor illustrated in the Guinness acquisition of La Cruz del Campo (see unit 6, **Change is Brewing**).

BANKING ON ACTION

Study Plan

SEQUENCE SUMMARY

NATWEST BANK IS HOSTING A RECEPTION TO MARK THE OPENING OF ITS NEW PREMISES IN MADRID. MEANWHILE, ACTION COMPUTERS – ONE OF THE BANK'S CUSTOMERS – PREPARES FOR AN IMPORTANT MEETING.

WHAT YOU WILL LEARN

Sección 1

- how to greet people you know
- how to introduce colleagues and acquaintances
- how to ask questions with *which?*, *when?*, *where?*, *who?* and *what?*

Business Notes

Banking in Spain
Foreign banks and opportunities in Spain
Opportunities in insurance
Obtaining finance

Sección 2

- how to use numbers
- how to announce yourself on arrival
- how to begin to talk about yourself and your company

LEARNING STRATEGY FOR EACH SECTION

Study the key words in the **Palabras y frases útiles** box and watch the video sequence, listening out for the key words. Make notes of what you have understood.

Then study the key phrases in the **Palabras y frases útiles** box and watch the video again.

Complete the **Comprensión** section that follows the **Palabras y frases útiles**.

Now you are ready to listen to the **Tutor cassette**. The cassette will take you through the exercises in this unit section by section.

When you have completed the language exercises in each section, study the **Business Notes** at the end of the unit for further information on business and industry in Spain.

1

BANKING ON ACTION

Sección 1

Banco NatWest abre una nueva oficina en Madrid.

PALABRAS Y FRASES UTILES

02.13   Lee estas palabras y frases antes de ver el vídeo.

noche = night	dirigir = to address	nueva = new
primero = first	palabra = word	sede = headquarters
dar = to give	todo = all	encantado = delighted
segundo = second	bienvenida = welcome	

Buenas noches	Good evening
dar las gracias	to thank
en segundo lugar	secondly
(Quisiera) presentarles a Lord Alexander	(I would like) to introduce you to Lord Alexander
. . . con motivo de la inauguración	. . . on the occasion of the inauguration
¿Qué tal?	How are things?
¿Cómo estás?	How are you?
Encantado	Delighted
¿Qué tal la visita con . . . ?	How was the visit with . . . ?
. . . aquel cliente	. . . that client
bastante bien/mal	quite well/bad

Elige la respuesta correcta.

1 El cóctel es por la mañana/por la noche.

2 En el cóctel, quiere dirigir unas palabras
el Presidente del banco./Lord Alexander.

3 El motivo del cóctel es la inauguración
de la sede del Banco NatWest
en Inglaterra./en España.

4 Manolo es el jefe de calidad de
servicios del Banco NatWest./
el secretario de Lord Alexander.

5 Manolo responde a la presentación de
Maribel: Hola. ¿Cómo estás Maribel?/
Buenas noches.

6 El nombre de la otra persona es
Fernando./José.

7 Fernando responde al saludo de Manolo:
¿Qué hay? Encantado./¡Adiós!

8 ¿Qué tal, Manolo? ¿Cómo estás? Bastante
bien./mal.

9 Manolo y Mariano hablan de
un cliente./un amigo.

10 ¿Qué tal la visita con aquel cliente?
Pues bastante bien./mal.

APLICACION

• E S   A S I •

G1 Masculino y feminino

In Spanish all nouns are either masculine or
feminine. A general rule of thumb is that nouns
ending in **o** are masculine while nouns ending in

a are feminine. The definite article (the) is **el** for
masculine nouns and **la** for feminine nouns. The
plural of **el** is **los**, and the plural of **la** is **las**.
Here are some examples from the sequence.

las visitas	el cálculo
la propuesta	los bancos
la bienvenida	el motivo

¿El, la, los o las?

Escribe el artículo correcto.

1	...... oferta	7	...... compañías
2	...... libro	8	...... factura
3	...... dinero	9	...... negocio
4	...... empresas	10	...... pedido
5	...... empleados	11	...... demanda
6	...... teléfono	12	...... mercado

Completa

Pon el artículo correcto. Usa estas palabras.

> del • El • la • los • la • del • al
> las • la • los • las • la

..... Presidente (de) .... banco NatWest da
.... gracias a .... invitados (a) ......
cóctel. Lord Alexander dirige ...... palabra a
.... señoras y .... señores en ...... fiesta
con motivo de ...... inauguración de ......
nueva sede (de) .... banco NatWest.

Completa

Mira el vídeo y escribe la palabra correcta.

> Qué• Buenas • Qué • Muy • Cómo • Hola

1 ¿ .... tal Mariano?
2 ¿ .... estás?
3 ¿ .... hay?
4 ...., ¿cómo estás Maribel?
5 .... bien.
6 .... noches

Relaciona

Ejemplo: **1f**
El cóctel es en la nueva sede del banco.

1 El cóctel es en . . .   **a** mal.
2 Hola, te presento . . .   **b** con aquel
                                     cliente?
3 ¿Qué tal?   **c** darles la
                                     bienvenida.
4 ¿Qué tal la visita . . .   **d** a María.
5 Pues, bastante . . .   **e** Encantada.
6 Es un honor . . .   **f** la nueva sede
                                     del banco.

• E S   A S I •

G2 In Spanish there are two verbs 'to be': **ser** and **estar**. Study these uses of the two verbs in the sequence:

*Lord Alexander **está** con nosotros . . .*
*Señores y señoras, **es** para mí . . .*
*Hola, ¿cómo **estás** Maribel?*
*Manolo **es** el jefe de calidad.*

estar   to be

Singular		Plural	
yo	**estoy**	nosotros	**estamos**
tú	**estás**	vosotros	**estáis**
él		ellos	
ella	**está**	ellas	**están**
usted		ustedes	

ser   to be

Singular		Plural	
yo	**soy**	nosotros	**somos**
tú	**eres**	vosotros	**sois**
él		ellos	
ella	**es**	ellas	**son**
usted		ustedes	

Completa

¿Ser o estar?   Pon la forma correcta del verbo *ser* o *estar*.

1 Yo .... el presidente de la compañía.
2 La sede de la compañía .... en Madrid.
3 Mi nombre .... Peter Weston.
4 ¿Cómo .... ustedes?
5 Alicia y Esther Koplovitz .... dos mujeres de negocios españolas.
6 Madrid .... la capital de España.
7 Lord Alexander .... en un cóctel.
8 El producto .... bueno.
9 ¿Vosotros .... los representantes?
10 Yo .... inglés.

Estudia

Lee el siguiente texto y estudia las preguntas.

Hoy el banco NatWest abre una nueve sede en Madrid, la capital de España. Lord Alexander, presidente de NatWest Bank plc, dirige unas palabras a los invitados al cóctel de inauguración.

♦ **¿Qué** banco abre una nueva sede?
• El Banco NatWest.

♦ **¿Cuándo** abre la nueva sede?
• Hoy.

♦ **¿Dónde?**
• En Madrid.

♦ **¿Quién** dirige unas palabras a los invitados?
• Lord Alexander.

♦ **¿Cuál** es su posición?
• Es presidente de NatWest Bank plc.

Completa

Pon la palabra correcta.

1 ¿................ banco abre una nueva sede?

2 ¿................... está la nueva sede del banco?

3 ¿................ es el presidente de NatWest Bank plc?

4 ¿................. está Lord Alexander ahora?

5 ¿................. es la posición de Lord Alexander en NatWest plc?

6 ¿................. es la presentación?

Repasa

Mira el vídeo otra vez y completa los díalogos.

1 ♦ H......... , buenos días.
  • Hola, ¿q...... tal?

2 ♦ Te p.................... a Maribel.
  • H......... , ¿cómo e............ ?
  ♦ E...................... .

3 ♦ ¿Q...... t...... , Mariano?
  • ¿Qué tal, Manolo? ¿C.........
    e............?
  ♦ B.................... bien.

Contesta

1 ¿Quién quiere dirigir unas palabras a las señoras y los señores del cóctel?

2 ¿Cuál es el motivo del cóctel?

3 ¿Quién es Manolo?

4 ¿Qué responde Manolo cuando le presentan a Maribel?

5 ¿Cuál es el nombre de la segunda persona que le presentan?

6 ¿Qué responde Fernando al saludo de Manolo?

7 ¿Cómo saluda Manolo a Mariano?

8 ¿Qué responde Mariano?

9 ¿De quién hablan?

10 ¿Qué tal la visita con él?

Sección 2

Una reunión en las oficinas de Action Computer para presentar un nuevo folleto.

PALABRAS Y FRASES UTILES

05.10 Lee estas palabras y frases antes de ver el vídeo.

fácil = easy	éxito = success	principal = main
reunión = meeting	copiar = to copy	tema = subject
último = last	catálogo = catalogue	peligro = danger
tríptico = form in three parts	lanzar = to launch	tamaño = size
ejemplares = copies	entrevista = interview	expediente = file

el propósito de esta reunión	the purpose of this meeting
deseamos lanzar ahora otro flyer	we now want to launch/distribute another flyer
Vamos a utilizar el mismo formato	We are going to use the same format
Damos un mensaje que es . . .	We are sending out the message that it is . . .
y también advertimos en cuanto al peligro	and we are also pointing out the danger
ya hemos estado hablando en otras reuniones	we've been discussing this in other meetings
. . . y lo ideal es que lancemos . . .	. . . and the best thing is to distribute . . .
He seleccionado diez sectores	I have chosen ten sectors
ya están comprando por nuestro catálogo	they are already buying through our catalogue
Tenemos una entrevista con el señor Breden	We have a meeting with Mr Breden
pueden subir al primero izquierda	you can go up to the first floor on the left
¿Me podrías traer el expediente de . . . ?	Could you bring me the file on . . . ?
¿Os apetece un café?	Would you like a coffee?

COMPRENSION

Elige la respuesta correcta.

1 El propósito de la reunión es considerar el último tríptico promocional./ catálogo.
2 Con el flyer anterior experimentaron un éxito tremendo./un fracaso tremendo.
3 El fin del flyer es dirigir atención a las impresoras láser./el catálogo principal.
4 El catálogo circulando es el número catorce./dos.
5 Lo ideal es que lancemos treinta mil ejemplares del flyer./diez ejemplares del flyer.
6 La entrevista con David Breden es por la mañana./por la tarde.
7 David Breden quiere el expediente de Action Computers./del Banco NatWest.
8 Francisco toma el café con leche sin azúcar./con leche con azúcar.

APLICACION

• E S   A S I •

G3 In Spanish, all verbs end in either **-ar**, **-er** or **-ir**. The formation of verbs depends on these endings. Verbs ending in **-ar** are formed as follows in the present tense:

hablar to talk/speak

Singular		Plural	
yo	habl**o**	nosotros	habl**amos**
tú	habl**as**	vosotros	habl**áis**
él		ellos	
ella	habl**a**	ellas	habl**an**
usted		ustedes	

Study the use of **-ar** verbs in the sequence:

*. . . o como lo **llamamos** normalmente . . .*
*Como sabéis **experimentamos** un éxito . . .*
*. . . te **presento** a Maribel*

Completa

Pon la forma correcta de los verbos que están entre paréntesis.

1 Yo no .... que es prudente. (*considerar*)
2 Juan .... a María por teléfono. (*llamar*)
3 ¿Vosotras .... comenzar la reunión a las tres? (*desear*)
4 Ellos .... impresoras láser. (*utilizar*)
5 Las compañías de automóviles .... nuevos modelos en septiembre. (*lanzar*)
6 Yo .... a una compañía inglesa de productos químicos. (*representar*)
7 El color rojo .... peligro. (*indicar*)

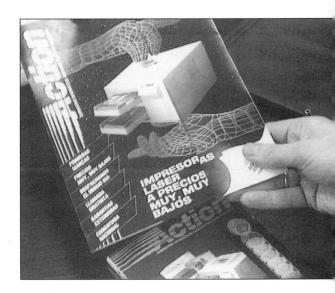

8 Lo siento, yo no .... español. (*hablar*)

9 Los competidores .... las ideas de Action Computer. (*copiar*)

10 Nosotros .... ordenadores por catálogo. (*comprar*)

• E S   A S I •

Numbers in Spanish are the following:

0	cero				
1	uno	11	once	21	veintiuno
2	dos	12	doce	22	veintidós
3	tres	13	trece	33	treinta y tres
4	cuatro	14	catorce	44	cuarenta y cuatro
5	cinco	15	quince	55	cincuenta y cinco
6	seis	16	dieciséis	66	sesenta y seis
7	siete	17	diecisiete	77	setenta y siete
8	ocho	18	dieciocho	88	ochenta y ocho
9	nueve	19	diecinueve	99	noventa y nueve
10	diez	20	veinte	100	cien/ciento

¿Verdadero o falso?

Mira el vídeo otra vez. ¿Aparecen estos números?

1 diez
2 cincuenta
3 treinta y siete
4 tres
5 dieciocho
6 catorce
7 cuatro
8 noventa y nueve
9 treinta
10 ochenta y tres

• E S   A S I •

Numbers from 200 in Spanish are the following:

200	doscientos
400	cuatrocientos
500	quinientos
700	setecientos
900	novecientos
1.000	mil
7.000	siete mil
12.000	doce mil
30.000	treinta mil
100.000	cien mil
500.000	quinientos mil
600.000	seis cientos mil
700.000	setecientos mil
900.000	novecientos mil
1.000.000	un millón

Números

Escribe las cantidades.

Ejemplos:
526 = *quinientos veintiséis*
Cinco mil cuarenta y uno = *5.041*

1 8.759
2 Novecientos tres
3 14.715
4 Setecientos uno
5 5.706.024
6 Seis mil trescientos ochenta y cuatro
7 150.014
8 Ciento sesenta y ocho
9 7.777
10 Noventa millones novecientos noventa mil nueve

Escribe el número

Mira el vídeo otra vez y completa cada frase con un número.

Ejemplo:
El catálogo ...... ya está circulando.
*El catálogo **catorce** ya está circulando.*

1 Es una impresión en tamaño A .....
  desplegable.
2 En un papel de ...... gramos.
3 Y lo ideal es que lancemos ...... ejemplares.
4 He seleccionado ...... sectores.
5 En empresas ¿eh? He seleccionado
  estos ....
6 Empleados de más de ......

● E S A S I ●

G1 The indefinite articles (a/an) in Spanish are **un** for masculine nouns and **una** for feminine nouns. The plural of **un** is **unos** and the plural of **una** is **unas**. Listen to the two video sequences again and notice how they are used.

*. . . perdón que interrumpa **un minuto***
*. . . les quiere dirigir **unas palabras***
*. . . experimentamos **un éxito** tremendo*
*Todos tenéis **una copia** de la agenda*

Repasa

Pon la forma correcta de los artículos definidos e indefinidos y de los verbos *(ser/estar)* en las siguientes frases.
Ejemplo:
Richard Branson y Lord Hanson ....
empresarios ingleses.
*Richard Branson y Lord Hanson **son unos** empresarios ingleses.*

1 Francisco .... director de ventas
  de .... compañía en Madrid.
2 .... oficina de ...... Calle Alcalá .... en
  .... edificio moderno.
3 Exporta SA .... compañía
  de exportación.
4 John Wright y Paul Giddings ....
  clientes ingleses.

5 .... Banco NatWest ofrece ....
  servicios inmejorables.
6 .... propuestas de la compañía
  inglesa .... muy interesantes.
7 Fernando y Roger .... en
  .... cóctel de NatWest.
8 María y Elena ....
  secretarias muy eficientes.

● E S A S I ●

In Spanish, telephone numbers are read either as single numbers or in pairs.
490386 = *cuatro-nueve-cero-tres-ocho-seis*
OR *cuarenta y nueve-cero-tres-ochenta y seis*

¿Dígame?

El servicio que permite comunicarse con España sin problemas de idiomas. Con ''España Directo'' su llamada será atendida directamente en castellano. Sin problemas de dinero, ni de cambio... ya que su llamada se abonará a cobro revertido.
Solamente marcando el número indicado desde:

ALEMANIA	0130 80 0034	ARGENTINA	0034 800 44 4111	
BELGICA	11 0034	CANADA	1800 463 8255	
DINAMARCA	800 1 0034	CHILE	00* 0334	
FINLANDIA	9800 1 0340	COLOMBIA	980 34 0057	
FRANCIA	19* 0034	EE.UU. (ATT)	1800 24SPAIN	
HOLANDA	060 22 0034	EE.UU. (MCI)	1800 9 ESPANA	
IRLANDA	1800 55 0034	GUATEMALA	191	
ITALIA	172 0034	MEXICO	*234	
NORUEGA	05 01 9934	REP. DOMINICANA	1800 333 0234	
PORTUGAL	05 05 0034	URUGUAY	000 434	
REINO UNIDO	0800 89 0034			
SUECIA	020 79 9934	AUSTRALIA	001 488 1340	
		FILIPINAS**	1 0534	
* Espere segundo tono.		INDONESIA	008 0134	
** Sólo ciudades importantes.		JAPON	003 9341	

¡Póngase al habla con España!

☎ Telefónica

Mira los números para llamar a España y contesta las siguientes preguntas.

1 ¿Qué número marco para llamar desde Alemania?
2 ¿El número 980 34 0057 corresponde a qué país?
3 Para llamar desde el Reino Unido, ¿qué número marco?
4 ¿En qué país estás si marcas el número 1800 55 0034?
5 Desde Francia, ¿qué debo esperar después de marcar el número 19?

• E S A S I •

G4 Verb endings of **-er** and **-ir** verbs change following a similar pattern to **-ar** verbs. However, many **-er** and **-ir** verbs are irregular.

creer to believe/think

Singular		Plural	
yo	cre**o**	nosotros	cre**emos**
tú	cre**es**	vosotros	cre**éis**
él		ellos	
ella }	cre**e**	ellas }	cre**en**
usted		ustedes	

subir to go up/raise

Singular		Plural	
yo	sub**o**	nosotros	sub**imos**
tú	sub**es**	vosotros	sub**ís**
él		ellos	
ella }	sub**e**	ellas }	sub**en**
usted		ustedes	

Study the use of **-er** and **-ir** verbs in the sequence.

*Como **sabéis** experimentamos un éxito*
*. . . **decimos**, es fácil de copiar,*
*. . . y también **advertimos** en cuanto . . .*
*Estos señores **tienen** una entrevista con . . .*
*Si pueden **subir** al primero izquierda . . .*

Completa

Pon la forma correcta de los verbos que están entre paréntesis.

1 Nosotros .... el pedido todos los meses. (*repetir*)
2 La secretaria .... los expedientes de Action Computer. (*traer*)
3 El director .... hablar español. (*saber*)
4 ¿Tú no .... al nuevo director? (*conocer*)

5 El director del banco .... que no .... el crédito. (*decir/conceder*)
6 ¿Qué .... vosotros? (*preferir*)
7 El señor Morton .... que España ...... un país ideal para invertir. (*creer/ser*)
8 Las tarifas de avión .... durante los meses de julio y agosto. (*subir*)
9 La compañía .... beneficios el 31 de diciembre. (*repartir*)
10 Las sucursales de Sevilla y Córdoba .... las facturas con mucho retraso. (*recibir*)

Apunta

1 Mira la solicitud de suscripción al catálogo de Action Computer y estudia las respuestas de Julio Bravo.
Hola. Mi nombre es Julio Bravo. Soy el jefe de ventas de la compañía El Lino SA. Soy el responsable de compras. La sede de la compañía está en la Avenida del Mediterráneo 106, Alcoy, en la provincia de Valencia. En la compañía trabajan 80 personas. Mi número de teléfono es el 37 3839. El número de fax es el 21 2265.

Nombre:	*Julio Bravo*
Cargo:	*Jefe de Ventas*
Empresa:	*Telas El Lino SA*
Dirección:	*Avenida del Mediterráneo 106, Alcoy*
Cód. Postal: *20112*	**Provincia:** *Valencia*
Nº Teléfono: *(96) 373839*	
Nº Fax: *(96) 212265*	
Nº de empleados: *80*	
¿Es usted el responsable de compras?	**Sí** **No**

2 Ahora lee este párrafo sobre Ana Márquez y rellena la solicitud con sus datos.
Buenos días. Soy Ana Márquez y soy la directora comercial de la compañía Ibertel SA pero no soy responsable de compras. Trabajo en las oficinas principales que están en la calle Raimundo Fernández Villaverde, 37, 20172 Madrid. La empresa tiene más o menos 350 empleados. El número de

*teléfono de mi oficina es el 321 45 39 y el
número de fax es el 321 45 45.*

Nombre:	
Cargo:	
Empresa:	
Dirección:	
Cód. Postal:	**Provincia:**
Nº Teléfono:	
Nº Fax:	
Nº de empleados:	
¿Es usted el responsable de compras?	**Sí No**

3 Ahora rellena la siguiente solicitud con
tus datos y escribe una breve descripción.

Nombre:	
Cargo:	
Empresa:	
Dirección:	
Cód. Postal:	**Provincia:**
Nº Teléfono:	
Nº Fax:	
Nº de empleados:	
¿Es usted el responsable de compras?	**Sí No**

Contesta

1 ¿Cuál es el propósito de la reunión?
2 ¿Cómo llaman normalmente al tríptico?
3 ¿Con qué flyer experimentan un éxito tremendo?
4 ¿Cuál es el fin del flyer que desean lanzar ahora?
5 ¿Cuál es el número del catálogo en circulación?
6 ¿Qué dice el mensaje?
7 ¿Quién tienen una entrevista con David Breden?
8 ¿Qué quiere ver el agente de seguridad?
9 ¿Qué expediente quiere David Breden?
10 ¿Cómo toma el café Francisco?

RECUERDA

In this unit you have studied:

- the use of definite and indefinite articles
  El *negocio es* **un** *éxito.*
- the use of some question words
  ¿Quién *es el inventor del teléfono?*
  Alexander Graham Bell.
- how to say numbers
  7.923. 574 = *siete millones novecientos veintitrés mil quinientos setenta y cuatro*
- the present tense of **ser** and **estar**
  ¿Dónde **está** *su oficina?*
  Está *en Madrid.*

  *¿***Eres** *inglés?*
  No, **soy** *americano.*

- the present tense of **-ar**, **-er** and **-ir** verbs
  Yo **hablo** *español.*
  El **vende** *casas.*
  Ellas **escriben** *los informes.*
- to give specific information about
yourself and your company
  Mi nombre *es . . .*
  En la compañía trabajan *20 personas.*
  El número de teléfono *es el 332 54 78.*

Before going on to the next unit, revise the
exercises and the vocabulary and make
sure you have not only understood all the
grammar points but that you know how to
use them.

Business Notes

BANKING IN SPAIN

The Bank of Spain (Banco de España) is Spain's central bank, responsible for supervising the country's banking and monetary system. In this role, it performs similar functions to central banks in other EC countries. Private banks have multiplied to approximately 140 since 1985, although half of these are regional or local rather than national in character. They are small by world standards but have been extremely profitable in recent years. There has, however, been a squeeze in margins in 1990 and 1991 as the Spanish boom calms down. Traditionally, the banks have not been internationally minded, but this has changed rapidly since 1986, with alliances being forged with foreign banks (as in the video sequence) as expansion has taken place into foreign markets, and with diversification into a broader range of financial services leading, for instance, to the establishment of investment banking divisions. The main strengths of Spanish banks have been their strong capital and healthy reserves, while their principal weakness is high labour costs through an overcapacity in branches, estimated by some to be as high as 30%.

Alongside the private banks are the savings banks *(cajas de ahorros)* which may be privately or publicly owned but are run as non-profit-making foundations, somewhat similar to the building societies in the UK. Their importance can be gauged from a comparison of the different banking institutions (see table).

Banking institutions in Spain

	NO. OF INSTITUTIONS	NO. OF OFFICES	% TOTAL DEPOSITS	% TOTAL LOANS
Banco de España	1	53	0.2	15.1
Banks	135	16,062	61.0	51.8
Cajas	80	11,787	34.7	23.0
Others (e.g. cooperative credit agencies)	155	3,221	4.1	10.1
Total	371	31,123	100.0	100.0

(Source: *Banco de España*)

The regional governments have been promoting the regional savings banks, and the trend is toward merger, with the biggest merger to date being between La Caixa and Caixa de Barcelona in July 1990, which created the largest financial entity in Spain and the second largest savings bank in Europe, by deposits, after La Cassa di Rispermo delle Provincie Lombarde in Italy.

In 1991, the private banks in Spain reacted in alarm at the creation by central government of a state 'megabank', the Corporación Bancaria de España (CBE). The CBE represents an attempt by government to establish a Spanish bank of European dimensions. In other EC countries, the state banks have had greater weight than in Spain (state banking represents only 13% of the system in Spain, compared with 30% in Germany). The private banks feared that the CBE would monopolise finance for the state sector in a country where 40% of GDP is controlled by the government.

Mergermania has taken hold of Spanish banks as the government pressurises link-ups by offering practical inducements, e.g. a 99% exemption on capital gains tax, payable after a revaluation of assets. The biggest merger to date, between Banco Central and Banco Hispanoamericano in 1991, has created the biggest bank in Spain, the Banco Central Hispanoamericano (BCH), which has overtaken the Banco Bilbao Vizcaya (BBV). BBV's profile typifies the leading Spanish banks: it has important stakes in three of Spain's principal electrical companies; it owns a variety of firms in the food industry, including Kas and the Savin wine group; BBV is the biggest client of INI, the state holding company; and in recent years it has been buying firms in strategically vital areas of industry.

Despite government pressure for greater concentration through mergers, Spanish banks continue to open new branches in an attempt perhaps to dissuade foreign penetration. Spain has roughly three times as many branches as Germany and twice as many as France.

FOREIGN BANKS AND OPPORTUNITIES IN SPAIN

The Spanish banks' extensive network of branches is, paradoxically, why foreign banks have been buying up or into Spain. The domestic banks are basically strong, have made large investments in new technology, but are still not internationally oriented. Restrictions on foreign banks in Spain have been gradually lifted to permit forty banks to operate (twenty from the EC), while ten Spanish banks are foreign controlled.

The opening of Banco NatWest's new headquarters, seen in the video sequence, represents a further stage in NatWest's penetration of the Spanish market. National Westminster Bank is a 99.4% shareholder in Banco NatWest España, and this sizeable interest provides banking facilities in over 200 branches throughout the Spanish mainland. Banco NatWest has over 120 of these, with the subsidiary organisation, Banco de Asturias accounting for the remaining branches.

The network is focused on Spain's major industrial and financial cities: Madrid, Barcelona, Valencia, Zaragoza, Bilbao and Seville. However, the bank is also well represented on the Costa del Sol and the Costa Brava, and has a growing presence in Alicante, Santander and the regions of Asturias and Galicia.

Banco NatWest España is primarily geared to providing a service to the retail, small and medium-sized business sectors of the market. In addition, it supplies a comprehensive facility for personal account holders through its wide branch network. It also has in-depth experience of mortgage finance and Spanish property purchase procedures, which can often be complicated.

A number of foreign banks had already acquired Spanish banks in the early 1980s when the Spanish banking system underwent a crisis. Citibank and Barclays bought into Spain at that time, and the Deutsche Bank also took complete control of the ailing Banco Comercial Transatlántico in 1989. The Barclays story is an interesting one. Having opened hundreds of small branches across the country, Barclays have succeeded in making headway in the profitable retail market by offering interest on a range of current accounts well ahead of their Spanish rivals. However, the launch in 1990 by the Banco de Santander, Spain's most aggressive and internationally oriented bank, of the *supercuentas*, or interest-bearing current accounts, which was quickly copied by other banks, has led to a highly competitive situation. Ironically, the Banco de Santander is linked with the Royal Bank of Scotland which, without the resources available to a giant like NatWest, sought a different solution to the problem of establishing itself in Europe.

The Royal Bank and Santander came into contact when each was looking for an equal partner with whom to expand in Europe. They knew they had no competing activities in each other's markets and soon discovered they were of similar size and outlook. The result, a highly informal partnership leading to closer ties as the two sides got to know each other, is a strategy that could be adopted by all sorts of companies that want a European network without exposure to risks. The scope of the agreement between the Royal Bank and Santander includes cooperation in Britain and Spain, linking up their computerised fund transfer network, joint ventures in other European territories and pooling information outside Europe. Their retail networks stay separate. The basis of the third country joint ventures was a couple of virtually inactive banks Santander owned in Belgium and Germany, CC Bank Belge and CC Bank. Royal Bank has taken stakes in them, and the partnership has bought into operations in Portugal and Gibraltar.

OPPORTUNITIES IN INSURANCE

There has been a convergence of banking and insurance interests in Spain as the growth of life insurance business has attracted banks, while the distribution networks of banks have attracted insurance companies. There are a large number of small insurance firms in Spain, many of them owned by the banks, although the insurance market, dominated by vehicle insurance, is quite small (total premiums in 1986 were only 2.2% of GDP compared with a UK figure of 8%). About one half of the industry is in the hands of foreigners, whether through overseas offices or participation in Spanish companies. Thus BUPA owns Sanitas; Norwich Union acquired Plus Ultra from BBV in 1990; Scottish Widows began a joint venture in 1990 with Spain's second largest private medical insurer, Previasa. Foreign accountancy firms have also begun to penetrate the Spanish market.

OBTAINING FINANCING

The video sequence shows Action Computers going to NatWest for advice and expertise and as a source of finance. Obviously, as in the UK, the Spanish private banks are the major source of short- and long-term financing for industry. They generally do not specialise; each is normally prepared to offer most of the usual banking services. They are grouped into 'industrial' and 'commercial' banks. Most of the principal banks are commercial banks that may have industrial bank affiliates. Industrial banks specialise in providing medium- and long-term financing to new and growth companies.

Commercial banks generally provide loans for periods ranging from three to six months, which are usually renewable. It is common business practice to discount unaccepted drafts with commercial banks and in this way obtain more or less permanent bank financing. The savings banks also operate this practice and provide much of the finance for blue-chip companies and for private housing purchases.

Apart from the central bank, there are four public banks under the control of the Ministry of Economy and Finance which provide loans at favourable rates of interest. They are as follows:

1 Banco Hipotecario de España: finances public works, construction, housing, ship-building, educational facilities, and lends businesses up to 70% of the cost of investment projects.
2 Banco de Crédito Industrial: lends to growth industries and grants loans for working capital.
3 Banco de Crédito Agrícola: lends to farmers and agricultural cooperatives.
4 Banco de Crédito Local: finances local authorities, public transport and water supply systems.

LAYING FOUNDATIONS

Study Plan

SEQUENCE SUMMARY

THE BRITISH PAVILION AT THE EXPO '92 SITE IS BEING BUILT BY TRAFALGAR HOUSE CONSTRUCTION MANAGEMENT. JOSÉ CARLOS, THE COMPANY'S LANGUAGE INSTRUCTOR IN SEVILLE, IS BEING SHOWN ROUND THE BUILDING UNDER CONSTRUCTION.

WHAT YOU WILL LEARN

Sección 1	*Sección 2*
• how to describe a product in simple terms • how to express dimensions, volume, capacity • how to use numbers in context	• how to give and check directions • how to say what you are going to do • how to ask some more questions
Sección 3	*Business Notes*
• how to name countries and nationalities • how to say where things are	The construction industry in Spain Other opportunities for larger companies Hotel groups

LEARNING STRATEGY FOR EACH SECTION

Study the key words in the **Palabras y frases útiles** box and watch the video sequence, listening out for the key words. Make notes of what you have understood.

Then study the key phrases in the **Palabras y frases útiles** box and watch the video again.

Complete the **Comprensión** section that follows the Palabras y frases útiles.

Now you are ready to listen to the **Tutor cassette**. The cassette will take you through the exercises in this unit section by section.

When you have completed the language exercises in each section, study the **Business Notes** at the end of the unit for further information on business and industry in Spain.

2

LAYING FOUNDATIONS

Sección 1

En el recinto ferial de Sevilla se reunen muchas naciones, formando así una nueva ciudad de pabellones. La compañía Trafalgar House construye el pabellón británico. José Carlos es un profesor de lengua y enseña a los empleados de la compañía.

PALABRAS Y FRASES UTILES

10.44 Lee estas palabras y frases antes de ver el vídeo.

pabellón = pavilion	trabajador = worker	cristal = glass
estructuras = structures	caída = fall	película = film
hormigón = concrete	cortina = curtain	construcción = building
de ancho = in width	grande = big	norte = north

¿Podemos echar un vistazo?	Can we have a look?
Toma un casco	Take a hard hat
ahora te lo enseño	I'll show it to you now
tiene setenta metros de largo	it's seventy metres long
tiene cuarenta de ancho	it's forty metres wide
Me han dicho	I've been told
va a ser . . .	it's going to be . . .
el agua estará cayendo	the water will be cascading
se ha traído desde el Reino Unido	it has been brought from Great Britain
por carretera desde allí	by road from there

COMPRENSION

¿Verdadero o falso?

1 La construcción tiene tres estructuras diferenciadas. *V/F*
2 Una estructura es de hormigón. *V/F*
3 El pabellón tiene setenta metros de largo. *V/F*
4 Tiene cuarenta de ancho. *V/F*
5 Los paneles solares están en la parte superior. *V/F*
6 Tienen cien trabajadores. *V/F*
7 Todos los trabajadores son españoles. *V/F*
8 La cortina de agua tiene veinte metros de largo y setenta de altura. *V/F*
9 El material de construcción viene del Reino Unido. *V/F*
10 El material viene desde Santander en barco. *V/F*

APLICACION

● E S   A S I ●

tener to have

Singular		Plural	
yo	**tengo**	nosotros	**tenemos**
tú	**tienes**	vosotros	**tenéis**
él		ellos	
ella	**tiene**	ellas	**tienen**
usted		ustedes	

Completa

Mira el vídeo otra vez. Identifica la forma del verbo *tener*.

1 .... dos estructuras diferenciadas.
2 El pabellón .... setenta metros de largo.
3 .... cuarenta de ancho.
4 ¿Cuántos trabajadores ....?

5 Ahora mismo .... setenta trabajadores.
6 .... setenta metros de largo y veinte de altura.

● E S   A S I ●

Watch the video again and note how Pedro Arozamena talks about the dimensions of the British pavilion. Look at these examples.

- *¿Cuánto mide de alto?/¿Qué altura tiene el pabellón británico?*
- *Mide 25 metros de alto./Tiene una altura de 25 metros.*
- *¿Cuánto mide de ancho?/¿Qué anchura tiene?*
- *Mide 40 metros de ancho./Tiene una anchura de 40 metros.*
- *¿Cuánto mide de largo?/¿Qué largo (longitud) tiene?*
- *Mide 70 metros de largo./Tiene 70 metros de largo (longitud).*

¿Cuánto mide?

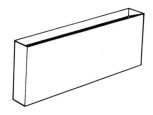

Esta caja tiene:
- 2 metros de alto.
- 50 centímetros de ancho.
- 4 metros de largo.

La piscina tiene:
- 80 centímetros de profundidad.
- 3 metros de profundidad.

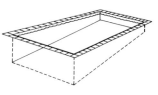

Este computador portátil pesa solamente 8 kilos.

Una moneda de 100 pesetas pesa 10 gramos.

El recinto ferial de la Expo '92 tiene una extensión de 2.150.000 metros cuadrados.

2,150,000

¿Cómo es?

Pregunta y responde sobre las dimensiones de los objetos que tienes en los dibujos.

Ejemplo:

- ¿Cuánto mide la Torre Eiffel de alto?
- ◆ Mide 320 metros de alto.

1 una lata de sardinas

2 una furgoneta

2m

5m

2m

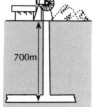

700m

3 una mina

Se venden Oficinas 300 metros cuadrados.

4 las oficinas

¿Sabías que . . . ?

Elige la respuesta correcta.

1 El canal de Panamá tiene una longitud de:
  a 100 kilómetros.
  b 37 kilómetros.
  c 64 kilómetros.

2 El océano Pacífico tiene una profundidad máxima de:
  a 5.098 metros.
  b 11.033 metros.
  c 9.547 metros.

3 España cubre una área de:
  a 450.983 kilómetros cuadrados.
  b 596.740 kilómetros cuadrados.
  c 504.750 kilómetros cuadrados.

4 La torre panorámica tiene:
  a 90 metros de alto.
  b 135 metros de alto.
  c 200 metros de alto.

5 Una onza son:
  a 20,06 gramos.
  b 28,35 gramos.
  c 30,10 gramos.

6 Un contenedor tiene:
  a 2 metros 40 de ancho.
  b 3 metros de ancho.
  c 3 metros 50 de ancho.

● E S A S I ●

G5 **poder**   to be able to (can)

Singular		Plural	
yo	**puedo**	nosotros	**podemos**
tú	**puedes**	vosotros	**podéis**
él		ellos	
ella	**puede**	ellas	**pueden**
usted		ustedes	

Look at the use of the verb **poder** in the sequence.

*¿**Puedo** ver al señor Arozamena?*
*¿**Podemos** echar un vistazo al pabellón británico?*

¿Puedes . . . ?

Pon la forma correcta del verbo *poder*.
Asocia cada frase con el dibujo apropiado.

a ¿ .... repetir su nombre por favor?
b El jefe de personal no .... venir a la reunión, está enfermo.
c ¿ .... ver?
d ¿ .... telefonear?
e Nosotros no .... llegar hasta la próxima semana, hay huelga de aviones.
f ¿ .... hablar más despacio? No entiendo nada.
g Lo siento, no .... aceptar su tarjeta. Está caducada.

Comprensión

1 ¿A dónde llega José Carlos?
2 ¿Qué quiere hacer?
3 ¿Todos los trabajadores son británicos?
4 ¿De dónde viene el material de la construcción?
5 ¿Cuál es la característica de la cortina de agua?
6 ¿Cómo se llama el ingeniero jefe del pabellón británico?
7 ¿De qué dos materiales son las dos estructuras?
8 ¿Cuántos metros de largo tiene el pabellón?
9 ¿Y cuántos de ancho?
10 ¿Cuántos trabajadores hay?

Sección 2

Desde el primer piso José tiene une idea de cómo va ser el pabellón una vez terminado.

PALABRAS Y FRASES UTILES

13.43 Lee estas palabras y frases antes de ver el vídeo.

explicar = explain	teatro = theatre	fuego = fire
abierto = open	medio = middle	elementos = elements
allí = over there	agujero = hole	conducto = pipe
puente = bridge	tierra = earth	aire acondicionado = air conditioning
rampa = ramp	aire = air	torre = tower

cómo va a funcionar el pabellón	how the pavilion is going to work
el público va a entrar por ese puente	the public are going to come in over that bridge
¿Y van a poder ver . . . ?	And are they going to be able to see . . . ?
una vez arriba . . .	once upstairs . . .
Allí van a ver una película sobre . . .	There they are going to see a film about . . .
¿ . . . para qué sirve esa estructura metálica?	. . . what is that metal structure for?
¿Y para qué son?	And what are they for?
eso de aquí ¿qué es?	what's this thing over here?

COMPRENSION

1 José Carlos y Pedro están en el área de recepción./el teatro.
2 El público va a entrar por ese puente./por la cortina de agua.
3 En el área de recepción el público va a ver unos vídeos sobre España./unos vídeos sobre el Reino Unido.
4 Van a ver los vídeos durante cinco minutos./quince minutos.
5 En los teatros hay una película sobre el Reino Unido./una representación de Romeo y Julieta.
6 Las dos exhibiciones están en el teatro./en la parte central.
7 La estructura de la parte central está dividida en dos partes./cuatro partes.

8 Hay exhibiciones sobre las cuatro estaciones del año./los cuatro elementos

9 Los conductos son para el aire acondicionado./el fuego

10 En total hay cuatro/tres torres para distribuir el aire acondicionado.

APLICACION

• E S   A S I •

G6 To express a future idea in Spanish, use the verb **ir** followed by **a** and the infinitive of another verb, very much like *to be going to + infinitive* in English. Look at the examples in the **Palabras y frases útiles** above and at the following:

¿Qué vas a hacer mañana? *Voy a celebrar el Año Nuevo.*

¿Cuándo vais a visitar Sevilla? *Vamos a visitar Sevilla en abril.*

ir to go

Singular		Plural	
yo	**voy**	nosotros	**vamos**
tú	**vas**	vosotros	**vais**
él		ellos	
ella	**va**	ellas	**van**
usted		ustedes	

Completa

Mira el vídeo otra vez y completa con la forma correcta del futuro intencional. Comprueba que la respuesta es correcta en la transcripción.

Este área en el que estamos es el área de recepción, y aquí se .... al público que .... por, ves allí el puente. . .
El público .... por ese puente y será recibido aquí y .... unos vídeos sobre el Reino Unido durante cinco minutos.
Bueno, pues ellos después de ser recibidos en este área, ... por esos andenes o rampas mecánicas que ves ahí hacia los teatros, los dos teatros que hay.
Allí ellos .... una película sobre, pues, el Reino Unido y diversos – todavía no está completamente diseñada, hecha la película – y después de visitar los teatros van hacia la parte central donde están las dos exhibiciones.

Responde

Ejemplo:

¿Qué va a hacer? (*visitar*)
Va a visitar el banco.

1 ¿Qué va a hacer?
(*escribir*)

2 ¿Qué va a hacer?
(*enviar*)

3
¿Qué van a hacer?
(firmar)

4
¿Que va a hacer?
(depositar)

5
¿Qué van a hacer?
(vender)

• E S   A S I •

During his visit, José Carlos says:

– *Sí, sí, y ¿**para qué sirve** esa estructura metálica que está ahí . . . ?*
– *Y ¿**para qué son** . . . bueno **esto de aquí qué es**?*

This is how you can ask the purpose of something.

¿Para qué sirve?

A Conecta cada nombre con el objeto.

Ejemplo:
El número siete es un busca.

> una fotocopiadora • un teléfono
> un TV y vídeo • una impresora • un fax
> un ordenador

La oficina portátil

B Con las pistas, di qué es cada objeto y para qué sirve. Usa las frases que están abajo.

Ejemplo:
El precio es de 180.000 a 210.000 pesetas y pesa aproximadamente 1,5 kilos.
Es un TV y vídeo y sirve para ver un programa.

1 El precio es de 150.000 a 1.000.000 pesetas y pesa aproximadamente 3 kilos.
2 El precio es de 50.000 pesetas aproximadamente y pesa 150 gramos.
3 El precio es de 150.000 a 230.000 pesetas y pesa aproximadamente 700 gramos.
4 El precio es aproximadamente 150.000 pesetas y pesa más o menos 3 kilos.
5 El precio es 100.000 pesetas y pesa aproximadamente 2 kilos.
6 El precio es aproximadamente 120.000 pesetas y pesa más o menos 1,4 kilos.

> hacer copias de documentos
> imprimir los documentos del ordenador
> avisar a una persona
> hacer cálculos y escribir informes
> hablar con otra persona
> enviar planos, documentos, etc.

Comprensión

1 ¿Por dónde va a entrar el público al pabellón británico?
2 ¿Qué puede ver el público en el área de recepción?
3 Una vez arriba ¿qué pueden ver?
4 ¿Cuántos teatros hay?
5 ¿Cuáles son los cuatro elementos que menciona el señor Arozamena?
6 ¿Dónde están las dos exhibiciones?
7 ¿Para qué sirven los conductos?
8 ¿Cómo son los conductos?
9 ¿Dónde están situadas las torres que suben el aire acondicionado?

Sección 3

Desde el piso de arriba tenemos una vista panorámica de la Expo y vemos cómo progresan las obras.

PALABRAS Y FRASES UTILES

15.38 Lee estas palabras y frases antes de ver el vídeo.

derecha = right	ahí = over there	allí = there
operativas = operative	mástil = mast	izquierda = left
aquí = here	cubierta = covering	ambos = both
este = this	sombra = shade	lados = sides

Está ya casi acabada	It's nearly finished
¿ . . . detrás del pabellón de Alemania?	. . . behind the German pavilion?
entre esa torrecita y el pabellón negro	between that little tower and the black pavilion
¿ . . . más a la izquierda, esas lonas o velas?	. . . over to the left, what are those pieces of canvas or sails?
. . . están distribuidos a ambos lados de la avenida	. . . are laid out on either side of the avenue
Me ha gustado mucho	I've really enjoyed it
Encantado de haberte conocido	Delighted to have met you

COMPRENSION

Completa.
1 La estación del tren está a la ......
2 La estación está casi ......
3 Por aquí tenemos la zona de pabellones ......
4 Este pabellón de aquí es el pabellón de ......
5 Detrás del pabellón de Alemania está el pabellón de ......

6 El tubo y la torre forman parte del pabellón de ......
7 A la izquierda está la Avenida de ......
8 La Avenida de Europa llega hasta el pabellón de ......
9 Todos los pabellones de la Comunidad Europea están distribuidos a ambos lados de la ......
10 Pues ya se ha terminado la ......

APLICACION

● E S A S I ●

Este es el pabellón de Alemania.
= Es el pabellón alemán.
Ahí está el pabellón de Noruega.
= Es el pabellón noruego
La Avenida llega hasta el pabellón de España.
= La Avenida llega hasta el pabellón español.

alemán, **noruego** and **español** are words which identify nationalities and the language people use. Like all adjectives, there must be agreement with the noun, so:

Helga Kreiser trabaja en el consulado alemán. Ella es alemana.
Kirsta Anderssen es editora de un periódico noruego. Ella es noruega.
Ana Márquez y María López son coordinadoras del pabellón español. Ellas son españolas.
Look up the countries and nationalities that you need to use in a dictionary.

¿Qué nacionalidad?

Empareja cada producto con su nacionalidad y di de qué país es.
Ejemplos:
La tequila El Cuervo es mejicana. Es de Méjico.
Las hamburguesas McDonald's son americanas. Son de los Estados Unidos.

> suizo • japonés • francés
> mejicano • irlandés • italiano
> americano (estadounidense)
> inglés • español • alemán

1 la ropa Benetton
2 los coches BMW

3 el queso Camembert
4 las hamburguesas McDonald's
5 las videocámaras Sony
6 el chocolate Cadbury's
7 la cerveza Guinness
8 el vino de Rioja
9 el reloj Swatch
10 la tequila El Cuervo

Así se dice

Observa el siguiente diálogo y haz lo mismo.

Ejemplo: Mrs Thatcher (francesa)

● _¿Es Mrs Thatcher francesa?_
◆ _No, es inglesa._

1 Pérez de Cuéllar (mejicano)
2 Esther y Alicia Koplovitz (polacas)
3 Jacques Delors (portugués)
4 El rey Juan Carlos y Doña Sofia (italianos)
5 George Bush (canadiense)
6 Anita Roddick (americana)

¿Dónde está?

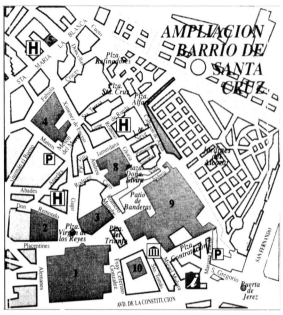

Monumentos:
1. Catedral y Giralda
2. Palacio Arzobispal
3. Convento de la Encarnación
4. Iglesia de Santa Cruz
5. Iglesia de Santa María la Blanca
6. Barrio de Santa Cruz
7. Monumento a Colón
8. Hospital de los Venerables
9. Reales Alcázares
10. Archivo de Indias

A Mira el plano y estudia las frases.

*La plaza Contratación está **en frente de** los Reales Alcázares.*

*La Puerta de Jerez está **al final de** la Calle San Fernando.*

*El Archivo de Indias está **a la derecha de** la Catedral y la Giralda.*

*El Convento de la Encarnación está **a la izquierda** de los Reales Alcázares.*

*La Plaza Virgen de los Reyes está **entre** el Convento de la Encarnación y el Palacio Arzobispal.*

*La Plaza Virgen de los Reyes está **detrás de** la Catedral y Giralda*

B Mira el plano de la planta de exhibición. Con los siguientes datos coloca los stands y servicios que no están.

- Archivosa, muebles de oficina, está en frente de Euroinversión.
- Los servicios están a la izquierda de Archivosa.
- Información está a la derecha de la entrada principal.
- Electrónica Edison está entre Archivosa y Transportes Mercurio.
- Márketing y Publicidad-Marcomás están detrás de Euroinversión.
- Química Curie está entre la entrada principal y Electrónica Edison.

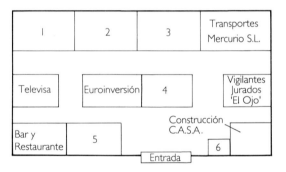

C Mira el plano en la página 63. Lee las pistas y relaciona cada pabellón con el número correspondiente

- El Hotel Príncipe de Asturias está detrás de los pabellones de las Comunidades Autónomas Españolas.
- El pabellón de España está al final de la Avenida de Europa.
- El pabellón de Méjico está a la izquierda de la Avenida de Europa.
- El aparcamiento está entre los edificios de servicios y el terminal del AVE.

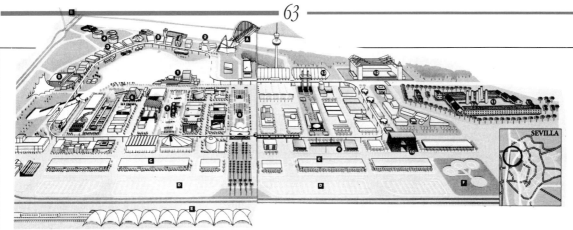

1.   **2.**   **3.**Pabellones de las comunidades autónomas españolas.   **4.**   **5.**Plaza de América.   **6.**
7.Avenida de Europa.   **8.**   **9.**Pabellón de la URSS.   **10.**Pabellón de Japón   **11.**Cartuja de Santa María de las Cuevas.
12. Auditorio   **13.**Pabellón del Futuro.   **A.**Puente de la Barqueta   **B.** Puente del Alamillo
C.Edificios de servicios.   **D.**   **E.**Terminal del AVE   **F.**Helipuerto

- El pabellón de Andalucía está a la derecha de los pabellones de las Comunidades Autónomas Españolas.
- La Avenida de las Palmeras está a la derecha de la Avenida de Europa.

Contesta

1 ¿Dónde está la estación del tren de alta velocidad?

2 ¿Ya está acabada la estación?

3 ¿En qué mes va a llegar el primer tren?

4 ¿Qué va a tener el mástil del pabellón de Alemania?

5 ¿Para qué sirve la cubierta?

6 ¿Qué pabellón está al final de la Avenida de Europa?

7 ¿Dónde están todos los pabellones de la Comunidad Europea?

8 ¿Qué es Siemens?

RECUERDA

In this unit you have studied:

- the present tense of the verb *tener*
  *¿Cuántos trabajadores **tenéis**?*
- how to describe the dimensions of an object
  *La caja **tiene un metro de largo, 50 centímetros de alto y pesa 500 gramos**.*
- the present tense of the verb *poder*
  *¿**Puedo** ver al señor González?*
- how to express a future idea
  ***Vamos a visitar** la fábrica mañana.*

- how to ask what something is and what it is for
  ¿Esto qué es?
  ***¿Para qué sirve** la caja electrónica?*
- how to talk about nationalities
  *SEAT es una compañía **española**.*
  *Coca Cola es un producto **americano**.*
- how to locate places
  *La oficina está **al final de** la calle **a la derecha**.*

Business Notes

THE CONSTRUCTION INDUSTRY IN SPAIN

The video sequence highlights the construction of the British pavilion at Expo '92 by Trafalgar House. The construction industry in Spain, after experiencing severe crisis between 1975 and 1985, is now more powerful than ever, with a workforce of one million and some of the top companies in Spain. The industry contributed a weighty 9% of GDP in 1990, the fifth successive year of significant growth. Companies have benefited from a property boom, especially in Madrid and Barcelona, and from increased government spending on infrastructure, particularly roads, and on public works generally. Housing, leisure and tourism facilities are still being expanded rapidly across the country, not just in the construction boom-towns of Seville, Barcelona and Madrid.

While Seville has witnessed the construction of the Expo pavilion buildings and major infrastructural works, including the high-speed rail link with Madrid, Barcelona has, if anything, been even busier. An estimated 430,000 m² of new office space will have been completed in the two-year period up to mid-1993, one third of which will be outside the city centre. The Olympic Village, built in the city's old industrial area by the waterfront, includes a new hotel and more than 100,000 m² of offices by developer G. Ware Travelstead. On the Avenida Diagonal, one of Barcelona's most famous up-market streets,

Swiss insurance company Winterthur is putting up 48,000 m² of offices in a development which includes a hotel, shops, apartments and parking for 2,300 cars. While opportunities for new development inside Barcelona's core area are restricted, several new business parks are taking shape on the outskirts. The largest is local developer Dorn's Augusta Business Park, which, at 500,000 m², also lays claim to being southern Europe's biggest. At San Cugat, where a new road tunnel was opened in 1991, UK developer Higgs and Hill is busy with a project which will offer 20,000 m² of space in four buildings, set in landscaped grounds.

Madrid has been equally frenetic. Following an office and housing construction boom between 1987 and 1990, an estimated 200,000 m² of top-quality new space was completed in the central business district in 1991, with a further 54,000 m² and 71,000 m² already in the pipeline for 1992 and 1993 respectively.

Opportunities for foreign penetration: construction

The principal opportunities for British companies in the construction industry which, until the late 1980s, proved difficult for foreign companies to penetrate, are through joint ventures, mergers or acquisitions. The main reason for this is the complex ownership structure of many Spanish companies, especially large ones, and the fact that, in the past, construction companies have financed their own work for up to six months in advance of payment.

Major companies in the construction industry (1988)

COMPANY	SALES (billion ptas)	EMPLOYMENT
Dragados	156.0	11,692
Focsa	101.2	13,300
Cubiertas	97.1	6,843
Entrecanales	95.0	7,500
Ferrovial	86.2	3,660
Hasa-Huarte	73.0	4,406
Agromán	69.4	5,623

Some of Spain's leading banks have large holdings in the top companies, e.g. Banco Central in Dragados and Banesto in Agromán. In addition, the tourism boom and the vast urban expansion of the 1960s and 1970s saw the emergence of many medium-sized companies and thousands of small companies (often in the black economy). Despite economic crisis in the late 1970s and early 1980s, the more recent construction boom has seen new companies springing up in the industry.

The late 1980s has, however, finally brought significant foreign penetration. Major holdings in Agromán and other Spanish companies have been taken by the German construction giant Philipp Holzmann. The French company Bouygues also has considerable holdings, as does Heron International.

The British company Butler Building Systems Ltd is currently undertaking the expansion of the Coca-Cola plant in Madrid as a result of a joint venture with a Spanish company. The British firm reports successful cooperation with their Spanish partners, founded upon the local firm's knowledge of the domestic market, a liberal attitude by the Spanish authorities to innovative design and the absence of any protectionism.

OTHER OPPORTUNITIES FOR LARGER COMPANIES

With Spain's rapid growth, opportunities have mushroomed for larger investors and multinationals, especially in the private sector, where long isolation has left few Spanish firms in a position to withstand competition. Spain's chemical, current and insurance industries have been the most popular sectors for foreign investors in the late 1980s. Arab and British companies have led the way in wholesale acquisition of Spanish firms in a variety of sectors, with, for example, the acquisitions of Alhambra Publishing by the Pearson Group, the olive oil giant José Guiu by Unilever and the Petromed refinery by BP.

The Spanish Government has also actively welcomed foreign investment in state-owned firms. Having spent the 1980s rationalising and streamlining many industries in the public holding company, the INI (National Institute for Industry), the government announced a further 150-billion-peseta restructuring plan in late 1991. The plan aims to capitalise and privatise the healthier companies in INI, while maintaining the chronically indebted ones under the government wing. It classifies public-sector companies by profitability and describes acceptable candidates for complete or partial privatisation as the 'nucleus of opportunities'. Companies forming this nucleus – the list to be drawn up in early 1992 is likely to include, amongst others, the electricity giant ENDESA, the aluminium manufacturers INESPAL, and the Spanish airline IBERIA – will receive 150 billion pesetas in the 1992 budget. Additional funding will be achieved by floating the stock of selected companies and by increasing the capital of those already quoted on the stock market. The expectation is that the sale of these companies, or the inclusion of private capital in them, will help boost their competitiveness and productivity.

HOTEL GROUPS

Large multinational hotel groups began to enter the Spanish market in a major way in the late 1980s. Holiday Inn opened its first hotel in Spain (Madrid) in 1985. It has since invested in the construction of hotels in Seville, Barcelona and in ten other large towns, offering low-priced, functional accommodation in direct competition with more traditional accommodation. In 1990, Trusthouse Forte concluded a joint-venture agreement with the oil company REPSOL to develop 100 Little Chefs and Travelodges in Spain, while the French hotel groups Accor and Air France are planning to create hotel chains in Spain through franchising arrangements. Clearly, the prospects for further inward investment are considerable.

TAPAS AND TECHNOLOGY

Study Plan

SEQUENCE SUMMARY

JOSÉ CARLOS, THE TRAFALGAR HOUSE SPANISH INSTRUCTOR, HOLDS AN EVENING CLASS IN A BAR TO INTRODUCE SOME OF THE COMPANY'S STAFF TO TAPAS. THE SECOND SEQUENCE SEES ANA VALLE DESCRIBING FUTURE PLANS FOR THE EXPO SITE.

WHAT YOU WILL LEARN

Sección 1

- something about food and drink
- how to describe something in simple terms
- how to say what you like and dislike

Business Notes

Cartuja '93
Spain's high-tech revolution
Competition and companies in the
   high-tech sector

Sección 2

- how to talk about future events
- how to prepare a report on the current state of affairs

Science parks
The tapas culture
Surnames in Spain

LEARNING STRATEGY FOR EACH SECTION

Study the key words in the **Palabras y frases útiles** box and watch the video sequence, listening out for the key words. Make notes of what you have understood.

Then study the key phrases in the **Palabras y frases útiles** box and watch the video again.

Complete the **Comprensión** section that follows the **Palabras y frases útiles**.

Now you are ready to listen to the **Tutor cassette**. The cassette will take you through the exercises in this unit section by section.

When you have completed the language exercises in each section, study the **Business Notes** at the end of the unit for further information on business and industry in Spain.

3

TAPAS AND TECHNOLOGY

Sección 1

Las tapas son un aspecto fundamental de la vida social en España. Esta noche José se reune con un pequeño grupo de empleados de Trafalgar House dentro de un bar para enseñarles cómo pedir tapas.

19.32 Lee estas palabras y frases antes de ver el vídeo.

camarero = waiter	cerveza = beer	boquerón = pickled anchovy
plato = dish	vino = wine	patata = potato
comida = food	calamares = squid	queso = cheese
bebida = drink	pescado = fish	

decimos, por ejemplo, 'Oiga!' para atraer su atención	we say, for example, 'Excuse me!' to attract his attention
Entonces le pedimos una lista de tapas	Then we ask him for a list of tapas
a ver si os gusta algo	let's see if you'd like something
Robin, dices 'Oiga!' y lo llamas, ¿eh?	Robin, you say 'Hello!' and call him, OK?
¿Qué tapas hay?	What tapas have you got?
Entonces ¿cuántas cervezas?	So, how many beers?
a ver qué nos dan . . .	let's see what they give us . . .
¿Cómo se llama esto?	What is this called?
falta el queso	the cheese is missing

● E S A S I ●

COMPRENSION

1 ¿Dónde van a dar la clase esta noche?
2 ¿Para qué?
3 ¿Qué dices para llamar a un camarero en España?
4 ¿Qué son 'tapas'?
5 ¿Quién llama al camarero?
6 ¿Qué son čalamares?
7 ¿Qué prefieren beber?
8 ¿Cuántas cervezas piden?
9 ¿Qué tapa falta?
10 ¿Cómo son los boquerones, grandes o pequeños?

APLICACION

● E S A S I ●

G7 As we saw in the last sequence, adjectives of nationality change their endings. In Spanish, adjectives must agree in gender and number with the noun.
Look at these examples from the sequence.

*. . . son pequeño**s** plato**s** con comida.*
*. . . **las** cervez**as** están casi llen**as**.*
*Calamares con patat**as** frit**as**.*

¿Qué adjetivo?

Completa las siguientes frases con la forma adecuada del adjetivo entre paréntesis.

Ejemplo:
La torre panorámica es muy ...... *(alto)*
*La torre panorámica es muy **alta**.*

1 El Ferrari X2 es un vehículo muy .... *(rápido)*
2 La Avenida de Europa es .... *(ancho)*
3 Los presupuestos son .... *(bajo)*

4 Las impresoras Apple son .... *(bueno)*
5 David Landry dice que las vacaciones son .... *(corto)*
6 El flyer tiene un éxito .... *(tremendo)*
7 Es una compañía .... *(nuevo)*
8 Las ideas de Carmen son .... *(práctico)*
9 Es un concepto .... *(estupendo)*
10 Prefiero viajar en avión. Los barcos son muy .... *(lento)*

● E S A S I ●

G8 One way to express likes and dislikes in Spanish is with the verb **gustar** which is formed as follows:

gustar to like

Singular		Plural	
me te le }	gusta/gustan	nos os les }	gusta/gustan

Notice that this verb needs an *object* pronoun (i.e. **me, te, le, nos, os, les**).
Look at how José Carlos asks if there is anything they fancy.

*bueno, a ver si **os gusta** algo, . . .*

¿Qué van a tomar?

Tú y dos amigos, Fernando y Marta, vais a un bar de tapas. Mira el menú y rellena los espacios en blanco.

Tú: →

Camarero: ¡Buenas noches!

Tú: →

Camarero: Aquí tiene el menú, así puede ver qué tapas hay hoy.

Tú: →

Fernando: No, los calamares no me gustan. Prefiero tortilla de patatas.

Tú: →

Fernando: No, el vino blanco no me gusta. Me apetece una caña.

Tú: →

Marta: No sé . . .

Tú: →

Marta: No, no, las sardinas no me gustan . .

Tú: →

Marta: Sí, sí, el jamón me gusta mucho.

Tú: →

Marta: No, el alcohol no me gusta. Prefiero agua.

Tú: →

Camarero: Sí, ¿qué van a tomar?

Tú: Para la señora →

Para el señor →

Y para mí de tapa, queso, y para beber un vaso de vino tinto.

Calcula

Cuando preguntas al camarero ¿Cuánto es? él responde .... pesetas.

★★★★ Tapas Bar El Sevillano ★★★★

Tapas

Tortilla de patatas..	125 ptas
Queso	200
Calamares..	250
Jamón...	375
Ensalada de tomates..	80
Ensalada de marisco..	145
Sardinas a la plancha..	115

Bebidas

Agua mineral...	60
Refrescos..	80
Cerveza de barril..	120
Caña de cerveza...	90
Vino blanco...	70
Vino tinto..	70

Una encuesta

Esta es una encuesta de una compañía distribuidora de automóviles para obtener datos sobre el mercado de automóviles de lujo. Lee las preguntas y termina las encuestas que no están completas.

Nombre: *Luis Alvarez* **Profesión:** *Arquitecto*
Edad: *38* **Estado Civil:** *Soltero*

Preguntas: **Respuestas:**

1 ¿Te gustan los coche deportivos? 1 *Sí.*
2 ¿Por qué te gustan? 2 *Porque son rápidos.*
3 ¿Te gusta los Ferraris? 3 *Sí.*
4 ¿Por qué? 4 *Porque tienen un diseño moderno.*
5 ¿Te gustan descapotables o con capota? 5 *Me gustan descapotables.*
6 ¿Te gusta conducir por la ciudad o por autopista? 6 *Me gusta conducir por autopista*

Informe:
A Luis Alvarez le gustan los coches deportivos porque son rápidos. Le gustan los Ferraris porque tienen un diseño moderno. Le gustan los coches deportivos descapotables y no le gusta conducir por la ciudad.

Nombre: *Antonio González / Carmen Rodríguez* **Profesión:** *Taxista / Ama de Casa*
Edad: *58/51* **Estado Civil:** *Casados*

Preguntas: **Respuestas:**

1 ¿Te gustan los coche deportivos? 1 *No, no nos gustan.*
2 ¿Por qué? 2 *Porque son peligrosos.*
3 ¿Les gustan los Ferraris? 3 *No, no nos gustan.*
4 ¿Por qué? 4 *Porque no son fuertes*
5 ¿Les gustan los BMW? 5 *Sí, nos gustan bastante.*
6 ¿Por qué? 6 *Porque son sólidos y seguros.*
7 ¿Te gusta conducir por la ciudad o por el campo? 7 *Nos gusta conducir por el campo*

Informe:
Al señor y la señora de González no les gustan los coches deportivas porque son peligrosos. Tampoco les gustan los Ferraris porque no son fuertes. Les gustan los BMW porque son sólidos y seguros. Les gusta conducir por el campo.

Nombre: *Isabel Ferrer* **Profesión:** *Bióloga*
Edad: *29* **Estado Civil:** *Casada*

Preguntas: **Respuestas:**

1 ¿Te gustan los coche deportivos? 1 *No, ...*
2 ¿Por qué? 2 *Porque... (consumir / mucha gasolina)*
3 ¿Qué marca de coche le gusta? 3 *Me... (Volvos)*
4 ¿Por qué? 4 *Porque... (fiables)*
5 ¿Le gusta conducir? 5 *No, ...*
6 ¿Le gusta viajar en coche? 6 *Sí.*

Informe:

Nombre: **Profesión:**
Edad: **Estado Civil:**

Preguntas: **Respuestas:**

1 ¿Te gustan los coche deportivos? 1
2 ¿Por qué? 2
3 ¿Qué marca de coche le gusta? 3
4 ¿Por qué? 4
5 ¿Le gusta conducir? 5
6 ¿Te gustan las multas de tráfico? 6

Informe:

• E S   A S I •

Verbos reflexivos

Note the verbs that José Carlos uses:

*¿Cómo **se** llama esto?*
***Se** llaman piquitos.*

There are some verbs in Spanish which always have a pronoun with them. They are called reflexive verbs and are formed exactly in the same way as other verbs.

llamarse to be called

Singular		Plural	
yo	**me** llamo	nosotros	**nos** llamamos
tú	**te** llamas	vosotros	**os** llamáis
él		ellos	
ella	} **se** llama	ellas	} **se** llaman
usted		ustedes	

Completa

Completa las siguientes frases con el pronombre reflexivo correspondiente.

Ejemplo:
El presidente nunca ...... quita la chaqueta en las reuniones.
*El presidente nunca **se** quita la chaqueta en las reuniones.*

1 ...... llama Luis.
2 ¿Generalmente, a qué hora ...... levantas?
3 ...... preparan para ir a la reunión.
4 Después de comer ...... lavamos los dientes.
5 Normalmente ...... voy de la oficina a las cuatro y media.
6 Los ordenadores nunca ...... equivocan.
7 Siempre ...... olvidáis del número de teléfono.
8 El director ...... siente muy optimista con los resultados.
9 ...... dedicamos a la fabricación de casas prefabricadas.
10 ¿ ...... acordáis del nombre de la calle?

Sección 2

El final del Expo '92 no va a ser el final de algunos de los edificios en la isla de Cartuja. Los organizadores tienen planes para el futuro. Ana Valle es un técnico del proyecto Cartuja '93.

PALABRAS Y FRASES UTILES

23.51 Lee estas palabras y frases antes de ver el vídeo.

proyecto = project	desarrollo = development	recursos = resources
tecnológico = technological	comunidad = community	investigación = research
inversión = investment	riqueza = wealth	fabricar = to manufacture
inovador = innovative	suelo = ground	prohibido = prohibited

la empresa se localiza aquí por dos razones	the industry is locating here for two reasons
tanto en recursos humanos como todo tipo de . . .	both in human resources and all types of . . .
El CESIC instalará seis institutos	The CESIC will set up six institutes
. . . que será el segundo centro	. . . which will be the second centre
. . . y aportarán un número importante de . . .	. . . and they will provide an important number of . . .
los edificios que quedan	the buildings that remain
y toda la banda de servicios	and all the range of services
del lado este de la isla	on the east side of the island
donde está prohibida la fabricación	where manufacturing is prohibited
los proyectos que están financiados por . . .	the projects which are financed by . . .

COMPRENSION

1 ¿Qué es Cartuja '93?

2 ¿Qué tipo de organizaciones participan en este proyecto?

3 ¿Qué va a aportar a la comunidad española?

4 ¿Por qué razones Cartuja '93 se localiza en Andalucía?

5 ¿Qué es el CESIC?

6 ¿Cuántos institutos de investigación instalará el CESIC?

7 ¿Qué no puede aclarar Ana Valle sobre los institutos de investigación?

8 ¿Qué aportarán los institutos de investigación?

9 ¿Qué compañías nacionales e internacionales menciona Ana?

10 ¿Qué diferencia existe entre el Centro de Innovación Tecnológica y Cartuja '93?

11 ¿Dónde está el Centro de Innovación Tecnológica?

12 ¿Por quién están financiados los proyectos?

APLICACION

• E S A S I •

G10 In the sequence, Ana Valle says:

Se considera que las inversiones . . .
La empresa **se localiza** aquí
. . . que **se encarga** de . . .

Spanish uses this form to emphasize that the action is more important than the person doing it. Notice that the verb is always in the third person singular or plural.

¿Dónde se pone?

Mira las frases y escribe cada una debajo del dibujo correspondiente. Tienes la primera.

Se venden oficinas • Se cierra a las dos
¿Cuándo se abre el Expo?
Se habla inglés. • Se prohibe fumar
¿Cómo se dice 'credit card' en español?
¿Dónde se celebra la Expo?

Relaciona

Ejemplo: **1c**

1 Las inversiones que realiza el departamento de producción son aprobadas . . .
2 El señor Blasco y la señorita Rosales son los . . .
3 Nosotros no estamos de acuerdo . . .
4 Las impresoras PX 256 . . .
5 Dentro de los sectores de mercado que nos interesan están . . .
6 La mercancía va a llegar por . . .
7 El camión tiene una longitud . . .

a . . . son modernas, rápidas y eficaces.
b . . . las empresas de más de cien empleados.
c . . . por el presidente de la compañía.
d . . . de ocho metros.
e . . . encargados de márketing y ventas.
f . . . con el nuevo presupuesto.
g . . . barco a Bilbao y desde allí por carretera hasta Madrid.

Completa

G1 Mira el vídeo y completa con el artículo adecuado.

La Exposición Universal de Sevilla tiene …… singularidad de ser …… última exposición universal del siglo XX. Va a aportar a …… región de Andalucía …… desarrollo económico importante. Para reutilizar …… inversiones que se generan con …… Exposición, se crea …… proyecto Cartuja '93. …… sociedad estatal es …… encargada de …… ejecución de este proyecto. …… innovación científico-tecnológica que se va a crear con Cartuja '93 va a modernizar …… comunidad española que no está muy desarrollada.
Cartuja '93 se situa en Andalucía porque es …… región, en …… continente europeo, que reune tres características importantes: …… localización geográfica, …… fertilidad del suelo en que se asienta y …… riqueza de todo tipo de recursos.

● E S A S I ●

El futuro

G11 In the previous unit, we saw how Pedro Arozamena described how the public was *going to* move around the British pavilion once it had opened. Notice now how Ana Valle talks about the future plans for the Cartuja site:

*El CESIC instala**rá** seis . . .*
*. . . y aportar**án** un número . . .*
*. . . que se**rá** el segundo centro*
*. . . esta**rá** el pabellón de España*

Completa

Pon el verbo en la forma correcta del futuro.

1 La economía española ………… un 3% en el año que viene. *(crecer)*
2 La política eonómica ………… a la inversión empresarial. *(ayudar)*
3 Nosotros ………… los pedidos mañana. *(mandar)*
4 Muchas empresas europeas ………… sucursales en España en el año que viene. *(establecer)*
5 La demanda de productos españoles ………… boyante. *(ser)*
6 Alemania y Francia ………… en nuevos negocios en España. *(invertir)*
7 Lo siento. Yo no ………… libre hasta mañana. *(estar)*
8 El gobierno ………… 700 millones en la nueva carretera. *(gastar)*
9 Segur SA y Mega Marketing plc ………… una joint venture. *(formar)*
10 ¿Cuántas empresas ………… presentes en la exposición? *(estar)*

¿Cuándo?

Lee la agenda y contesta las preguntas.

ENERO

Portugal accede a la Presidencia de la Comunidad Europea.
Referéndum sobre la autodeterminación del Sahara occidental.
Puesta en marcha del acuerdo de libre cambio entre Colombia, México y Venezuela.
Reunión de los gobiernos de la Asociación de países del Sudeste de Asia (ASEAN), en Singapur.
Convención nacional del Partido Demócrata Liberal de Japón.
Cumbre de Ministros de Asuntos Exteriores de la Conferencia de Seguridad y Cooperación Europea en Praga.
Fusión de los mercados de futuros y opciones de Londres.
Gran Premio de Montecarlo de automovilismo.
Primera vuelta de la Copa de América en California. España se enfrenta al San Diego Yacht Club.
Quinto centenario de la expulsión de los árabes en España.

FEBRERO

El Parlamento canadiense debatirá un nuevo marco constitucional.

Elecciones presidenciales primarias, en Iowa y New Hampshire, para la presidencia de Estados Unidos.
Forum sobre la Economía Mundial en Davos, Suiza.
Reuniones de la Comisión de Derechos Humanos de la ONU en Génova.
Conferencia de la ONU sobre Comercio y Desarrollo en Cartagena, Colombia.
Se inicia el Año del Mono en el calendario chino.
Juegos Olímpicos de Invierno en Albertville, Francia.
Se celebra el 40 Aniversario de la coronación de la reina Isabel II de Inglaterra.

MARZO

Elecciones generales en Tailandia.

Elecciones locales y regionales en Francia.
Elecciones presidenciales en Estados Unidos.
Reunión de la Conferencia de Seguridad y Cooperación Europea en Helsinki.
Chad y Libia discuten sus problemas fronterizos en el seno de la ONU.
Entrega en Los Angeles de los Oscars cinematográficos.
Entrará en funcionamiento la primera prisión privada de Gran Bretaña.

ABRIL

Elecciones generales en Rumania.
En Japón, el Gobierno introduce una normativa sobre Medio Ambiente para las empresas niponas ubicadas en el extranjero.
Cumbre hispano-portuguesa.
Asamblea conjunta del FMI y el Banco Mundial en Washington.
Primera asamblea anual del Banco Europeo para la Reconstrucción y el Desarrollo.
Apertura del Disneyworld europeo en las afueras de París.
Trofeo de golf de St. Andrews.
Inauguración de la EXPO'92 en Sevilla.
Grand National, en el hipódromo de Aintree, cerca de Liverpool.
Regata Oxford-Cambridge en Londres.
Maratón de Londres.

MAYO

Elecciones presidenciales en Filipinas.
Elecciones locales en Inglaterra.
Festival de Cine de Cannes.

Certamen de Música de Eurovisión.
Muestra floral de Chelsea, en Londres.
Congreso Mundial sobre Meteorología en Génova.

JUNIO

Cumbre Mundial de Medio Ambiente en Río de Janeiro.

Elecciones generales británicas.
Elecciones generales en Italia.
Elecciones presidenciales en Austria.
Elecciones generales en Las Bahamas.
Elecciones generales en Checoslovaquia.
Primeras elecciones generales libres en el Congo.
Conferencia sobre Desarme de la ONU.
Reunión de los Jefes de Estado de la Comunidad Europea en Luxemburgo.
Reunión de los ministros de Exteriores y Defensa de la OTAN.
Cumbre de los líderes de la Organización para la Unidad Africana.

JULIO

Gran Bretaña toma posesión de la presidencia de la CEE.
Convención Nacional del Partido Demócrata en Nueva York.
Cumbre de los líderes del Grupo de los Siete.
Elecciones presidenciales en Italia.
Elecciones generales en Fiji.
Juegos Olímpicos en Barcelona.
Tour de Francia.

AGOSTO

Convención Nacional del Partido Republicano de Estados Unidos en Houston, Texas.
Conferencia Internacional sobre el SIDA en Amsterdam.

Festival de Salzsburgo.
Conmemoración del apresamiento de Ricardo I de Inglaterra en Austria.

SEPTIEMBRE

Elecciones al Senado francés.
Cumbre anual del Movimiento de Países No Alineados, en Accra, Ghana.
Estados Unidos retira sus fuerzas de la base aérea de Zaragoza, en España.
Cumbre de la Commonwealth en Nueva Delhi.

OCTUBRE

Quinto Centenario del Descubrimiento de América.
Elecciones parlamentarias en Kuwait.

Brasil cancela la prohibición de importar ordenadores.
Se dan a conocer los premios Nobel.

NOVIEMBRE

Elecciones presidenciales y al Congreso en Estados Unidos.
Reunión de ministros de la CE y Japón.
Asamblea de los líderes de la Asociación Surasiática para la Cooperación Regional.
Cumbre CEE-EE.UU., en La Haya.
Reunión de ministros de la OPEP en Viena.

DICIEMBRE

Cumbre de los líderes de la CE para lanzar el Mercado Unico.
Reunión del Consejo de Cooperación del Golfo.
Elecciones presidenciales en Corea del Sur.

---

1 ¿Cuándo se celebrará la Conferencia de la ONU sobre Comercio y Desarrollo? ¿Dónde?

2 ¿Quienes se reunirán en Viena? ¿Cuándo?

3 ¿Qué país accederá a la Presidencia de la Comunidad Europea en enero?

4 ¿Dónde discutirán Chad y Libia sus problemas fronterizos? ¿Cuándo?

5 ¿Cuándo cancelará Brasil la prohibición de importar ordenadores?

6 ¿Qué país tomará posesión de la presidencia de la CEE en julio?

7 ¿En qué mes los Estados Unidos retirarán sus fuerzas de la base aérea de Zaragoza?

8 ¿Cuándo se reunirán los Jefes de Estado de la comunidad europea en Luxemburgo?

9 ¿Qué dos organizaciones celebrarán una asamblea conjunta en Washington en abril?

10 ¿Qué se celebrará en Davos, Suiza? ¿Cuándo?

11 ¿Cuándo será la cumbre de los líderes de la CE para lanzar el Mercado Unico?

12 ¿Dónde se celebrarán los Juegos Olímpicos?

13 ¿A dónde irás para asistir a la reunión de la Conferencia de Seguridad y Cooperación Europea en marzo?

14 ¿Cuándo habrá elecciones presidenciales y al Congreso de los Estados Unidos?

15 ¿En qué país introducirá el gobierno una normativa sobre el Medio Ambiente para sus empresas en el extranjero?

• E S A S I •

G12 Look at the video again and notice how Ana uses the following expressions:

. . . es un centro de investigación donde **está prohibida** *la fabricación . . . la producción.*
. . . los proyectos **están financiados** *por la misma administración que es la Junta de Andalucía*

Un banco nuevo

Completa el siguiente texto con la forma correcta del verbo *estar* y el participio de los verbos que están debajo.

Desde diciembre de 1991 Banco 21 .... Esta entidad bancaria .... por Juan Manuel Urgoiti quien está decidido a cambiar la banca comercial en España. El señor Urgoiti, presidente y consejero delegado de la entidad, ... a introducir elementos nuevos en cuanto a la calidad y la relación con los clientes. El capital social .... en 4.000 millones de pesetas. Banco 21 .... por un equipo humano de amplia experiencia.

La revolución que pretende hacer Banco 21 .... en la eficacia. Lo importante es que los clientes van a .... bien .... Los servicios del banco .... para atender al cliente 24 horas al día, 365 días al año.

> basar • valorar • diseñar • abrir • crear
> componer • disponer • atender

R E C U E R D A

In this unit you have studied:

- that nouns and adjectives agree in gender and number
  Los platos *son* **pequeños**.
  La avenida *es* **larga**.
- the verb **gustar** to express likes and dislikes
  No me gusta *el café*.
  Nos gusta hacer *negocios en España*.
- how to order a meal in a restaurant or bar
  ¿Qué quiere tomar?
  Para mí *una cerveza*.
- the use of the passive in Spanish
  Se vende *esta casa*.
  ¿A que hora **se abren** *las tiendas?*
- the use of the future tense
  La reunión **se celebrará** *en julio*.
  Yo **llegaré** *mañana*.
- how to describe a state or condition
  El banco **está abierto**.
  Lo siento, pero **estamos ocupados** *todo el día*.

Business Notes

CARTUJA '93

The video sequence shows how Spain, and particularly the region of Andalusia, hopes to use Expo '92 as an infrastructural springboard to create a high-tech 'supersite' known as Cartuja '93. Universal expositions are meant to reflect the latest technological advances and cultural trends, and act as a stimulus for change in the future. In the same way that the last Universal Exposition in Osaka in 1970 marked Japan's emergence as a power to be reckoned with, Expo '92 is intended to mark Spain's 'coming of age' as an advanced democratic nation.

At the end of Expo in October 1992, after attracting twenty million visitors and vast sums of money, Expo officials hope to have broken even. Their main aim in staging the coveted world fair, however, is to attract long-term investment to southern Spain and raise Andalusia's profile in the European business arena. Buildings and roads will be re-used in what will rank as Spain's first World Trade Centre and a showpiece scientific and technological research complex. Hosting six research centres, the complex, or *Centro Superior de Investigaciones Científicas* (CESIC), combines public and private investment and is designed to draw a string of international names to Seville. Cartuja '93, as the overall project is called, has already won contracts from multinationals such as IBM, Siemens, Phillips and Rank Xerox. Others are expected to follow suit. The end result will be a remarkable marriage of the old with the new; Cartuja Island, only five years ago

an arid wasteland surrounding an ancient Carthusian monastery from which Columbus set off to discover America, is destined to become the symbol of a new high-tech age of discovery.

SPAIN'S HIGH-TECH REVOLUTION

Whereas firms engaged in the new technologies have been shedding staff throughout the world at the start of the 1990s, in Spain the rapid expansion continues. The number of firms in this sector has increased from virtually nil at the start of the 1980s to fifty-eight in 1987 and over 100 in 1992, with further rises in companies and employment projected, just as other countries in Europe experience contraction.

The Spanish high-tech boom is deliberate government policy, embodied in the National Electronics and Information Technology Plan, which, over a three-year period ending in December 1993, allocates an overall budget of 158,000 million pesetas to the sector, 45% from public funds, 38% from the Centre for Technological and Industrial Development and 17% from the EC. The prime aim of the Plan, which provides continuity with previous plans, is to give priority to advanced technologies that improve the competitiveness of the production system and the efficiency of infrastructure and services. The Plan is subdivided into seven main areas:

1 electronics and data processing
2 advanced automation
3 stimulation of research in the pharmaceutical industry
4 development of biotechnologies, and chemicals and materials technology
5 support for basic industries and transformers
6 technological infrastructure
7 industrial and technological modernisation in firms.

The telecommunications industry has also grown rapidly, supported by a National Telecommunications Plan for 1989–1992 which envisaged continuing government investment in the industry of the level of 500,000 million pesetas annually, equivalent to between 1.1% and 1.5% of GDP. Spain's first communications satellite, Hispasat, was placed in orbit in 1991, one of its first major tasks being to support transmission of the Olympic Games in Barcelona.

COMPETITION AND COMPANIES IN THE HIGH-TECH SECTOR

This sector has always seen Spanish firms linked with foreign multinationals, following the pattern of the link between Spain's main telecommunications and electronics company, Telefónica, and ATT. There has been little indigenous development, and increasing foreign investment has been promoted by the government. Foreign multinationals now completely dominate production in Spain, especially in electronics and information technology. Consumption of personal computers and software is largely through import. Even Telefónica, one of Spain's biggest companies, has lost its tele-communications monopoly (except for the basic telephone service) and foreign participation in the company has increased from 3% in 1982 to almost 30% in 1992.

The major foreign multinationals in Spain include Alcatel-Standard Eléctrica (a subsidiary of the Compagnie Générale d'Electricité de France), ATT Network Systems and LM Ericsson-Intelsa. Another Scandinavian firm, Electrolux, bought two firms in Catalonia in 1988, while a number of electronics industry giants have plants in Spain, e.g. IBM, Olivetti and Rank Xerox, mostly in the Madrid and Barcelona regions (although Fujitsu and Siemens also have plants in Malaga). The government favours European networks or joint ventures in this sector. An example is Spain's flight simulation company, CASA, which is engaged in an initiative to develop high-speed computers with other EC companies which form part of a pan-European consortium linking industry and research institutes, supported by the EC Esprit programme.

In terms of domestic retail consumption, Spain has recently experienced rapid growth, and demand remains very strong. For example, the home computer market expanded nearly ten-fold between 1986 and 1989, from a total value of 204 million pesetas to 1,900 million pesetas. Also, the sales value of personal computers rose from a total of 33.5 billion pesetas in 1986 to 37 billion pesetas in 1989. Both markets are set to continue growing as Spanish consumers catch up with their EC neighbours. The scope for penetration by foreign companies is equally great.

SCIENCE PARKS

The video sequence refers to Spain's plans for developing science and technology parks and makes specific reference to the Malaga Science Park. The Malaga area is a logical choice for the first major initiative designed to attract European investment, with 100,000 foreigners legally resident in the Malaga area. The 415-acre science park cost 4.2 billion pesetas, and Hughes Microelectronics (part of General Motors) has committed itself to an 8-million-peseta investment in the park.

Malaga is selling itself as southern Europe's high-tech boom town. With Spain's fifth largest metropolitan area and third largest airport, Malaga claims to be Europe's fastest growing city below the Madrid–Rome axis. The city's university has recently opened a Computer Science and Telecommunications Faculty which will assist in the training of the 2,500 high-tech personnel, mostly local people, who will be working in the park by the year 2000. Inducements to foreign companies to set up bases in the area are considerable, with subsidies and incentives offered to cover 100% of all running expenses and up to 50% of a company's investment. In addition, Malaga is an area designated by the EC and the regional government of Andalusia as a priority development zone. Despite the frantic activity in Spain during 1992, Malaga is in no hurry to fill the park but is determined to find the right occupants in specified fields, i.e. telecommunications, microelectronics, industrial and office automation, IT, lasers, new materials, renewable energies and biotechnology. Though the city suffers from poor land communications, the completion of the dual-carriageway link to the new Seville–Granada motorway will assist industry.

THE TAPAS CULTURE

An ever-present theme of the video sequences is the desire of Spaniards to preserve their own distinctive traditions and characteristics as a people, while equally ambitious to modernise their country.

In the first sequence, the vital business of ordering drinks and *tapas* (small snacks) in bars is depicted. The Spanish tradition of spending time with people in social situations such as in this sequence is of crucial importance in developing business relationships. Business people in Spain do not appreciate the more formal, desk-bound approach to discussion and decision-making characteristic of the Anglo-Saxon executive. In Spain, the development of a good business relationship is very much tied up with the development of a good personal relationship. Mutual trust and understanding are regarded as very important, and social situations facilitate their development.

Misunderstanding or even conflict between Spanish and British business people tends to revolve around a different interpretation of time. Despite their *mañana* image, Spaniards are very time-conscious; they do not, however, regard it as a waste of time to take a lengthy mid-morning break at the cafeteria with colleagues or to eat a full two-hour lunch or to spend an evening sampling tapas before eating an evening meal, which may not start until after 10pm. On the contrary, such social occasions both cement the personal relationship and often provide the informal forum where formal decisions are forged. This people-friendly, apparently time-consuming approach, can frustrate non-Spaniards, who often like to move more directly to a decision-making situation; Spaniards, on the other hand, may prefer a series of preliminary meetings over a period of months to establish the integrity of potential partners. In addition, considerable stamina and enthusiasm are recommended for the 'night on the town' which may follow the evening meal that finished at midnight! A working lunch with sandwiches is therefore not appropriate in Spain, where there is also no custom of dinner parties or home entertainment of business colleagues or clients.

In Spain, friends, families and colleagues go out together to eat and drink in hotels, bars and restaurants. That you are not invited home is no slight, merely the norm. Naturally, there are dos and don'ts in terms of topics of conversation. The Spanish will appreciate the demonstration of real interest in and knowledge of any aspect of Spanish life, politics included, by the visitor. However, despite the fact that most Spaniards are very liberal-minded, the subjects of religion and Franco, irrespective of the irreligious nature of the hosts, are best avoided.

SURNAMES IN SPAIN

Spaniards have two surnames, the father's and the mother's. When a woman marries, she keeps her father's surname and then adds (usually with a *de* in front of it) her husband's last name. For example, the fictitious couple in the exercise entitled **Una encuesta** in Sección 1 of this unit are called Antonio González and Carmen Rodríguez de González. Rodríguez is Carmen's father's surname, and de González is her husband's last name. In everyday speech, however, only one surname tends to be used, as with Antonio in the example above. Also, when signing a document, a woman uses both her parents' surnames. It is worth noting that a wife's signature is necessary in addition to the husband's on many transactions.

STARTING UP IN SPAIN

Study Plan

SEQUENCE SUMMARY

ANDY AND KAREN RAMAGE ARE THE OWNERS OF CURZON DIRECT, A MAIL-ORDER COMPANY SPECIALISING IN QUALITY BRITISH LEISUREWEAR, OPERATING FROM A BASE IN SEVILLE. ANDY IS ARRANGING A VISIT TO THE PRINTERS, AND KAREN HAS AN APPOINTMENT WITH THE COMPANY'S LEGAL AND FINANCIAL ADVISER.

WHAT YOU WILL LEARN

Sección 1

- how to use the telephone
- how to talk about time
- how to arrange and rearrange appointments
- how to give instructions

Business Notes

Small companies
Mail order in Spain
Small companies and new technology

Sección 2

- how to compare two things
- how to make an appointment by phone
- more times and dates
- some common abbreviations
- how to express obligation

LEARNING STRATEGY FOR EACH SECTION

Study the key words in the **Palabras y frases útiles** box and watch the video sequence, listening out for the key words. Make notes of what you have understood.

Then study the key phrases in the **Palabras y frases útiles** box and watch the video again.

Complete the **Comprensión** section that follows the **Palabras y frases útiles**.

Now you are ready to listen to the **Tutor cassette**. The cassette will take you through the exercises in this unit section by section.

When you have completed the language exercises in each section, study the **Business Notes** at the end of the unit for further information on business and industry in Spain.

STARTING-UP IN SPAIN

Sección 1

Andy arregla una visita a la compañía impresora para hablar de un nuevo anuncio.

PALABRAS Y FRASES UTILES

| 29.15 | Lee estas palabras y frases antes de ver el vídeo. |

tarde = late	ampliar = to enlarge
almacén = warehouse	gratis = free
boceto = design	gente = people
anuncio = advert	talla = size
diseñar = to design	datos = data
ordenador = computer	

un pedido acaba de llegar	an order has just arrived
nuestro horario de trabajo por la tarde es . . .	our working hours in the afternoon are . . .
Bueno, hasta las cinco	Fine, until five
Bueno, quedamos en eso	Fine, we'll agree to that then
Les encanta	They really like it
hemos puesto la foto más alta	we have moved the photo up
Es más grande que antes	It's bigger than before

COMPRENSION

1 ¿Por qué Andy va a llegar un poco tarde?
2 ¿A qué hora dice que va a llegar a la reunión?
3 ¿Cuál es el horario de trabajo por la tarde?
4 ¿A qué hora va a llegar Andy?
5 ¿Qué va a llevar Andy?
6 ¿Con quién quiere hablar Andy?
7 ¿Por qué quiere Andy la palabra 'gratis' mucho mayor?
8 ¿Cómo quiere Andy la foto?
9 ¿Qué es muy importante?
10 ¿Por qué es muy importante el cupón?

APLICACION

• ES ASI •

Notice how Andy and Verónica arrange a time for Andy's visit to the printers.

*Mira, voy a llegar **un poco tarde** . . .*
*. . . voy a llegar **a las cuatro***
. . . nuestro horario de trabajo por la tarde es
de **cinco a ocho**
*Bueno, **hasta las cinco***

To ask the time you say: **¿Qué hora es?**
Now look at the watches to know how to respond.

Son las cinco de la tarde.

Son las siete y cinco de la mañana.

Son las once y diez de la noche.

Son las nueve y cuarto de la mañana.

Son las cuatro y veinte de la madrugada.

Es la una y veinticinco de la tarde.

Son las diez y media de la noche.

Son las doce menos veinticinco de la mañana.

Son las siete menos veinte de la tarde.

Es la una menos cuarto de la tarde.

Son las nueve menos diez de la mañana.

Son las cinco menos cinco de la tarde.

Son las tres de la madrugada.

¿Qué hora es?

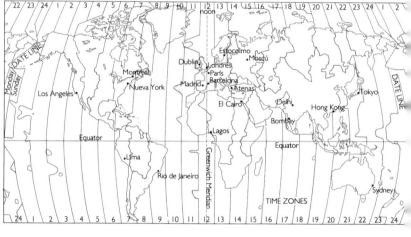

1 ¿Qué hora es en Bombay cuando en Madrid son las cinco y media de la tarde?
2 ¿Qué hora es en Los Angeles si en Londres es la una y cuarto de la mañana?
3 ¿Qué hora es en Sydney si en París son las cuatro menos cuarto de la tarde?
4 ¿Qué hora es en Moscú cuando en Barcelona es la una y diez de la tarde?
5 ¿Qué hora es en Lima si en Río de Janeiro son las siete menos veinticinco de la tarde?
6 ¿Qué hora es en Hong Kong cuando en Montreal son las diez menos cinco de la noche?

Jornada sobre
Instituciones de Inversión Colectiva

PAPELES DE ECONOMIA ESPAÑOLA

SUPLEMENTO FINANCIERO Número 35

- COLABORACIONES: Luis Carlos Croissier Batista, Gonzalo Azcoitia y Jesús Borque, Ignacio Garrido, Carlos Contreras, Sebastián Albella y Juan Antonio Mayorga, y Eduardo Ramírez Medina.

- APENDICE LEGISLATIVO

- OPINIONES: Manuel Conthe, José Pérez, José Luis Méndez, José María García Alonso, Pedro Fernández-Rañada, Raimundo Ortega, Fernando de Roda, José Antonio Sánchez-Rico e Iñigo Sangro.

Programa

9,30:	APERTURA. D. FERNANDO DE RODA LAMSFUS, PRESIDENTE DE SAFEI.
9,45:	CONFERENCIA INAUGURAL. D. LUIS CARLOS CROISSIER, PRESIDENTE DE CNMV.
10,15:	*"CONSECUENCIAS PARA EL SISTEMA FINANCIERO ESPAÑOL DEL BOOM DE LOS FONDOS DE INVERSIÓN."* D. JOSÉ PÉREZ, DIRECTOR GENERAL DEL BANCO DE ESPAÑA.
10,45:	*"LOS FONDOS INMOBILIARIOS."* D. GREGORIO ARRANZ. SUBDIRECTOR GENERAL DE LEGISLACIÓN DE LA DGTPF.
11,15:	*"COMPORTAMIENTOS DEL MERCADO ESPAÑOL DE FONDOS DE INVERSIÓN: UNA COMPARACIÓN INTERNACIONAL."* D. LUIS DE GUINDOS, CONSEJERO DELEGADO DE ASESORES BURSÁTILES EUROINVEST SGIIC.
11,45:	COLOQUIO. MODERADO POR: D. JESÚS MARTÍNEZ VÁZQUEZ, DIRECTOR DE EXPANSIÓN Y PRESIDENTE DE LA APIE.
12,15:	COFFE - BREAK.
12,30:	*"LOS FONDOS DE INVERSIÓN EN EL EXTRANJERO."* D. GABRIEL HERRERA, VICEPRESIDENT INVESTMENT RESEARCH DE SUISSE BANK CORPORATION.
13,00:	*"LA FISCALIDAD DE LOS PRODUCTOS DE AHORRO: PLANES DE AHORRO POPULAR."* D. MIGUEL CRUZ, DIRECTOR GENERAL DE TRIBUTOS.
13,30:	COLOQUIO. MODERADO POR: D. ANDREU MISSÉ, REDACTOR JEFE SECCIÓN DE ECONOMÍA DE EL PAÍS Y VOCAL DE LA APIE.
14,30:	ALMUERZO.
17,00:	MESA REDONDA. *"EL BOOM DE LOS FONDOS DE INVERSIÓN".* INTRODUCTOR: D. ENRIQUE FUENTES QUINTANA. COMUNICANTES: D. FELIPE ECHEVARRÍA HERRERÍAS, SUBDIRECTOR GENERAL DEL BBV. D. IGNACIO GARRIDO, SUBDIRECTOR GENERAL DE DEUDA PÚBLICA. D. JOSÉ CARLOS GÓMEZ BORRERO, DIRECTOR GENERAL DE SOGEVAL. D. JOSÉ LUIS MÉNDEZ, PRESIDENTE DE AHORRO CORPORACIÓN FINANCIERA. D. XAVIER MARTÍ, PRESIDENTE DE SAFEI-BARCELONA, AGENCIA DE VALORES.
18,00:	COLOQUIO. MODERADO POR: D. ENRIQUE FUENTES QUINTANA, DIRECTOR GENERAL DE LA FUNDACIÓN FIES.
19,00:	CONFERENCIA DE CLAUSURA. D. MANUEL CONTHE, DIRECTOR GENERAL DEL TESORO Y POLÍTICA FINANCIERA.

¿A qué hora . . . ?

Mira el programa para la *Jornada sobre Instituciones de Inversión Colectiva* y responde.

1 ¿A qué hora va a comenzar la Jornada?

2 ¿A qué hora va a ser la conferencia de don Luis de Guindos?

3 *La conferencia sobre los fondos de inversión en el extranjero, ¿es a las doce?*

4 ¿A qué hora es la conferencia sobre *La fiscalidad de los productos de ahorro: Planes de ahorro popular*?

5 ¿A qué hora se sirve el almuerzo?

6 ¿A qué hora se celebra el coloquio moderado por don Enrique Fuentes Quintana?

7 ¿A qué hora se va a celebrar la última conferencia?

• E S   A S I •

While on the phone to Verónica, Andy says:

*un pedido **acaba de llegar** al almacén*
(=an order has just arrived in the warehouse)

The expression **acabar de** + infinitive refers to something that has just happened.

Responde

Mira los ejemplos y haz el ejercicio.

Acaba de ganar
un millión
de pesetas

Acaban de comprar una casa

1 ¿A qué hora llega el tren de Madrid?
   (llegar)
2 ¿Dónde están Antonio y Jorge? *(salir)*
3 ¿Cuándo vas a terminar el informe? No sé,
   . . . *(empezar)*
4 ¿Está el director en su oficina? Sí, . . .
   (entrar)
5 ¿A qué hora sale el avión para Londres?
   Lo siento, . . . *(despegar)*
6 ¿Sabe algo de nuestro representante en
   París? Sí, . . . *(enviar un fax)*
7 ¿Cómo sabes que Juan va a dimitir?
   (hablar con él)

8 ¿Por qué estáis tan contentos? (*recibir un aumento de sueldo*)
9 ¿Cuándo van a pagar estas facturas? (*ingresar un cheque*)
10 ¿Cuándo vais a finalizar las negociaciones? (*firmar el contrato*)

• E S   A S I •

G13 In the sequence, Andy tells Carlos to change the text of the coupon. This way of asking people to do things is more usual in Spanish than in English Look at these examples of the imperative.

*Y **amplía** la palabra 'gratis'*
*No, **déjalo** ahí*
*Y bueno, **sácame** una copia*

¿Qué hago?

La próxima semana vas a ir en viaje de negocios a Inglaterra. Aquí tienes una lista de asuntos pendientes. Por teléfono explica a tu secretaria qué hacer.

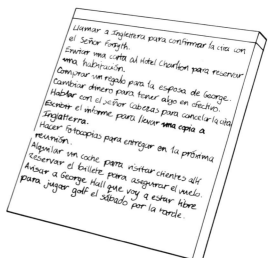

Llamar a Inglaterra para confirmar la cita con el Señor Forsyth.
Enviar una carta al Hotel Charlton para reservar una habitación.
Comprar un regalo para la esposa de George.
Cambiar dinero para tener algo en efectivo.
Hablar con el señor Cabezas para cancelar la cita
Escribir el informe para llevar una copia a Inglaterra.
Hacer fotocopias para entregar en la próxima reunión.
Alquilar un coche para visitar clientes allí
Reservar el billete para asegurar el vuelo.
Avisar a George Hall que voy a estar libre para jugar golf el sábado por la tarde.

Ejemplo:
Llama a Inglaterra para confirmar la cita con el señor Forsyth.

Notice how Andy and Carlos compare things.

*. . . la foto **más alta***
***Más ancha** también*
*Ahora es **más grande que** antes*

Compara

Se puede viajar entre Madrid y Sevilla por avión o en tren. Mira la tabla y compara las dos formas de viajar. Usa las palabras que están abajo.

Ejemplo:
El tren es más barato que el avión.

Tren

Precio: 6.800ptas
Comodidad: ★★★
Rapidez: 2h30m
Frecuencia: 3 salidas por día
Proximidad al centro de la ciudad:
    en el centro
Servicio: ★★
Puntualidad: ★★★
Categorías de billete: turista/preferente/club

Avión

Precio: 7.000ptas
Comodidad: ★★
Rapidez: 1h15m
Frecuencia: 2 vuelos diarias
Proximidad al centro de la ciudad:
    a 10km del centro
Servicio: ★
Puntualidad: ★★
Categorías: turista/club

> Leyenda
> ★★★ excelente
> ★★ bueno
> ★ regular

---

cómodo • rápido • frecuente • cerca
bueno • puntual
variedad de categorias

While on the phone, Verónica says to Andy:

*Bueno, Andy, **nuestro** horario de trabajo por la tarde es de cinco a ocho.*

This is how you say who something belongs to. Remember that adjectives in Spanish must agree in gender and number with their noun. The possessive adjectives are as follows.

Singular	Plural
mi	mis
tu	tus
su	sus
nuestro/a	nuestros/as
vuestro/a	vuestros/as
su	sus

Transforma

Usa el adjetivo posesivo adecuado para transformar las siguientes frases.

Ejemplos:
Tengo un coche nuevo. =
Mi coche es nuevo.
Tenéis una profesora muy agradable. =
Vuestra profesora es muy agradable.

1 Luisa tiene una secretaria muy eficiente.
2 Tienes unos diseños estupendos.
3 Tenemos una fábrica muy moderna.
4 Tenéis un horario de trabajo muy flexible.
5 España y Portugal tienen productos muy baratos.
6 Tenéis unas oficinas muy céntricas.

Sección 2

Karen llama para pedir una cita con Don Manuel. Cuando llega a la oficina Chari le da unos documentos.

PALABRAS Y FRASES UTILES

33.59 Lee estas palabras y frases antes de ver el vídeo.

libre = free	pago = payment	seguridad = security
ocupado = occupied	pago = payment	terminar = to finish
despacho = office	impuesto = tax	llamada = call
dar = to give		

tengo unos temas aquí pendientes	I've got some points which need to be dealt with
mañana tiene todo el día ocupado	he's busy all day tomorrow
Las seis quizás sea un poco difícil	Six o'clock might be a little difficult
tengo cita a las siete con Manuel	I've got an appointment at seven with Manuel
el calendario fiscal de octubre	the tax deadlines for October
aquí te detalla cuando es el plazo del IVA	here it tells you the time limit for VAT
. . . del impuesto de sociedades y el pago fraccionado	. . . of company tax and payment by instalments
Este es sobre kilometraje y las dietas	This is about mileage allowance and expenses
también eso hay que repasarlo	that also needs to be checked

COMPRENSION

1 ¿Por qué quiere Karen pedir una cita con Manuel?
2 ¿Dónde estará Manuel todo el día mañana?
3 ¿Qué día va a tener la cita Karen?
4 ¿A qué hora?
5 ¿De qué mes es el calendario fiscal?
6 ¿En qué circular pone lo del IVA?
7 ¿Qué tendrá que explicar don Manuel?
8 ¿En qué cartilla está incluida Karen?
9 ¿Por qué Karen tiene que esperar un momentito?

APLICACION

• E S   A S I •

To make appointments, you need to be able to talk about times and dates. In Spanish, the months of the year and days of the week are as follows.

Los doce meses del año son: **enero, febrero, marzo, abril, mayo, junio, julio, agosto, septiembre, octubre, noviembre, diciembre.**
Los siete días de la semana son: **domingo, lunes, martes, miércoles, jueves, viernes, sábado.**

Escucha

Vuelve a ver el vídeo e identifica los días y el mes que citan.

¿Cuándo?

Así decimos las fechas en español.
12 octubre 1492: **El doce de octubre de mil cuatrocientos noventa y dos**

Estas son unas fechas importantes en la historia de España. Lee cada fecha y después asocia esa fecha con el hecho histórico correspondiente.

Ejemplo:
El doce de octubre de mil cuatrocientos noventa y dos Colón llega a América.

12.10.1492	España entra como miembro del Mercado Común.
02.05.1808	El rey don Juan Carlos I sube al trono.
18.07.1936	Colón llega a América.
22.11.1975	Empieza la Guerra de Independencia en España.
01.01.1986	Se abre la Expo '92 en Sevilla.
01.04.1992	Empieza la Guerra Civil española.

Crucigrama

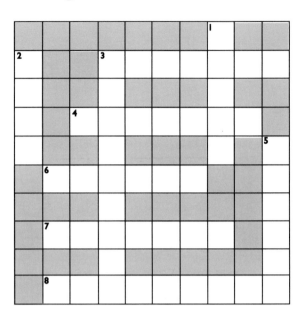

Horizontales:
3 Está después del sábado.
4 El 12 de ese mes, en 1492, Cristóbal Colón llega a América.
6 El día que don Manuel está fuera de la oficina.
7 El día de San Valentín se celebra en ese mes.
8 Dos días después del lunes.

Verticales:
1 Es el primero de los meses.
2 El 1 de ese mes se celebra el Día del Trabajo.
3 Es el último mes del año.
5 Entre el lunes y el miércoles.

¿Dígame?

Mira el vídeo otra vez y completa la conversación telefónica.

Secretaria: ¿Dígame?
Tú: →
Secretaria: Hola, buenas tardes. ¿Qué desea?

Tú: →

Secretaria: El señor Cameselle está en una reunión. ¿Quiere dejar un recado?

Tú: →

Secretaria: Bueno, si quiere hablar con él personalmente ¿por qué no lo llama más tarde?

Tú: →

Secretaria: Lo siento, pero a las ocho no va a poder ser. Nuestro horario de trabajo es de tres y media a siete.

Tú: →

Secretaria: Sí, muy bien.

Tú: →

Secretaria: De nada. Hasta luego.

¿Hoy o mañana?

Son las diez de la mañana

Mañana es el 9 de septiembre.
Pasado mañana es el 10 de septiembre.
Dentro de un mes/El mes que viene/El próximo mes es el 9 de octubre.
Dentro de un año/El año que viene/El próximo año es el 9 de septiembre de 1994.
Dentro de una hora son las once de la mañana.
Dentro de una semana/La semana que viene es el 15 de septiembre.

Elige la expresión adecuada.

1 • ¿Cenamos juntos esta noche?
   ♦ De acuerdo.
   • Entonces, hasta luego./Entonces, hasta el año que viene.

2 • Los planes para la nueva fábrica están aprobados.
   ♦ ¿Y cuándo entrará en funcionamiento?
   • Dentro de una hora./El año que viene

3 • Necesito hablar con el señor Ramírez urgentemente.
   ♦ Ahora está ocupado. ¿Puede llamar más tarde?
   • Bueno, llamaré el próximo mes./Bueno, llamaré después.

4 • ¿Cuándo es la reunión?
   ♦ Dentro de dos días.
   • Entonces. hasta pasado mañana./Entonces, hasta 1995.

5 • Pagarán las facturas a 30 días.
   ♦ Entonces tendremos el ingreso en el banco dentro de un mes./Entonces tendremos el ingreso en el banco mañana.

6 • Roger, June dice que el restaurante está lleno.
   ♦ Bueno, comeremos más tarde./Bueno, comeremos el año que viene.

¿El IVA?

En España se emplean mucho las siglas. En la secuencia anterior Chari da a Karen unas planillas donde se habla del *plazo del IVA, del IRPF, ...* El IVA significa 'Impuesto sobre el Valor Añadido'.

Cuando todas las palabras están en plural se repite la letra inicial.

Ejemplo: los EEUU = *los Estados Unidos.*

Averigua el significado de las siguientes siglas. Usa las palabras de abajo.

IRPF	.... sobre la .... de las ....
INI	.... Nacional de ....
PSOE	....
SEAT	.... de .... de Turismo
CEOE	.... de Organizaciones ....
INH	Instituto .... de ....
UGT	.... de ....
CCOO	....
NIF	.... de Identificación ....

Automóviles • Comisiones
Confederación • Empresariales • Español
Española (x2) • Fiscal • Físicas
General • Hidrocarburos • Impuesto
Industria • Instituto • Nacional
Número • Obrero • Obreras • Partido
Personas • Renta • Socialista • Sociedad
Trabajadores • Unión

• E S   A S I •

G15 In the sequence, Chari and Karen talk about what Karen has to do with the forms. Look at how they express this obligation.

. . . no lo **tienes que hacer** tú.

. . . lo **tendrá que explicar** don Manuel.

. . . eso hay **que repasarlo.**

Responde

Mira el ejercicio **¿Qué hago?** en la Sección 1 y contesta las preguntas.

1 ¿Por qué tiene que llamar a Inglaterra?
2 ¿Qué tiene que comprar para la esposa de George?
3 ¿Dónde tiene que enviar una carta y por qué?
4 ¿Por qué tiene que alquilar un coche?
5 ¿Qué tiene que llevar a Inglaterra?

Deberes

Usa la expresión *hay que* o la forma correcta de *tener que* o *deber* en las siguientes frases.

1 Esta reunión es muy importante, nosotros .... estar presentes.
2 En los vuelos internacionales .... estar en el aeropuerto 90 minutos antes de la salida del vuelo.
3 Si vas a hacer negocios en España, ... aprender algo de español.
4 En España no .... usar el cinturón de seguridad cuando conduces en la ciudad.
5 Si el equipaje pesa más de 20 kilos, ... pagar exceso de equipaje.
6 Para constituir una Sociedad Anónima en España, ... tener un mínimo de tres socios.
7 Mañana viene el director, y yo .... presentar el informe.
8 Los miembros de un Consejo de Administración .... ser elegidos por la Junta General.

• E S A S I •

G8 When Karen and Chari are talking about the forms, Chari says:

. . . *no **lo** tienes que hacer tú.*

. . . ***lo** tendrá que explicar don Manuel.*

. . . *eso hay que repasar**lo**.*

Note the positions of these object pronouns.

Completa

Coloca el pronombre adecuado en las siguientes frases.

Ejemplos:

• Tengo cita con don Manuel.

♦ *¿A qué hora **la** tienes?*

• Aquí tengo los impresos.

♦ *¿Dónde **los** tienes?*

1 • ¿Tiene la cartilla de la Seguridad Social?
   ♦ Sí, también ...... tiene.

2 • ¿Ampliamos el texto?
   ♦ Sí, ... quiero más grande.

3 • ¿Justifico el texto?
   ♦ Sí, ... quiero a la izquierda.

4 • ¿Quién no conoce el nuevo reglamento?
   ♦ Elena no ...... conoce.

5 • ¿Quieres las copias?
   ♦ Sí, ... quiero.

6 • ¿Elena sabe algo del asunto?
   ♦ No, no ...... sabe.

R E C U E R D A

In this unit you have studied:

• how to tell the time
  ¿Qué hora es?
  Son las cinco.
  *La reunión comienza **a las diez de la mañana**.*

• how to talk about something that has just happened
  ¿Conoce la ciudad?
  *No, **acabo de llegar**.*

• how to ask people to do things and give orders
  *Por favor, **avisa** al señor González que estoy aquí.*
  *Bueno, **sácame** una copia.*

• how to compare things
  *El avión es **más rápido que** el tren.*

• how to express dates and use expressions to talk about future events
  El doce de octubre de mil cuatrocientos noventa y cuatro
  Colón llega a América.
  *Ahora estoy ocupado, te llamaré **después**.*

• the meaning of some acronyms
  *¿Qué quiere decir **PIB**?*
  Producto Interior Bruto.

• how to express an obligation
  *No puedo salir a cenar. **Tengo que** terminar este trabajo.*

Business Notes

SMALL COMPANIES

The video sequence introduces two small companies: Curzon Direct, run by Andy and Karen Ramage, who use mail order to sell imported English country leisurewear; and a small Spanish family business of printers.

For a small British company, starting up in Spain need not be difficult as long as a number of sensible steps are followed. These were referred to in Business File 3, but it is worth making a brief checklist:

- allocate a member (or members) of staff with the time and interest to research the Spanish market;
- approach organisations with the expertise and the willingness to help, e.g. the Department of Trade and Industry, the local Chamber of Commerce;
- consider joining a trade mission to Spain to take advantage of group reductions on travel and accommodation;
- be prepared to commit finances to researching the Spanish market;
- consider producing promotional material, e.g. leaflets, in Spanish so as to facilitate contacts in Spain;
- remember that the regions offer start-up incentives and financial concessions which may vary;
- use organisations such as the DTI and Chambers of Commerce to find a suitable local agent if required and/or a Spanish lawyer who understands the UK;
- plan well ahead to learn or improve Spanish language skills if intending to establish a permanent presence in Spain.

Another way into the Spanish market which should be considered is a tie-up with another small Spanish company or companies. This does not necessarily imply a full joint venture or networking arrangement, but may be a strategic alliance in a particular market or sector, i.e. a specific agreement to cooperate within defined parameters. Spanish small companies, known as PYMES (*Pequeñas y Medianas Empresas*) have traditionally been very reluctant to link up, but in recent years, many small companies have been forging strategic alliances in order to survive. The message coming from increased EC competition is 'ally or die', and companies have combined to cooperate over specific programmes, for instance export, purchase of materials, product development, shared research, etc. In this respect, it could be said that the PYMES are emulating the large companies in Spain, which have increasingly transnational operations, e.g. the Repsol–Agip link, the Nunni automobile alliance which links General Motors with Toyota, and the EC Airbus project.

Examples abound of successful alliances involving small, often family companies such as those seen in the video sequence. For instance, Carlos Velasco e Hijos, Conservas Antonio Echevarría and Conservas Dufer are three Cantabrian companies involved in the packaging of fish. They have formed a consortium for the purposes of fish purchase and export but continue as competitors in the domestic market. In Spain, the Institute of Foreign Trade (*Instituto de Comercio Exterior* or ICEX) and the Chambers of Commerce have taken a leading role in forming export consortia of PYMES. More importantly for any small company starting up in Spain, the Institute of Small and Medium-sized Firms (*Instituto de Pequeñas y Medianas Empresas* or IMPI) provides concrete aid to consortia of small companies. Within the Plan for the Promotion of Design, Quality and Fashion (*Plan de Promoción de Diseño, Calidad y Moda*), IMPI promotes agreements in the sectors of confection, jewellery, footwear, furniture, ceramics, toys, etc. Toy manufacturers in particular display the trend toward strategic alliances.

Strategic alliances are not without financial implications, of course. Additional management costs may be incurred, but again organisations such as IMPI can help. IMPI participates, for example, in collectives formed by PYMES, usually for a three-year period and often in research, quality control and design. Alliances which cross national boundaries may also be eligible for support from a variety of EC programmes. The most relevant perhaps to small companies is the EC BRITE programme, which awards subsidies for research and development and includes a sub-programme, CRAFT, which is specifically designed to assist consortia of small companies.

MAIL ORDER IN SPAIN

In the video sequence, Curzon Direct's main source of sales is direct mail via a catalogue which they need to keep updated. Mail order in Spain is a tiny sector, representing less than 1% of retail sales. The sector is dominated by Spanish subsidiaries of European mail-order firms, with turnover

estimated at 40 billion pesetas in 1989, the last year for which reliable information is available at the time of writing. The principal mail-order operators are as shown in the following table.

Mail order in Spain

FIRM	ULTIMATE CONTROL	TURNOVER (billion pesetas)
Venta Catálogo (Venca)	Otto Versand (Germany)	10.2
Damart España	Damart (France)	8.0
Beyela	Damart España	1.0

(Source: *Consumer Spain '91*)

The market leader, Venca, lists mainly women's wear and has 400 local suppliers. Venca is expecting a 10% yearly growth up to the mid-1990s. Damart España sells mainly thermal underwear through mail order and also has twenty-five retail outlets. Beyela sells mainly clothes for young people but has added baby clothes and health products in recent years.

The Spanish mail-order scene has developed differently from most other European countries in that mail order preceded catalogue sales. This helped consumers to accept the concept of buying by mail which, until quite recently, was unfamiliar to most. Prospects for Curzon Direct look promising, since it is estimated that only 15% to 20% of the potential market in Spain is being exploited, and it is known that other European firms have been considering entry.

SMALL COMPANIES AND NEW TECHNOLOGIES

Despite their size, the Spanish family firm of printers seen in the video sequence employ an advanced graphics system. Although many family firms in Spain do not have the money for technological updating, the interest in employing the latest technologies is usually great and is backed up by a number of national and regional initiatives targeted at small firms. An example of the kind of help that may be provided at regional level is to be found in the low-interest loans, R&D concessions and cash grants made available to small and medium-sized companies by the Madrid Economic and Development Agency (*Instituto Madrileño para el Desarrollo Económico* or IMADE). IMADE, which services the Madrid regional government, also provides subsidies for training programmes to new ventures, whether Spanish or foreign.

It is also possible for small companies to take on new employees who can bring to the firm expertise in the new technologies. The central government National Institute for Employment (*Instituto Nacional para el Empleo* or INEM) has been devoting considerable resources in recent years to training for the unemployed. Centres have been established throughout Spain, and emphasis has been put on training in the new technologies. Since half of INEM's budget derives from the European Social Fund, it works in close conjunction with regional governments and the European Commission.

ON THE FAST TRACK

Study Plan

SEQUENCE SUMMARY

THE AVE, SPAIN'S HIGH-SPEED TRAIN, WILL EVENTUALLY PROVIDE A FAST RAIL LINK ALL OVER SPAIN AND BEYOND, WITH THE INITIAL STAGE BETWEEN MADRID AND SEVILLE. DAMIAN HERNANDEZ TALKS ABOUT THE DEVELOPMENT OF THE PROJECT AND THE DESIGN OF THE TRAIN. HE ALSO MEETS WAYNE ROSEMIN OF THE BRITISH DESIGN CONSULTANTS ADDISON, TO DISCUSS ASPECTS OF THE TRAIN'S DESIGN AND THE NEW STATION IN SEVILLE.

WHAT YOU WILL LEARN

Sección 1	*Sección 2*
• how to talk about events in the past • to use dates and expressions of time • how to expand the Spanish you already know	• how to put across your point of view • how to agree and disagree • how to say you're hungry/thirsty/in a hurry/hot/cold/etc.
Business Notes Spain's transport and communications system The railway system and AVE	Design in Spain Opportunities in other service industries

LEARNING STRATEGY FOR EACH SECTION

Study the key words in the **Palabras y frases útiles** box and watch the video sequence, listening out for the key words. Make notes of what you have understood.

Then study the key phrases in the **Palabras y frases útiles** box and watch the video again.

Complete the **Comprensión** section that follows the **Palabras y frases útiles**.

Now you are ready to listen to the **Tutor cassette**. The cassette will take you through the exercises in this unit section by section.

When you have completed the language exercises in each section, study the **Business Notes** at the end of the unit for further information on business and industry in Spain.

5

ON THE FAST TRACK

Sección 1

Damián Hernández, un representante de AVE, habla de los progresos tecnológicos, el desarrollo de la línea Madrid – Sevilla y del diseño del nuevo tren de alta velocidad.

PALABRAS Y FRASES UTILES

39.11 Lee estas palabras y frases antes de ver el vídeo

ferroviaria = railway	etapa = stage	encuesta = survey
alcanzar = to reach	asiento = seat	arista = edge
velocidad = speed	morro = nose	asesoramiento = advice

hemos acortado en cien kilómetros la distancia	we've cut the distance by one hundred kilometres
se han construido diecisiete túneles	seventeen tunnels have been built
se han utilizado las técnicas más importantes	the most important techniques have been used
Addison se ha encargado del diseño exterior y . . .	Addison has looked after the exterior design and . . .
cuando hicieron los estudios de márketing . . .	when they did the marketing studies . . .
. . . salió unas encuestas donde . . .	. . . some surveys came out in which . . .
. . . que debíamos suavizarlo más	. . . that we should make it smoother
parece que tiene el morro de un Boeing	it looks like it has the nose of a Boeing

COMPRENSION

1 ¿Cuántos kilómetros tiene la línea del AVE entre Madrid y Sevilla?
2 ¿Cuántos viaductos se han construido?
3 ¿Qué técnicas se han utilizado?
4 ¿Cuánto tiempo durará el viaje entre Madrid y Sevilla en la primera etapa?
5 ¿De qué se ha encargado Addison?
6 ¿De dónde es la compañía que colaboró con Addison?
7 ¿Qué diferencia fundamental tiene el AVE con el TGV Atlantique?
8 ¿Cómo es el morro del TGV Atlantique según las encuestas realizadas por los franceses?
9 ¿Qué pensaron que debían hacer?
10 ¿A qué se parece el morro del AVE?

APLICACION

● E S A S I ●

El pretérito perfecto
haber + -ado (**-ar** verbs)
         -ido (**-er** and **-ir** verbs)

haber to have

Singular		Plural	
yo	**he**	nosotros	**hemos**
tú	**has**	vosotros	**habéis**
él		ellos	
ella	**ha**	ellas	**han**
usted		ustedes	

In this sequence, Señor Hernández talks about what has been done recently. Notice how he does this:

hemos acortado en cien kilómetros . . .
se han construido . . .
Addison **se ha encargado** del diseño . . .

¿Ahora o antes?

Fíjate en las siguientes expresiones antes de hacer el ejercicio:

Hoy por la { mañana / noche / noche

Esta { mañana / tarde / noche / semana

Este { fin de semana / mes / año / verano, otoño, etc.

Ejemplo:

Yo me encargo de la correspondencià.
Este mes **me he encargado de la correspondencia**.

1 El trabaja mucho.
  Esta mañana . . .
2 Ellas trabajan en el departamento de contabilidad.
  Este mes . . .
3 La directora está de viaje por Galicia.
  Esta semana . . .
4 Nosotros leemos las cartas de presentación de los nuevos representantes.
  Esta tarde . . .
5 Vosotros venís al trabajo en taxi.
  Hoy por la mañana . . .
6 Las ventas aumentan.
  Este año . . .

Forma frases

Usa las siguientes expresiones para hacer el ejercicio:

aún
todavía } negativas/interrogativas

ya   positivas/interrogativas

Ejemplo: **2f**
*No, ellos **todavía** no han terminado el diseño del tren.*

1 Sí, el dólar . . .

2 No, ellos . . .

3 No, nosotros . . .

4 Sí, Rodrigo . . .

5 No, el gobierno . . .

6 Sí, Aurora y Julio . . .

7 Sí, yo . . .

a . . . ha leído el anuncio.

b . . . no ha dicho nada sobre los nuevos impuestos.

c . . . he reparado el coche.

d . . . no hemos comprado acciones de Repsol.

e . . . se ha devaluado.

f . . . no han terminado el diseño del tren.

g . . . han resuelto el problema.

Nunca mejor

Lee el siguiente texto y contesta las preguntas.

GRUPO HISPANO-SUIZA, S.A.

Velázquez, 150 · 28002 Madrid · Tel. 261 29 00 · Fax 563 87 21

	1989	1988
Ingresos	18.625	11.773
Beneficio antes impuesto	1.912	1.165
Beneficio neto atribuible	1.164	743
Dividendos	63	48
Beneficio por acción	1.452	929

RESUMEN DE RESULTADOS (Millones de Pesetas)

1 ¿Cómo ha sido el ejercicio del año 1989?

2 ¿Qué metas han alcanzado?

3 ¿Qué ha experimentado un crecimiento del 58%?

4 ¿A cuánto han ascendido los beneficios por acción?

5 ¿Qué cantidad ha invertido el grupo durante el año?

6 ¿Qué división ha consolidado su posición como la segunda fuerza del país?

7 ¿Por qué se ha optado?

8 ¿A qué empresa se ha dado un nuevo enfoque?

9 ¿Qué les ha animado a extender esta iniciativa?

10 ¿Qué confirma todo ello?

¿Verdadero o falso?

Nunca hemos estado en mejor forma

Extracto del informe del Presidente D. Charles Burdett

El año 1989 ha sido otro ejercicio de importante expansión y crecimiento de nuestra Sociedad, en el que hemos alcanzado metas fijadas para un tiempo más lejano. Nuestros ingresos consolidados han experimentado un crecimiento del 58 % hasta alcanzar 18.625 millones de pesetas. Asimismo, los beneficios por acción han sido de 1.452 pesetas que, comparados con las 929 pesetas de 1988, representan un avance del 57 %. De este modo, el crecimiento anual compuesto del beneficio por acción durante los últimos cinco años se sitúa por encima del 100 %.

El grupo consolidado ha realizado a lo largo del año inversiones por 1.425 millones de pesetas tanto en activos fijos como en la adquisición de los intereses minoritarios de Movinord S. A. y Mecanización de obras, S. A.

Nuestra División de distribución de maquinaria para la construcción, obras públicas y limpieza vial ha consolidado su posición como la segunda fuerza del país en este sector, alcanzando una cuota de mercado de un 20 % tras incrementar las ventas netas en un 45 %. La modernización de nuestra red de distribución así como la construcción de nuevas delegaciones, proceso que continuará durante el ejercicio en curso, son factores fundamentales de la creciente cobertura del territorio nacional por parte de nuestra organización.

En nuestra División de interiorismo cabe destacar la adquisición en Marzo de 1989, de Tecfloor, S. A., uno de los mayores fabricantes y distribuidores de la Península

Ibérica de suelos técnicos sobreelevados, que viene a complementar a Movinord, S. A. en la dimensión fabril de esta División. Las inversiones realizadas incluyen la adquisición de una nueva fábrica, terrenos y una moderna línea de producción para Tecfloor así como terrenos y dos líneas de fabricación nuevas para Movinord.

Por otro lado, se ha optado por separar la actividad de fabricación de elementos de interiorismo de la de instalación y servicios. Con este objeto, se ha dado un nuevo enfoque a Cador Centro, S. A. en Madrid destinado a ofrecer un servicio integral de interiorismo y soluciones llave en mano para la instalación de oficinas y otros locales comerciales e industriales. El indudable éxito obtenido nos ha animado a extender esta iniciativa a otras ciudades importantes de la Península Ibérica.

En Enero del presente año se adquirió Eurobags, S. A. sociedad que diseña, produce y distribuye bolsas publicitarias de alta calidad que crean para el cliente no sólo embalaje, sino también una imagen publicitaria propia y duradera. Estamos seguros de que esta nueva División de imagen contribuirá al crecimiento de nuestros resultados en los próximos años.

Entramos en 1990 con un balance sólido y una situación patrimonial envidiable que, unida al previsible crecimiento de los sectores en los que desarrollamos nuestra actividad nos hace confiar en una nueva progresión de los resultados durante el año en curso.

Todo ello confirma que nuestro Grupo nunca ha estado en mejor forma que en la actualidad.

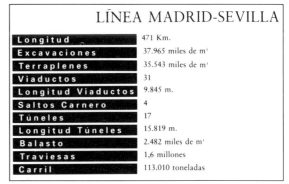

LÍNEA MADRID-SEVILLA	
Longitud	471 Km.
Excavaciones	37.965 miles de m³
Terraplenes	35.543 miles de m³
Viaductos	31
Longitud Viaductos	9.845 m.
Saltos Carnero	4
Túneles	17
Longitud Túneles	15.819 m.
Balasto	2.482 miles de m³
Traviesas	1,6 millones
Carril	113.010 toneladas

Di si las siguientes afirmaciones son verdaderas o falsas. Si son falsas, corrígelas.

1 Hay veintiún viaductos.
2 El largo de la línea es de cuatrocientos setenta y un kilómetros.
3 El número de traviesas es de uno coma seis millones.
4 Tiene nueve mil ochocientos cuarenta y cinco metros de viaductos.
5 Existen veintisiete túneles.
6 El carril tiene un peso de ciento trece mil ciento diez toneladas.
7 Hay treinta y cinco mil quinientos tres miles de metros cúbicos de terraplenes.
8 Hay cuatro saltos carnero.
9 La longitud total de los túneles es de cinco mil ochocientos diecinueve metros.
10 Tiene un balasto de dos mil cuatrocientos ochenta y dos miles de metros cúbicos.

• E S   A S I •

 El pasado

hablar to speak/talk

Singular		Plural	
yo	**hablé**	nosotros	**hablamos**
tú	**hablaste**	vosotros	**hablasteis**
él		ellos	
ella	**habló**	ellas	**hablaron**
usted		ustedes	

vender to sell

Singular		Plural	
yo	**vendí**	nosotros	**vendimos**
tú	**vendiste**	vosotros	**vendisteis**
él		ellos	
ella	**vendió**	ellas	**vendieron**
usted		ustedes	

recibir to receive

Singular		Plural	
yo	**recibí**	nosotros	**recibimos**
tú	**recibiste**	vosotros	**recibisteis**
él		ellos	
ella	**recibió**	ellas	**recibieron**
usted		ustedes	

While Damián Hernández talks about the development of the AVE, he refers to events which took place in the past. Look at how he does this.

colaboró con una empresa catalana, ADE.
. . . cuando ***hicieron*** los estudios de márketing . . .
nosotros ***pensamos*** en aquellos momentos que . . .

¿Qué tal el viaje?

La directora comercial de CCB acaba de regresar de un viaje promocional. Ahora está con el presidente de la compañía para hablar sobre el viaje.

Pon los verbos entre paréntesis en la forma correcta del pretérito indefinido (pasado). ¡Atención! ¡Hay verbos irregulares!

Presidente: ¿Qué tal el viaje?
Directora: Muy bien. *Estuve* en Caracas y Maracaibo y luego (*volar*) a Méjico donde (*visitar*) al Director de Operaciones Internacionales de PEMEX.
Presidente: ¿Qué (*hacer*) en Caracas?
Directora: (*Estar*) con Gisela Tinoco que me (*llevar*) a ver la refinería que tienen en Puerto La Cruz. Ellos (*construir*) un nuevo depósito el año pasado y ahora quieren otro.
Presidente: Le (*decir*) que estamos interesados en participar, ¿verdad?
Directora: Sí, claro. Yo creo que ellos no (*estar*) muy contentos con la actuación de la otra compañía. De todos modos voy a

preparar un presupuesto y ya veremos.

Presidente: De acuerdo. ¿A quién (*ver*) en Maracaibo? Javier Miranda ya no está, ¿verdad?

Directora: No, él (*marcharse*) a trabajar a los Estados Unidos. Yo (*hablar*) con Marco Betancourt. Nosotros (*firmar*) el contrato para los oleoductos. Luego (*dar*) una vuelta por el lago y yo (*poder*) ver el estado de las plataformas.

Presidente: ¿(*Estar*) en Maracaibo muchos días?

Directora: No. Yo (*ir*) a Méjico el día siguiente. Allí los representantes de PEMEX y yo (*empezar*) a negociar la entrega de material.

Presidente: ¿Cuándo (*pagar*) ellos la última entrega?

Directora: El mes pasado. Yo (*escribir*) a Méjico antes de salir de viaje y (*tener*) una reunión con nuestro contable. Están al día.

Presidente: En resumen (*ser*) un buen viaje. Bien hecho.

Fechas que hacen historia

Fechas que hacen historia

1986
— *11 de octubre*
Anuncio por parte del Vicepresidente del Gobierno de la decisión de construir el Nuevo Acceso Ferroviario a Andalucía (NAFA).
— *11 de noviembre*
Presentación del avance del Plan de Transporte Ferroviario (PTF).

1987
— *30 de abril*
Aprobación de PTF.
— *5 de octubre*
Comienzo de las obras del tramo Brazatortas–Córdoba.

1988
— *11 de enero*
Comienzo de las obras del tramo Getafe–Brazatortas
— *21 de octubre*
El Consejo de Ministros encarga a Renfe un informe sobre la posibilidad de introducir el ancho de vía internacional.
— *9 de diciembre*
El Consejo de Ministros acuerda que las nuevas líneas de alta velocidad que se construyan en España sean de ancho internacional.
— *23 de diciembre*
Adjudicación del AVE

1989
— *11 de julio*
Adjudicación de las obras de señalización y electrificación de los tramos Madrid–Getafe y Córdoba–Sevilla.

— *Julio*
Adjudicación de las otras del tramo Córdoba–Sevilla.

— *Agosto*
Adjudicación de las obras del tramo Madrid–Getafe.

— *2 de octubre*
Los Reyes de España asisten al montaje del primer tramo de vía, en ancho internacional, de la nueva línea.

1990
— *2 de abril*
Adjudicación de las obras de electrificación y señalización del tramo Getafe–Córdoba.

1991
— *Primavera*
Entrega de las primeras unidades AVE
Comienzo de pruebas en línea

1992
— *Abril*
Puesta en servicio comercial del tren de Alta Velocidad Madrid–Sevilla.

Lee la historia del desarrollo de la nueva línea ferroviaria entre Madrid y Sevilla y vuelve a escribir las frases en el pasado.

Ejemplos:

11 de octubre

El 11 de octubre de mil novecientos ochenta y seis el Vicepresidente del Gobierno anunció la decisión de construir el Nuevo Acceso Ferroviario a Andalucía.

11 de noviembre

El 11 de noviembre de mil novecientos ochenta y seis se presentó el avance del Plan de Transporte Ferroviario (PTF).

30 de abril
5 de octubre
21 de octubre
11 de julio
agosto de 1989
2 de octubre
2 de abril
primavera de 1991
abril de 1992

Todo a su tiempo

Estos sustantivos son del informe del ejercicio **Nunca mejor**. Busca el verbo relacionado con cada sustantivo y, después, completa las frases con el pasado correcto.

Ejemplo:
avance: La tecnología española ...... mucho en los últimos diez años.
avanzar *La tecnología española **ha avanzado** mucho en los últimos diez años.*

1 adquisición: El Grupo Hispano-Suiza ...... acciones de la compañía Movinord SA el año pasado.
2 distribución: Action Computers ...... 30.000 flyers este mes.
3 construcción: Nosotros ...... nuestra primera fábrica en España en 1951.
4 venta: Los nuevos modelos se ...... muy bien este año.
5 organización: La Xunta de Galicia ...... una feria de muestras para el próximo otoño.
6 fabricación: La compañía ...... su primer coche un 1953.
7 embalaje: ¿Vosotros aún no ...... los ordenadores?
8 división: Los padres ...... sus bienes entre los hijos.
9 progresión: El nivel empresarial ...... mucho en España en los últimos años.
10 crecimiento: En 1991 el Producto Interior Bruto ...... un 2,7% en España.

Sección 2

Wayne Rosemin y el señor Hernández discuten sobre algunos detalles del tren y la estación de Santa Justa.

PALABRAS Y FRASES UTILES

`42.36` Lee estas palabras y frases antes de ver el vídeo.

reunión = meeting	consigna = left luggage	maqueta = mock-up
acuerdo = agreement	mirada = look	arreglar = to fix
estación = station	sitio = place	franja = strip
señal = sign	rótulos = sign	puerta = door
fuerza = strength	explanada = concourse	

llegamos a acuerdos con el gerente	we reached agreements with the manager
dimos una vuelta	we walked round
Yo creo que falta fuerza	I think effect is lacking
A lo mejor no tengo razón, pero . . .	I might not be right, but . . .
No sé, quizás en el momento en que haya más cosas . . .	I don't know, perhaps when there are more things . . .

COMPRENSION

1 ¿Cuándo fue la reunión?
2 ¿Qué tal fue la reunión ayer?
3 ¿De qué hablaron?
4 ¿Con quién llegaron a acuerdos?
5 ¿Por dónde dieron una vuelta?
6 ¿Qué problema tienen las señales?
7 ¿Qué puede ser un error?
8 ¿Dónde van a seguir la conversación?
9 ¿Qué otra cosa quiere aclarar Wayne Rosemin?
10 ¿Cuál es uno de los primeros puntos que quieren revisar?
11 ¿Dónde piensa Wayne Rosemin que deben colocar el nombre de RENFE?
12 ¿Pondrán el símbolo, el logo, en los vagones?

APLICACION

● E S   A S I ●

Notice how Wayne and señor Hernández argue through a point, agreeing and contesting the other's viewpoint.

No sé, quizás . . .
No, yo creo que a no ser . . .

Opino igual que tú . . .
Sí, yo creo que es buena idea . . .
Muy bien, de acuerdo.

Here are a series of expressions which are used in Spanish to express agreement and disagreement.

Acuerdo

Tienes razón.
Opino igual que tú.
Sí, yo creo que es una buena idea.
Muy bien, de acuerdo.
Muy bien, me parece estupendamente.
(Sí,) Bueno.
(Sí,) Desde luego.
(Sí,) Claro que sí.

Desacuerdo parcial

A lo mejor no tengo razón.
No sé, quizás.
No lo sé.
Yo creo que . . .
No estoy seguro/a.
No estoy muy convencido/a.

Desacuerdo

No, yo creo que a no ser . . .
¿Por qué, cuál es el problema?
No estoy de acuerdo.
Pues, no estoy en absoluto de acuerdo.
De ninguna manera.
No es cierto.
Estás equivocado/a.
Estoy (completamente/absolutamente) en contra.

¿Qué opinas tú?

A Elige una de las expresiones (**a** - **j**) para responder a las siguientes frases.

Ejemplo: **1c**

1 • El gobierno debe gastar más en educación.
   ♦ . . . La preparación de los jóvenes es vital para el futuro del país.
2 • ¿Tú crees que Ramón será nombrado director comercial?
   ♦ . . . otros que también quieren el puesto.
3 • Yo estoy seguro de que el Mercado Unico beneficiará a España.
   ♦ . . . traerá problemas.
4 • España siempre ha sido una monarquía.
   ♦ . . . Ha habido dos repúblicas.
5 • No te preocupes. El banco nos dará un crédito.
   ♦ . . . debemos 10 millones de pesetas.
6 • Quiero invitarte a cenar esta noche. ¿Nos vemos en 'El Sevillano' a las 9.30?
   ♦ . . . parece estupendamente.
7 • Creo que podemos entrar en el mercado latinoamericano.
   ♦ . . . , porque la demanda de nuestros clientes actuales es superior a nuestra capacidad de producción.
8 • ¿Qué te parece si firmamos el contrato mañana?
   ♦ . . . mañana entonces.
9 • Me ofreciste un descuento de 10%.
   ♦ . . . ofrecí un 8%.
10 • ¿Estás segura de que el documento va a llegar a tiempo?
   ♦ . . . ya ha salido.

a No estoy de acuerdo, . . .
b Bueno, yo creo que también . . .
c Opino igual que tú.
d Muy bien, de acuerdo. Hasta . . .
e No sé, quizás. Hay . . .
f Estás equivocado.
g Desde luego. El mensajero . . .
h No es cierto, te . . .
i Muy bien, me . . .
j No estoy seguro. Ya . . .

B Organiza la siguiente discusión.

1 No estoy en absoluto de acuerdo con la elección de Sara para el puesto de vicepresidenta ejecutiva.

2 Sara es muy joven y atractiva, creará problemas . . .

3 Pues, que entre el personal femenino se creará un ambiente de envidia y crítica.

4 Sí, bueno, ¿y los hombres . . . ?

5 ¿Qué no?

6 Bueno, no estoy muy convencido, pero quizás tienes razón.

a No. Opino que el personal femenino verá en esta elección un estímulo para avanzar en sus propias carreras.

b Claro que sí.

c ¿Qué quieres decir con eso, por qué no estás de acuerdo?

d ¿Por qué? ¿Qué problemas?

e No, de ninguna manera.

f Yo creo que para ellos será positivo también. Sara es una persona muy inteligente y sabrá demostrar que el sexo no tiene nada que ver con la capacidad de trabajo.

● E S A S I ●

Look at these expressions with the verb **tener** used in the video:

Tengo la sensación de que *ha quedado pequeña.*

A lo mejor **no tengo razón** *. . .*

Sí, **tiene razón** *. . .*

Expresiones con tener

Tiene suerte.

Tiene prisa.

Tienen calor.

Tengo frío.

Tiene 100 años.

Tienen hambre.

Tiene sed.

Tiene sueño.

Tienen miedo.

Tiene dolor de cabeza.

Completa

Completa los siguientes diálogos con la forma y expresión correcta del verbo *tener*.

Ejemplos:
- ¿Por qué no conduces?
- *Porque solamente tengo quince años.*

- El mercado inmobiliario está congelado.
- *Tengo la sensación de que los precios de las casas bajarán.*

1 ¿Por qué abre Micaela las ventanas?
2 ¿Qué pasa con Alfonso?, tiene una cara terrible.
3 ¿Por qué van Luis y Rosa al bar?
4 ¿Por qué enciendes la calefacción?
5 Ahora que España está dentro del Sistema Monetario Europeo, yo creo que la peseta no se devaluará.
6 Covadonga y Fernando ganaron un millón de pesetas en las quinielas.
7 ¿Qué te pasa? ¿Por qué corres?
8 Pareces cansado, ¿no has dormido bien?
9 ¿Por qué no viajas en avión?
10 ¿Por qué no vienes a comer?

Completa

Completa las frases con el tiempo correcto del verbo entre paréntesis.

1 Ayer, el jefe de personal y el jefe de ventas .... una reunión con la directora de publicidad. (*tener*)
2 El avión para Bilbao .... todos los días a las ocho de la mañana. (*salir*)
3 Ellos todavía no .... el informe. (*haber/terminar*)
4 Nosotros .... los cheques en el banco todos los viernes. (*ingresar*)
5 Yo .... la exposición la semana que viene. (*visitar*)
6 Este mes, Carlos .... mucho. (*haber/trabajar*)
7 El representante sindical .... con los empleados esta tarde. (*ir/hablar*)
8 Yo .... la mercancía ayer a las tres de la tarde. (*enviar*)
9 Pues, nosotros aún no la .... (*haber/recibir*)
10 ¿Qué tal .... la conferencia de ayer por la mañana? (*ser*)

RECUERDA

In this unit you have studied:

- the use of the perfect tense and expressions you can use with this tense
  He trabajado *mucho este mes.*
  Aún no han reparado *la calle.*
- how to talk about some past events
  ¿**Mandaste** *la carta?*
  Yo **llegué** *ayer por la noche.*

- expressions with the verb tener
  Yo voy a dormir. **Tengo sueño**.
- how to argue a point
  Yo creo que *debemos invertir en Bonos del Estado.*
  No estoy de acuerdo. *Los intereses son muy bajos.*

Business Notes

SPAIN'S TRANSPORT AND COMMUNICATIONS SYSTEM

The video sequence introduces Spain's new high-speed train, the Alta Velocidad Española, or AVE. The new train will not only revolutionise rail travel in Spain but in an important sense symbolises a desire to elevate Spain's transport and communications system to the level of other European countries.

Spanish geographical realities have always hindered industrial development. Spain stands at a higher average altitude above sea level, 650 metres, than any other country in Europe except Switzerland. Madrid, focal point of road and rail networks, has the highest altitude of any capital city in the EC and, surrounded by mountains, has never been easily accessible from any part of the Peninsula. Communications and transport have been underdeveloped for a number of reasons: the many mountain ranges which have made road and rail construction difficult; extremes of climate in some parts of the country which may close roads in winter and ruin surfaces; seasonal rivers; the *rías* or fjords in the north-west, etc. In other European countries, such as the UK, an improvement in transport systems in the last century was due to the needs of the Industrial Revolution. In Spain, there was no Industrial Revolution until the 1960s, so when the economy and industry picked up to get on terms with other European competitors, the transport system could not cater adequately for the needs of business. Also, government was slow to respond to obvious infrastructural deficiencies, and after the first oil shock, investment in transport actually declined in real terms.

However, since 1982 and the advent of the first González government, the trend has been reversed. A 1980 Plan to extend the motorway network in Spain by 7,000 kilometres in ten years had only achieved half its objective by 1990. As a result, the government launched a major programme to build 1,700 extra kilometres of motorway and a further 1,200 kilometres of trunk roads by the end of 1992.

One major transport success in the 1980s was the development of domestic air travel, in line with the recommendations of another 1980 Plan to strengthen regional airports and facilitate commercial travel. Thus an initial 57,000 million pesetas' investment for the period 1981–1986 improved facilities at the airports of Madrid, Barcelona, Seville, Valencia, Malaga, Tenerife, Palma de Mallorca and Santiago. Five other airports important to the tourist trade – Alicante, Ibiza, Lanzarote, Las Palmas and Menorca – also received infrastructural subsidies. The resulting improvements and consequent increase in domestic air travel have been of enormous benefit to the Spanish business community, faced with lengthy alternative journeys by road or rail.

The railway system and the AVE

The Spanish national railway network, RENFE (*Red Nacional de Ferrocarriles Españoles*), under state ownership since

1941, has received significant government investment in the past decade. Recent improvements include the laying of more double track in mountainous terrain, a central computerised ticket booking system, more electrification and the introduction of better, faster trains. Since 1988, railway investment has risen at a yearly rate equivalent to 1% of GDP. The major part of this expenditure involves the introduction of high-speed trains, the AVE, on the Madrid–Seville and Madrid–Barcelona routes as well as the commencement of an operation which will go well into the next century, to narrow the gauge to that of Spain's EC partners. Spain's wider gauge of 1.668 metres compares with 1.435 metres in France, and the discrepancy has always hindered freight transport.

The high-speed line from Madrid to Seville is the first stage of a new international rail network, with two connections planned to France and one to Portugal by the year 2000. The Spanish aim is to link into a high-speed European rail network that is currently mapped out only on paper but which has a number of significant pieces slotting into place. There is the successful example of the French high-speed train, the TGV; the two-hour, 427-kilometre Paris–Lyon service alone carries 13,000 passengers a day, 90% of the market. The Channel Tunnel link, opening in 1994, will mean a three-hour journey from London to Paris and two hours forty minutes from London to Brussels. The UK business community may soon be witnessing a passenger or freight journey from the UK to Spain which could be equated with current journey times from London to the outer reaches of Britain.

The AVE Madrid–Seville service, opened in April 1992, has become a symbol of the Spanish desire to project themselves as a rich, progressive European nation. Constructed in great haste and at a cost which could rise to 500,000 million pesetas, six times the original budget, the AVE route has attracted great controversy, with environmentalists speaking of an 'ecological tragedy'. Despite such criticisms, twenty-four high-speed trains have been commissioned from the French company Alsthon, a new railway station has been built in Seville, as seen in the video sequence, and Madrid Atocha station has had fifteen new platforms constructed to take the train. Journey times will be within the timescale of three and a half hours, which is calculated to be the maximum time that business travellers are prepared to sit on a train.

The regional government of Cantabria, which wanted the link to France to be built first, accepted the argument that the route south of Madrid was a priority to ensure the connection of both halves of the country, but have exacted a promise from central government of an immediate start on the Madrid–Barcelona–French–border AVE. The Basque Country is also pressing for an extension of the high-speed track, but this is not expected until 2002. The AVE will have a dramatic impact on communities hitherto considered distant from Madrid. Ciudad Real, at 200 kilometres, is widely expected to become a dormitory town of Madrid. Apart from expanding the commuter network, the extremely competitive fare prices (tickets ranged from 6,000 to 16,500 pesetas when advertised in early 1992) are bound to appeal to the business and wider community.

The real cost of the AVE project is unknown, and, although many European governments, including Britain's, have been pouring money into their rail networks in recent years, the cost of putting a Europe-wide high-speed rail network in place is extremely high. (The Paris-based Community of European Railways estimates at least £85 billion, at 1985 prices, between now and 2015.) Spain, after centuries of isolation, is at the forefront of political and governmental pressure within the EC to transform the vision of a high-speed rail network from southern Europe to Scandinavia into reality.

DESIGN IN SPAIN

Addison's involvement in the AVE project is an indication both of opportunities for foreign companies in this service sector and of the Spanish interest in design. The world-wide 'fashionableness' of Spain since the mid-1980s has generated a desire on the part of Spanish designers to display their wares on a wider international stage and at the same time a willingness to import ideas from abroad. Spanish fashion (*diseño*) and the complex socio-cultural phenomenon of the *movida* – an explosion of the plastic and fine arts combined with a youth pop cult – were exported successfully to other EC countries in the 1980s. Spanish designers became famous across the world, and a proliferation of fashion shows and exhibitions in the major cities of Europe (e.g. Harrod's one-month 'Made in Spain' exhibition in 1988) was accompanied by renewed enthusiasm for Spanish artists, writers and film directors such as Pedro Almodóvar.

RENFE, as shown in the video sequence, has worked alongside Addison to design the AVE, seen as the flagship of Spain's new railway system. The project team has included ergonomists, transportation and interior designers and design specialists from other consultancies in Britain and Spain. Addison's Spanish experience also encompasses the Spanish dry pet foods manufacturer Purina, which came to Addison for help in creating the identity packaging and merchandising that would launch it successfully in the Spanish and other European markets. In both cases, Addison's ability to work in and manage multicultural, multiskilled teams was regarded as their greatest strength. Above all, the ability to communicate in Spanish and show an understanding of Spanish culture, as seen in the video sequence, has been a fundamental factor in the company's success in Spain.

OPPORTUNITIES IN OTHER SERVICE INDUSTRIES

The services sector in Spain is the most dynamic sector of the economy and the most significant component of GDP (54.6% in 1991). Foreign investments have been directed mainly at the financial institutions, insurance, transport and the hotel and catering trade. Many Spanish firms in this sector are small and require innovation, organisation and management. Opportunities are therefore abundant, particularly in insurance and advertising. The insurance market, while expanding rapidly, has obvious room for further growth when 40% of Spaniards have not yet taken out an insurance policy. Similarly, the advertising industry has been growing by an average of 20% per year since 1988, with all forms of media increasing turnover.

CHANGE IS BREWING

Study plan

SEQUENCE SUMMARY

THE BREWING COMPANY LA CRUZ DEL CAMPO HAS RECENTLY BEEN TAKEN OVER BY GUINNESS. VARIOUS SENIOR MANAGERS DESCRIBE THE COMPANY, THE BREWING PROCESS AND THE WAY IN WHICH THEIR OWN FUNCTIONS HAVE BEEN AFFECTED BY THE TAKEOVER.

WHAT YOU WILL LEARN

Sección 1

- to talk about the stages of a process
- to express quantities and percentages
- to use words like *of, with, for, between,* etc.

Business Notes

Acquisition of a Spanish company
Changing management structures
Changing work practices

Sección 2

- to talk about the history of your company
- some common job titles
- to describe a process of change
- to make some more comparisons
- to say what you are doing

LEARNING STRATEGY FOR EACH SECTION

Study the key words in the **Palabras y frases útiles** box and watch the video sequence, listening out for the key words. Make notes of what you have understood.
Then study the key phrases in the **Palabras y frases útiles** box and watch the video again.
Complete the **Comprensión** section that follows the **Palabras y frases útiles**.
Now you are ready to listen to the **Tutor cassette**. The cassette will take you through the exercises in this unit section by section.
When you have completed the language exercises in each section, study the **Business Notes** at the end of the unit for further information on business and industry in Spain.

6

CHANGE IS BREWING

Sección 1

Varios ejecutivos de la compañía La Cruz del Campo hablan sobre el proceso de producción y del desarrollo de la empresa.

PALABRAS Y FRASES UTILES

48.20 Lee estas palabras y frases antes de ver el vídeo.

cebada = barley	mosto = unfermented juice	cocción = cooking
malta = malt	mezcla = mixing	lúpulo = hop
caliente = hot	estrato = layer	amargor = bitterness
almidón = starch	bagazo = pulp	levadura = yeast
barato = cheap	ganado = cattle	cantidad = quantity
corregir = to correct		

La cebada, previamente germinada y tostada . . .	The barley, previously germinated and toasted . . .
. . . se muele y se mezcla con agua caliente . . .	. . . is ground and mixed with hot water . . .
Además de esta fuente de almidón . . .	Apart from this source of starch . . .
ya que su finalidad será . . .	since its purpose will be . . .
. . . que se va a vender posteriormente para . . .	. . . which is going to be sold afterwards for . . .
A continuación . . .	Next . . .
Inmediatamente finalizado este proceso . . .	Immediately this process is over . . .

COMPRENSION

1 Cebada germinada y tostada y malta, ¿son la misma cosa?
2 ¿Qué se hace con la malta?
3 ¿Qué porcentaje del contenido de la malta se verá disuelta?
4 ¿Por qué dos razones se pueden usar otras fuentes de almidón?
5 ¿Cuál es el proceso siguiente al de la mezcla?
6 ¿De qué se trata?
7 ¿Qué se hace después de enfriar el mosto?
8 ¿Cuántos grupos de producción de mosto hay en La Cruz del Campo?
9 ¿Cuántos litros de cerveza produce La Cruz del Campo al día?
10 ¿La producción anual coloca a La Cruz del Campo como la fábrica más importante de España?

APLICACION

• E S A S I •

Los procesos

In this sequence, Rafael talks about the process of making beer. Notice the phrases he uses to do this.

. . . *la cebada* **previamente** *germinada* . . .
En **el siguiente proceso** . . .
A continuación . . .
Inmediatamente **finalizado este proceso** . . .

¿Cómo se hace?

Fíjate en las expresiones que se utilizan en castellano para describir un proceso.

Primero • En la primera etapa • En primer lugar • Para empezar

Previamente • Anteriormente • Antes de esto

Al mismo tiempo • A la vez • Simultaneamente

Después • Seguidamente • En segundo lugar • Entonces • A continuación • Luego

Finalmente • En la última etapa • Por último

A El proceso de fabricación de la cerveza.

Aquí tienes un resumen de la explicación que Rafael da sobre el proceso de fabricación de la cerveza. Vuelve a ver el vídeo otra vez y escribe, en cada espacio en blanco, las expresiones adecuadas para describir este proceso

.... , la cebada .... germinada y tostada, más conocida con el nombre de malta, se muele y se mezcla con agua caliente, en un proceso en el que, aproximadamente, el 75% de su contenido se verá disuelto por la acción de las enzimas que se formaron .... en el malteado.

.... está la filtración. Mediante este proceso separamos el estrato soluble, conocido como mosto, de la parte insoluble, también llamada orujo bagazo, que se va a vender, ... , para alimentación de ganado vacuno. .... , se somete el mosto a un proceso de cocción más o menos prolongado en el que se le añade el lúpulo, que va a transmitir a la cerveza su típico y peculiar amargor y aroma. .... , una vez finalizado este proceso, el mosto se enfría, se oxigena y se siembra con la levadura de cultivo.

B El proceso de elaboración de vino tinto.

Coloca cada frase en el espacio correcto.

El vino se obtiene fermentando el zumo de uvas frescas. Primero .... Después, ... y al mismo tiempo

.... A continuación .... En la primera cuba los sedimentos son depositados en el fondo de la cuba. Una vez limpiado .... En la última etapa .... y, finalmente, ...

1 se deja fermentar el zumo con las cáscaras de las uvas
2 se llevan las uvas a la pisa donde se prensan
3 se extrae el mosto cn cl prensado y el vino está depositado en las cubas
4 después de un tiempo prudente, se embotella
5 de sedimentos se pasa el vino a la segunda cuba donde se añade sustancias para que se aclare
6 se añade anhídrido sulfuroso
7 se pasa a barriles de madera para su maduración

C Y ahora, con tus propias palabras y usando las expresiones dadas para describir un proceso, describe cómo se construyó la línea ferroviaria entre Madrid y Sevilla. Utiliza la forma pasiva del verbo y los datos del ejercicio **Fechas que hacen historia** en la página 101.

G10 Ejemplo:
Primero se anunció la decisión de construir el Nuevo Acceso Ferroviaria a Andalucía en octubre de 1986 y seguidamente se presentó el avance de Plan de Transporte Ferroviario.

● E S   A S I ●

In this sequence, Rafael says that the annual production of beer is **tres millones y medio de hectolitros**. In units 1 and 2 we saw how to express numbers and some measurements. Here are some more.

I   un . . .

I kg.	un kilo	de café
I gr.	un gramo	de oro
I l.	un litro	de aceite
I hl.	un hectolitro	de disolvente
I m.	un metro	de espesor

¹/₂   medio . . .

¹/₂ kg.	medio kilo	de plata
¹/₂ l.	medio litro	de vino
¹/₂ mm.	medio milímetro	de separación

¹/₄   un cuarto de . . .

¹/₄ l.	un cuarto de litro	de leche
³/₄ kg.	tres cuartos de kilo	de grasa

I%   uno por cien/ciento

35%	el treinta y cinco por cien/ciento de la producción
2,5%	el dos coma cinco por cien/ciento de interés

Conecta

Ordena y escribe las dos columnas lógicamente.

Ejemplo: **7d**
un cuarto de la población.

1	28,35 gr.	a	ancho
2	¹/₂ l.	b	interés
3	¹/₂ m.	c	oro
4	³/₄ kg.	d	la población
5	75 cc.	e	cerveza
6	8%	f	cebada
7	¹/₄	g	capacidad

Organiza y escribe

En estas frases las cantidades son mezcladas. Organiza y escribe las frases correctamente.

Ejemplo:
El tren español AVE va a alcanzar una velocidad de más de 300 km/h.

1 La distancia aproximada por carretera entre Madrid y Vigo es de 28,35 gr.

2 El 45.1. de las exportaciones españolas va a países de la CE.

3 En el centro de Madrid se vende un local de 650 km.

4 En 1993, el grupo Zannier-Poron, líderes de la ropa infantil en Francia, facturará 240 m² en el mercado español.

5 La capacidad del depósito de gasolina de un Honda Civic LSi es de 3.000 millones de pesetas

6 El tren español AVE va a alcanzar una velocidad de más de 68%

7 Una onza equivale a 300km/h

Completa

Entre las preposiciones que están abajo, elige la adecuada para completar cada frase.

Ejemplo:
Las llaves están ...... la mesa.
*Las llaves están **sobre** la mesa.*

1 La capital ...... España es Madrid.

2 Voy a hablar ...... el director mañana.

3 El otro centro está ...... Málaga.

4 Vendemos ...... catálogo.

5 Para mí un café solo ...... azúcar.

6 Estas dos rampas son ...... acceder al garaje.

7 El tren llegará ...... las ocho de la mañana.

8 La empresa está establecida ...... el año 1952.

9 Los sábados trabajamos ...... las dos de la tarde.

10 El Banco Gallego está ...... Correos y la farmacia.

> sin • en • de • a • desde • hasta
> entre • para • por • con

Sección 2

Don Eduardo Osborne y otros ejecutivos describen sus funciones dentro de la empresa y los cambios que han sucedido después de la fusión con Guinness.

PALABRAS Y FRASES UTILES

50.54 Lee estas palabras y frases antes de ver el vídeo.

asunto = affair	consumidor = consumer	fiscalidad = taxation
clima = climate	financiero = financial	tratado = agreement
accionista = shareholder	ventas = sales	imposición = taxation
empleado = employee	mercado = market	pagar = to pay
trabajador = worker	reclutar = to recruit	ejercicio = financial year
común = common	carrera = career	

Yo soy el vicepresidente de la compañía	I'm the deputy-chairman of the company
el Subdirector General de Asuntos Corporativos	the Deputy Director General of Corporate Affairs
. . . que tenía un consejo de administración	. . . which had a board of directors
. . . pensó que era importante. . .	. . . (the company) thought it was important
. . . que nos íbamos a encontrar una vez el Acta Unica . . .	. . . which we were going to find once the Single European Act . . .
hemos pretendido fusionar todos los elementos de márketing	we have endeavoured to amalgamate all the marketing elements
. . . centraliza absolutamente todas las marcas	. . . centralises the whole range of brands
estamos intentando efectuar algunos cambios	we are trying to make some changes
seguimos funcionando como una sociedad anónima sometida a las leyes españolas	we continue to work as a limited liability company subject to Spanish laws
. . . y una vez se reparten dividendos . . .	. . . and once dividends have been distributed . . .
. . . de los tratados internacionales de doble imposición	. . . of the international agreements on double taxation

COMPRENSION

1 ¿Cuáles son los cargos que don Eduardo Osborne ocupa en La Cruz del Campo?

2 ¿Qué tipo de compañía era La Cruz del Campo?

3 ¿Cuál fue la fórmula que La Cruz del Campo eligió para entrar en el mercado común?

4 ¿Cuál es la posición de Javier Personaga en el grupo Cruz Campo?

5 ¿Cuáles son las funciones de un departamento de márketing según Javier Personaga?

6 ¿Cuántas compañías formaban parte del grupo Cruz Campo antes de la entrada del grupo Guinness?

7 ¿Qué están tratando de establecer en la empresa?

8 ¿En qué dos mercados tiene que pensar la compañía?

9 ¿Cómo sigue funcionando La Cruz del Campo desde la fusión con Guinness?

10 ¿En qué país está la casa matriz de Guinness?

APLICACION

• E S   A S I •

G18 In this sequence, don Eduardo Osborne talks about the history of Cruz Campo.
*Cruz Campo **era** una compañía eminentemente familiar...*
*... **era** una sociedad anónima que **tenía** un consejo de administración...*
*... los consejeros **representaban** a los grupos familiares...*

Antes ...

A Contesta la pregunta.

Ejemplo:
¿Dónde vivían ustedes antes? (*en Madrid*)
Vivíamos en Madrid.

1 ¿Dónde trabajabas antes? (*en una fábrica textil*)

2 ¿Cómo era tu jefe anterior? (*muy serio*)

3 ¿A qué hora salíais de la oficina? (*a las ocho de la tarde*)

4 ¿Qué había en la isla de la Cartuja antes de la Expo? (*una fábrica de cerámica*)

5 ¿Teníais muchos empleados antes de la quiebra? (*diez*)

B Cambia al imperfecto.

Ejemplos:

● Ahora Juan siempre llega temprano. (*tarde*)
◆ *Antes siempre llegaba tarde.*
● Actualmente voy a todas las reuniones. (*no/ninguna*)
◆ *Antes no iba a ninguna.*

1 Ahora son millonarios. (*pobre*)
2 Ahora trabajas mucho. (*no/nada*)
3 Actualmente los medios de transporte son rápidos. (*muy lentos*)
4 Ahora vamos a España frecuentemente. (*no/nunca*)
5 Los precios de los alquileres de oficinas son muy caros. (*baratos*)

Un pasado histórico

D. Roberto Osborne Guezala, fundador de La Cruz Campo, Fábrica de Cervezas y Maltas, en 1904.

De los verbos que están abajo, elige el correcto para relatar la historia de La Cruz del Campo. Escribe los verbos en el pasado imperfecto. Tienes uno (. . . *era de 1.500.000 litros* . . .).

producir • salir • terminar • mantener
~~ser~~ • conmemorar • celebrar
venir • comenzar

La Cruz del Campo fue fundada en el año 1904 por don Roberto Osborne Guezala. Se estableció la primera fábrica de cervezas de Andalucía y una de las primeras de España. El nombre con que se designó a la sociedad .... de la ubicación de la factoría en las proximidades de un histórico monumento del siglo XIV. Este monumento .... el final de una procesión religiosa que todos los años se .... en Sevilla. Esta procesión .... del centro de la ciudad y .... en este monumento. Y así se convirtió en el logotipo de la fábrica.

En 1937 se constituye en Sociedad Anónima, y a partir de la década de los años cincuenta, ... la época de expansión.

La capacidad de producción en susinicios, *era* de 1.500.000 litros anuales, en 1987 se .... esta cantidad en un sólo día.

Antes de la asociación con Guinness, en diciembre de 1990, La Cruz del Campo .... una importante colaboración con el Grupo Cervecero norteamericano Stroh Breweries.

¿Puedo hablar con . . . ?

En esta secuencia hemos visto como se presentan algunos de los ejecutivos de la compañía.

Yo soy el **vicepresidente** *de la compañía.*
Mi posición es **subdirector general de márketing**.
Soy el **jefe de servicios de los estudios económicos y financieros** *del grupo Cruz Campo en España.*

A Mira el organigrama del equipo directivo de AVE en la página 118 e identifica la persona y su cargo.

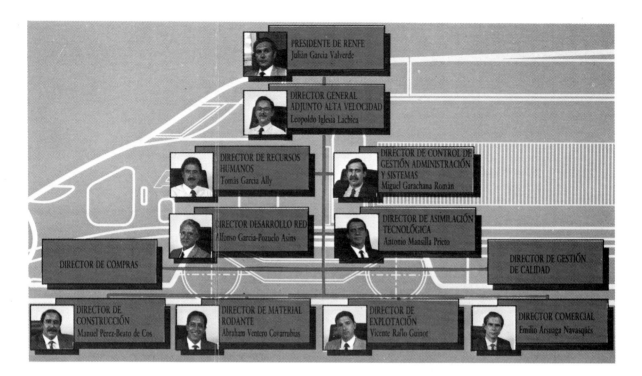

Ejemplo:

Está encargado del tren, de los vagones etc.
Es el director de material rodante y se llama
Abraham Ventero Covarrubias.

1 Está encargado de la construcción del
  ferrocarril, las estaciones etc.
2 Está encargado del personal.
3 En su trabajo tiene que estar al día con
  los avances tecnológicos.
4 Está encargardo de la compra y venta de
  bienes.
5 Es el segundo más responsable de la
  organización.

B Lee la información sobre los directivos de
  las compañías y contesta las preguntas.

AGUAS DE **F**UENSANTA, Ctra. Nal. 634, Km. 201,9. 33199
Meres Siero/Asturias. Tfno.: 98/792050. Telex: 84013.
Fax: 98/794552. Presidente: Rodrigo de Rato Figaredo.
Consejero Delegado: José María Fernández del Río.
Director General: Jesús Serafín Pérez Díaz. Director
Comercial: José Luis Nieto Senosiaín. Dtor.
Financiero-Administrativo: Enrique Aza Conejo. Subdirector
General: Pedro Isidro Riesco.

BODEGAS **C**APEL. Molino Alfatego s/n. 30100
Espinardo/Murcia. Tfno.: 968/830700. Telex: 67728. Fax:
968/830820. Consejero Delegado: Federico Muguniza
Unda. Director General: Axel Rucker. Director Comercial:
José Gomariz Romero. Director Administrativo: Ramón
Cascales López. Director de Producción: Francisco Rubio
Sebastián. Directora de Exportación: Sevi Rodríguez.
Director Financiero: José Tomás Vercher.

BODEGAS Y **B**EBIDAS. Paseo del Urumea, 21. 20014 San
Sebastián/Guipúzcoa. Tfno.: 943/468455. Fax:
943/462377. Presidente: José Domingo de Ampuero.
Vicepresidente: Manuel Azpilicueta Ferrer. Director General:
Pedro Casamitjana. Director Comercial: Jesús Trujillo
Ramos. Dtor. Financiero-Administrativo: Jesús Chocarro
Azcona. Director Técnico-Enológico: Francisco Díaz
Yubero. Director de Comunicación: Adolfo de Dios. Director
de Exportación: Victor Redondo. Director Asuntos Sociales:
Eduardo Manzano. Director Logística: Iñigo Ezcurra.
Director de Producción: Fernando Pozo.

Ejemplo:

¿Quién es el Director de Asuntos Sociales de
Bodegas y Bebidas?
Es Eduardo Manzano.

1 ¿Qué puesto ocupa Jesús Chocarro
  Azcona?

2 ¿Quién es el Director de Producción de Bodegas Capel?
3 ¿Sevi Rodríguez es la Directora de Exportación de qué compañía?
4 ¿Adolfo de Dios es un . . . ?
5 ¿En las tres compañías hay dos puestos comunes. ¿Cuáles son?

• E S   A S I •

G19 Juan de la Torre Fabre talks of the changes the managers in the Personnel Department are making to adapt to the new company structure. Look at how he does this.

. . . **estamos intentando** *efectuar algunos cambios* . . .

. . . **estamos trabajando** *en temas de remuneración* . . .

. . . **estamos tratando** *de establecer un nuevo sistema* . . .

Estamos trabajando

Mira los dibujos y contesta las preguntas.
Ejemplo:
¿Qué están haciendo? (*embotellar cervezas*)
Están embotellando *cervezas.*

1 ¿Qué está haciendo? *(hablar con)*
2 ¿Qué están haciendo? *(comprar)*
3 ¿Qué estáis haciendo? *(reorganizar)*
4 ¿Qué están haciendo? *(construir una fábrica nueva)*
5 ¿Qué está haciendo? *(esperar/ver)*
6 ¿Qué estás haciendo? *(redactar)*

Antes . . . pero ahora . . .

Contrasta el pasado con el presente.

Ejemplo:
Antes .... coches pero ahora .... autobuses. *(ellos/ producir/fabricar)*
*Antes **estaban produciendo** coches, pero ahora **están fabricando** autobuses.*

1 Antes .... para Megamárketing, pero ahora .... mi propia compañía. *(yo/trabajar/dirigir)*
2 Antes .... cada mes, pero ahora .... los pagos con letra a noventa días. *(nosotros/pagar/efectuar)*
3 Antes .... comprar nuestras acciones, y ahora .... de conseguir nuestros clientes. *(ellos/intentar/tratar)*
4 Antes .... de desarrollar una nueva fórmula, pero ahora .... las viejas. *(él/tratar/adaptar)*
5 Antes .... barcos de madera, pero ahora los .... de fibra de vidrio. *(nosotros/construir/hacer)*
6 Antes .... Digitalina, pero ahora me .... en comer mejor. *(yo/tomar/esforzar)*

• E S   A S I •

G14 In unit 4 we saw how Andy and Carlos compared things. In this sequence don Eduardo talks about the directors representing the most important family groups as

shareholders in Cruz Campo and the most useful formula for getting into Europe. Notice how he says something is the biggest and the best.

*. . . representaban a **los** grupos familiares **más importantes** . . .*
*. . . una de las formulas que era **la más útil** . . .*

El más grande del mundo

Forma el superlativo.

Ejemplo:
Este trabajo es .... de todos los que he hecho hasta ahora. *(difícil)*
*Este trabajo es **el más difícil** de todos los que he hecho hasta ahora.*

1 El Banco Central-Hispano es .... de España. *(importante)*
2 La región de Cataluña es .... de todas las regiones autónomas. *(rica)*
3 Este año ha sido .... de toda la historia de la compañía. *(malo)*
4 Las empresas alemanas son .... *(competitiva)*
5 Nuestra empresa es .... importadora de productos informáticos. *(grande)*
6 Nuestros tipos de interés son .... del mercado. *(bajo)*
7 Su oferta es .... que hemos recibido. *(interesante)*
8 Julio y Santiago son .... vendedores que tenemos. *(bueno)*
9 ¡Felicidades! Tu departamento es .... de toda la compañía. *(eficiente)*
10 Aunque su producto es .... , no quiere decir que es el mejor. *(caro)*

R E C U E R D A

In this unit you have studied:

- how to describe processes
  Primero la cebada es germinada y tostada y **después** se muele y se mezcla con agua. **A continuación** se separa el mosto del orujo bagazo y se somete a un proceso de cocción. **Al final** se añade el lúpulo y se deja enfriar.
- more ways of expressing numbers and quantities
  Se exporta **tres cuartos** de nuestra producción.
  En España se consume **28 millones de hectolitros** de cerveza al año.
  Tiene un espesor de **23 milímetros**.
- the use of some key prepositions
  Un café **sin** azúcar, por favor.
  Quiero hablar **con** el señor Juan Bravo.
  Voy a estar en la oficin **hasta** las cinco.
- another past tense (the imperfect)
  Antes ellos **trabajaban** en una compañía inglesa.

El año pasado yo no **podía** hablar español.
Cuando era niño **vivíamos** en Canadá.

- different positions in a company
  El señor Osborne es el **vicepresidente** de la compañía.
  David Breden es el **director de márketing** del Banco NatWest.
  El **jefe de ventas** es un inglés.
- how to express what people are and were doing
  Lo siento, pero él no está. **Está visitando** la fábrica en Sevilla.
  Estoy pensando en invertir en bonos del estado. El año pasado **estaban ganando** una fortuna.
- how to use superlatives
  Es **el mayor** productor de cerveza en España.
  Madrid es la ciudad **más grande** de España.
  De todos en la oficina ellas son **las más trabajadoras**.

Business Notes

ACQUISITION OF A SPANISH COMPANY

The video sequence illustrates some of the early consequences for a well-established family brewing firm from the south, La Cruz del Campo SA, arising from takeover by Guinness in late 1990. The impact on management and workforce is dealt with in later sections, although it is obvious that the underlying philosophy behind Guinness's penetration of the Spanish market is to allow the Spanish company to continue to employ local knowledge and expertise.

The Spanish brewing industry dates back to the 1500s when the King of Spain was Emperor Charles V, born in Ghent in Belgium. Although wine has traditionally been the chosen drink of Spaniards, recent years have nonetheless seen rapid growth in the consumption of beer, at the cost of wine. In acquiring La Cruz del Campo, Guinness have bought into a highly competitive market in which six major brewing groups, all dominated by foreign interests, control over 90% of the market.

Major brewing groups (1990)

NAME	OWNERSHIP/ PART OWNERSHIP	% MARKET SHARE
La Cruz del Campo	Guinness	21.6
El Aguila	Heineken (Holland)	17.7
Damm (Germany)	Oetker/Henninger	16.9
Mahou	Kronenbourg (France)	16.1
San Miguel	San Miguel (Philippines)	13.9
Unión Cervecera	Carlsberg (Denmark)	6.5
All six major brewers		92.7
Others		7.3
		100.0

(Source: *El País*)

Guinness's interest in buying into an expanding Spanish market, worth almost 300 billion pesetas in 1990, is also consistent with a recent internationalisation policy which has seen a Guinness link-up with LVMH, the Paris-based group which makes Moët et Chandon and Dom Pérignon champagnes, and Hennessy cognac. The Cruz del Campo acquisition may also assist Guinness's drive to promote sales in Spain of Johnnie Walker and Bell's whiskies as well as Gordon's and Booth's gins. With light taxes on spirits in Spain, whisky sales in particular have been accelerating in recent years.

The food, drink and tobacco industry in Spain is generally ripe for foreign intervention. The industry contains mostly small companies but is one of the most important manufacturing sectors, with almost 400,000 employees. About one quarter of Spain's largest 200 companies are to be found in this sector, which has seen strong penetration by foreign multinationals. The bread market, for instance, is dominated by Bimbo, (owned by Annhauser Busch, the US drinks firm) and Panrico (owned by Allied Lyons from the UK). Similarly, the meat industry is controlled by Unilever, Nestlé and Oscar Mayer from Germany.

Opportunities for UK and foreign companies rest precisely in the failings and limitations of many Spanish firms in this industry. Their lack of experience of international markets has meant little export success. Failure to invest sufficiently in product research and development has often led to a poor quality product with a poor image. If one combines this with poor distribution networks and lower levels of training among the workforce, it is easy to see the attraction of linking with a stronger European neighbour.

Changing management structures

The challenge for La Cruz del Campo as it faces up to a future within the Guinness organisation is to transform its philosophy from that of a leading regional company to that of a post-1992 international company with a Spanish arm. The implications for the management structures of La Cruz del Campo are outlined in the video sequence, but in the case of this company, are not so revolutionary as for many Spanish companies which have hitherto failed to put into place a marketing management team or responsive financial reporting, or paid attention to corporate identity.

The advent of a marketing-oriented philosophy has come later to Spanish companies, with marketing not taken seriously by most Spanish firms until the late 1970s, a decade or more behind competitors in the UK, Germany and France. La Cruz del Campo is a company with a background in marketing, and the firm's main task, as depicted in the video, is to streamline the marketing operations of the company's constituent parts into one cohesive marketing department, above all in an endeavour to improve brand image (*imagen de marca*). In many Spanish firms, the challenge is to introduce new managers trained in modern management techniques, or to acquire such skills by liaising with a foreign company.

Company image and corporate identity have not been high on the list of priorities of Spanish companies generally, although La Cruz del Campo, which claims to have management structures similar to the UK, is the exception which proves the rule, since the *vice presidente* of the company (equivalent to Deputy Chariman of the Board) states in the video sequence the importance of the firm's presentation of itself both to the outside world and to its own employees. Again, financial practices of Spanish firms are bound to change – and are changing – as a result of link-ups with foreign firms or as a consequence of the need to compete efficiently. As described in the video, the main thrust of the changes is the need for more reliable and more regular financial monitoring and reporting. The example provided is that of taxation changes, especially corporate tax (*impuestos sobre sociedades*), which may accrue from greater internationalisation.

Changing work practices

In the video sequence, La Cruz del Campo are concerned to review work practices in the light of the company's absorption into an international giant. The Spanish firm stress a number of points: the good employer/employee relations in the past; the need for new communications with the workforce, both vertical and horizontal; the need for review of remuneration and for job evaluation generally; and the shortage of workforce skills training.

The Spanish labour market has traditionally been characterised by a rigid legal framework and work practices. Job security was very tight, and large redundancy payments necessary if a contract was broken. Unitl the mid-1980s, it was difficult for employers to use part-time or fixed-term contracts. In addition, there was, and still is, a substantial black, or submerged, economy (*economía sumergida*) with perhaps two million people employed in a variety of sectors, but especially service industries, construction, and manufacturing industries such as textiles, food, toys and shoes.

Since 1984, the Spanish government has been gradually introducing greater flexibility into the labour market, perceiving the need for Spain to come into line with other EC countries over employment legislation. The advent of the Single Market has accelerated this trend. The period up to 1992 has thus seen the introduction of fixed-term contracts, usually for six months, the spread of part-time employment, especially for the under twenty-fives and over forty-fives, and expansion of training schemes and more provision for early retirement. These have been accompanied by special employment programmes to promote small industry and self-employment, which include employment and training grants, relief from social security contributions, fiscal measures and soft loans

The result has been an explosion in temporary jobs, with an estimated one in three of the workforce on such contracts in 1992. Four in five of workers under the age of twenty fall into this category. Whereas in 1985, one year after the first major measures to improve flexibility in employment laws had been implemented, only 11% of employees were on temporary contracts, in 1992 the figure was over 30%. The government claims that new flexibility has created two million jobs.

Further flexibility in the labour market has ensued from a government report in 1990, which made a number of recommendations. Temporary posts may now be for a minimum of three months instead of six and a maximum of two years instead of three. A new kind of apprenticeship, known as a *contrato en prácticas*, is available for a minimum of six months for those with further educational qualifications. Training centres (*centros de formación*) have been set up nationally to assist the unemployed, while temporary posts have been created for the over-forty-five age group and for the disabled. Part-time employment has been on the increase in an effort to alleviate redundancies and cuts in full-time employment. Most strikingly, as companies like La Cruz del Campo invest in new plant and technology, the training emphasis in Spain has switched dramatically to training for young people in the new technologies.

RETAIL IN SPAIN

Study Plan

SEQUENCE SUMMARY

MARKS AND SPENCER HAVE OPENED A LARGE STORE IN MADRID. THE M&S STYLE OF DOING BUSINESS IS NEW TO SPANISH CUSTOMERS, WHO TRADITIONALLY EXPECT A FAIR DEGREE OF PERSONAL ATTENTION. AT THE WEEKLY MEETING, THE MANAGEMENT TEAM REVIEWS PROGRESS ON THE SALES OF LADIES' CLOTHING AND PLANS A SPECIAL PROMOTIONAL EVENT TO BOOST SALES OF MENSWEAR. FINALLY, WHILE THE MANAGERS MUNCH THEIR WAY THROUGH SOME NEW FOOD LINES, THERE IS A BRIEF LOOK AT METHODS OF PAYMENT AVAILABLE TO THE CUSTOMER.

WHAT YOU WILL LEARN

Sección 1

- how to present a product – 1
- how to express your reactions and preferences
- some colours
- how to make a purchase

Sección 3

- how to describe the way things are done, e.g. *certainly, urgently, easily,* etc.
- how to complete your purchase and pay for it

Sección 2

- how to give your opinion and advice
- how to brief colleagues on future events
- how to say *everybody/nobody/some/none/* etc.
- how to present a product – 2

Business Notes

The retail revolution
Marks and Spencer–Cortefiel joint venture
A different approach to retailing

LEARNING STRATEGY FOR EACH SECTION

Study the key words in the **Palabras y frases útiles** box and watch the video sequence, listening out for the key words. Make notes of what you have understood.

Then study the key phrases in the **Palabras y frases útiles** box and watch the video again. Complete the **Comprensión** section that follows the Palabras y frases útiles.

Now you are ready to listen to the **Tutor cassette**. The cassette will take you through the exercises in this unit section by section.

When you have completed the language exercises in each section, study the **Business Notes** at the end of the unit for further information on business and industry in Spain.

7

RETAIL IN SPAIN

Sección 1

En la nueva tienda de Marks and Spencer en Madrid.

PALABRAS Y FRASES UTILES

`00.00` Lee estas palabras y frases antes de ver el vídeo.

adquirir = to acquire	planchar = to iron	prefiero = I prefer
sábana = bedsheet	lavar = to wash	tarjeta = card
cama = bed	estampado = printed	en efectivo = in cash
algodón = cotton	raya = stripe	

¿Le puedo ayudar?	Can I help you?
Quisiera adquirir un conjunto de sábanas	I would like to buy a set of sheets
Compone la sábana de arriba, sábana bajera y cubrecanapé	It is composed of the upper sheet, the lower sheet and bedspread
Es cincuenta poliéster y cincuenta algodón	It's 50% polyester and 50% cotton
Prefiero el liso en tonos pasteles o el estampado	I prefer the plain pastel shades or the printed one
puede pasar aquí a caja	would you come this way to the cash desk
¿Cómo lo va a abonar, en efectivo o con tarjeta?	How are you going to pay, in cash or by credit card?

COMPRENSION

1 ¿Qué quiere comprar la señora?
2 ¿Para qué tamaño de cama quiere las sábanas?
3 ¿En qué consiste el conjunto de sábanas?
4 ¿Cuál es la composición del material?
5 ¿Es difícil de lavar y planchar?
6 ¿Qué otros colores y tipos de estampado hay?

7 ¿Qué clase de material no tienen?
8 ¿Qué prefiere la señora?
9 ¿Cómo va a pagar?
10 ¿Cuánto tiene que pagar la señora?

¿Qué es?

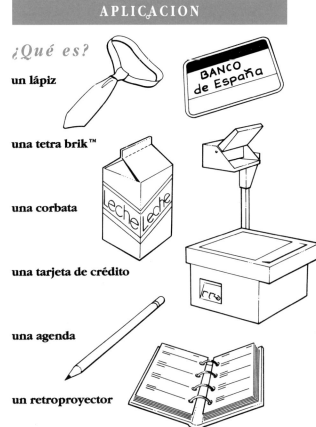

un lápiz

una tetra brik™

una corbata

una tarjeta de crédito

una agenda

un retroproyector

Relaciona cada objeto con su descripción.
1 Es rectangular.
  Es de plástico.
  Es plana.
  Tiene un código numérico.
  Es ....
2 Es tridimensional.
  Es de cartón.
  Generalmente se fabrica en dos tamaños
  estándar.
  Es para contener líquidos.
  Es ....

3 Es de metal y cristal.
  Tiene una lámpara potente.
  Sirve para proyectar imágenes.
  Tiene un interruptor.
  Es ....
4 Es cilíndrico.
  Es de madera.
  Sirve para escribir.
  Tiene punta.
  Es ....
5 Puede ser de lana, de seda, acrílica o de
  algodón.
  Generalmente la usan los hombres.
  Es más ancha en un extremo que en el
  otro.
  Se lleva en el cuello.
  Es ....
6 Las tapas pueden ser de cuero, de
  plástico o de cartón.
  Dentro, las hojas son de papel.
  Sirve para anotar citas.
  Se cambia cada año.
  Es ....

Organiza

Tu jefe acaba de abrir una oficina en
España y necesita comprar algunas cosas.
Ha dejado la lista de lo que hay que
comprar en el ordenador, pero hay un
'virus' y todo está mezclado. Organiza la
lista de la compra.

Ejemplo: **5f**
Un teléfono portátil

1 Un ordenador de	a bolsillo
2 Una silla de	b porcelana
3 Una mesa de	c algodón
4 Una calculadora de	d madera con cuatro cajones
5 Un teléfono	e plástico
6 Tres cortinas de	f portátil
7 Seis tazas de	g cuero

● E S   A S I ●

Prefiero . . .

Notice how the customer expresses preferences:

*No, rayas **no me gustan, prefiero** los lisos . .*
Prefiero el liso en tonos pasteles . . .

We saw how to express likes and dislikes in Sección I of **Tapas and Technology**. Here are some more ways to express your feelings about something:

Entusiasmo (++)

Me encanta(n) ⎫ mucho
Me gusta(n)   ⎬ bastante
               ⎭ muchísimo

Agrado (+)

Está bien
No está mal

Desagrado (-)

No me gusta(an) ⎰ mucho
                ⎱ nada

Es horrible

Reacciona

Ejemplos:

* ¿Qué te parece la nueva tarjeta de crédito BXT?
♦ **Me gusta muchísimo**, *tiene muchas ventajas y el interés es muy bajo.*
* ¿Qué le parecieron los acuerdos a los que llegó el sindicato?
♦ **No me gustan nada**. *Nos harán perder dinero.*

1 • ¿Qué te parece el nuevo horario de trabajo?
  ♦ .... , porque ahora tengo que levantarme más temprano.

2 • ¿Qué opinas de los nuevos ordenadores que tenemos en la oficina?
  ♦ .... ¡son fantásticos!
3 • ¿Le gustan los diseños de los envases?
  ♦ .... , son horribles.
4 • ¿Qué te pareció la exhibición?
  ♦ .... , pero tampoco fue nada especial.
5 • ¿Le gusta el catálogo que acabamos de lanzar?
  ♦ .... Es muy aburrido.
6 • ¿Qué opinas del jefe de personal que tenemos ahora?
  ♦ .... , parece inteligente.

¿Cuál te gusta más?

Di cuál de las dos opciones te gusta más y explica por qué.

Ejemplo:

♦ Tenemos camisas de algodón o de nailon. *(gustar/fibras naturales)*
● *Prefiero camisas de algodón porque **me gustan las fibras naturales**.*

1 Tenemos el modelo con motor diesel o de gasolina. *(no gustar/diesel)*
2 Hay cerveza con o sin alcohol. *(tener que conducir)*
3 Podemos hacer paquetes de 100 o de 1.000 unidades. *(1.000 unidades son excesivas)*
4 Puede viajar en tren o en avión. *(no gustar/volar)*
5 En tu viaje puedes llevar dinero en efectivo o cheques de viajero. *(dar/más seguridad)*
6 Podemos invertir en letras del tesoro a un 11,85% o pagarés del INI a un 12,15%. *(ser/más rentable)*

¿Qué color?

En esta sección el cliente dice:
. . . *acabo de pintar la habitación de* **rosa**.

Mira las definiciones de los colores.

rosa	Nombre de una flor y también de mujer.
azul	Color de fondo de la bandera de la Comunidad Europea.
azul marino	Color de los uniformes de la policía en Inglaterra.
blanco	Color de una hoja de papel antes de escribir en ella. Nombre de la casa donde vive el Presidente de los EEUU.
negro	Color de los coches Ford Modelo T.
verde	Nombre de un movimiento ecologista. Color de las hojas de los árboles.
marrón	Color de la tierra
gris	Una mezcla de negro y blanco. El color de los vehículos de British Telecom.
amarillo	El color de las líneas pintadas en las calles donde está prohibido aparcar. El color del submarino de los Beatles.

Completa el crucigrama con las pistas y descubre el color escondido en la línea horizontal.

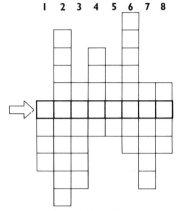

1 Es el color del cielo. Una época temprana de Picasso.
2 Color de fondo de la bandera de Escocia.
3 El color de la madera.
4 En una tabla de ajedrez hay dos colores, blanco y ......
5 El color del plomo.
6 El mismo color que está en la línea horizontal.
7 Como la nieve.
8 En esta sección la señora pintó su habitación en este color.

Sección 2

Alan Cooke dirige una reunión en castellano.

PALABRAS Y FRASES UTILES

03.30 Lee estas palabras y frases antes de ver el vídeo.

departamento = department	sección = division	dependiente = shop assistant
abrigo = coat	caballeros = gentlemen	gambas = prawns
chaquetón = three-quarter coat	pantalones = trousers	ajo = garlic
camisa = shirt	ropa interior = underwear	jamón = ham
traje = suit	niños = children	té = tea
manga = sleeve	promoción = promotion	

. . . la semana pasada y esta semana serían difíciles este año	. . . last week and this week would be difficult this year
es una camisa de poliéster de manga corta	it's a polyester, short-sleeved shirt
el blázer azul marino de lana	the navy blue woollen blazer
estoy super contenta de lo bien que va	I'm extremely pleased with how well it's going
la sección de caballeros	the menswear department
para esta promoción vamos a tener excepciones	for this sales promotion we are going to have special offers
Vamos a tener doce dependientes	We are going to have twelve shop assistants
estos son gambas con ajo	these are prawns with garlic
llevan bastante ajo	they've got quite a lot of garlic
casi todas las líneas	nearly all the lines
es para hacerlo directamente en la taza	it's to make it directly in the cup

COMPRENSION

1 ¿Cuál es el primer departamento que cita Alan Cooke?

2 ¿Qué semanas serán difíciles este año?

3 ¿Qué incremento tuvieron al final?

4 En el departamento de señoras, ¿qué número tiene la sección de abrigos y chaquetones?

5 ¿Qué porcentaje hace el stock sesenta y ocho cero cero?

6 ¿Cómo es la camisa?

7 ¿Qué número de stock le corresponde al blázer azul marino?

8 ¿Qué van a ampliar para esta promoción? Cita las seis prendas que van a tener en esa sección.

9 ¿Cuándo van a hacer el cambio?

10 ¿Qué días de la semana son para los clientes de M&S?

APLICACION

• E S   A S I •

G20 Notice how Alan Cooke acknowledged that they knew the last two weeks would be difficult:

Sabemos que la semana pasada y esta semana **serían** *difíciles . . .*

We can use the conditional in Spanish, as in English, to give advice and suggestions.

Completa

Rellena los espacios con la forma adecuada del potencial.

• El jefe me va a despedir después del fracaso de las negociaciones.

♦ ¿No puedes hacer nada?

• ¿Qué me (*aconsejar*)?

♦ Bueno, (*poder*) tratar de hablar con el director de recursos humanos. Estoy seguro de que te (*agradecer*) la posibilidad de resolver el asunto. Lo que tú (*deber*) hacer es pedir una cita con él.

• No (*ser*) una mala idea, pero ¿cuándo hablo con él?

♦ Yo (*hablar*) con él lo antes posible.

• Sí, tienes razón.

¿Qué hago?

¿Qué consejo darías en estas situaciones?

Ejemplo:

• Y ¿qué pasa si te quedas sin dinero? (*pagar con Visa*)

♦ **Pagaría** *con Visa.*

1 • No sé dónde invertir la herencia de la tía Julia.

♦ Yo .... con tu asesor fiscal. (*hablar*)

2 • ¿Cuándo debo mandar la confirmación del envío?

♦ .... hacerlo cuanto antes. (*deber*)

3 • ¿Qué pasa si viene el inspector y no tengo los libros de contabilidad al día?

♦ .... que pagar una multa. (*tener*)

4 • Y si hay una huelga. ¿Qué .... Vd? (*hacer*)

♦ .... la mercancía por carretera. (*mandar*)

5 • ¿Y si decimos a los sindicatos que no podemos aumentar los sueldos este año?

♦ Me parece que .... un error. (*ser*)

Todo o nada

En esta sección oímos como Julio Hernanz habla de cantidades indefinidas. Mira como lo hace.

casi todas *las líneas*

Vamos a ver cómo expresar cantidades sin usar números:

FORD   SEAT   RENAULT   CITROEN
Valencia   Barcelona   Valladolid   Vigo

Todas *estas compañías tienen fábricas en España.*

En la venta directa **casi todos** *los vendedores son independientes.*

Fuente: Federación Mundial de Venta directa

Muchas *de las exportaciones suizas son de maquinaria.*

LA RELIGION EN OCCIDENTE

Van a la iglesia al menos una vez a la semana

Francia	10
G. Bretaña	13
Alemania	19
Holanda	21
Suecia	4
Italia	40
España	33
Irlanda	65
EE.UU.	43
Canadá	33

Pocos *suecos van a la iglesia.*

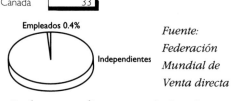

Fuente: Federación Mundial de Venta directa

En la venta directa **casi ningún** *vendedor es empleado.*

Algunos *de los empleados de Marks and Spencer en Madrid son ingleses.*

Ningún *empresario puede ignorar el Mercado Unico.*

Completa

Mira la lista de hoteles en Madrid y la guía. Ahora coloca el adjetivo más apropiado según el sentido de la frase.

GUIA DE HOTELES

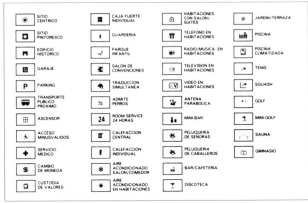

Categoría y grupo	Mod.	ESTABLECIMIENTO	Temporada Alta Media Baja	N.º habit.	Habitación doble	
1	2	3	4	5	Baño 6	Lavabo 7
		MADRID (Cont.)				
HR ****		**Tryp Fenix** ◉ 🛏 ⊞ $ 🔒 📺 ☎ 🐕 24 🍴 I ✱ ❄ 🏠 🖥 Hermosilla,2 ☎4316700 ☎45639tryps 🖥 🍴 ❄ 🎾 RAMOS D'ANGELO, IGNACIO J. ☎5760661	1/1-31/12	216	22900	
HR ****		**Tryp Menfis** ◉ ⊞ $ 🔒 📺 🍴 I ✱ ❄ 🖥 🏠 🖥 ⊟-V Gran Vía 74 ☎2470900 ☎48773phtoe BARRIO MOYA DOMINGO DEL ☎2475199	1/1-31/12	122	14000	
H ****		**Tryp Velázquez** ◉ 🅖 P ⊞ $ 🔒 📺 🔒 🍴 I ✱ Velázquez 62 ☎5752800 ☎22779hovee 🖥 🏠 🖥 LLANO URIARTE JOSE FELIPE ☎5752809 ⊟-V ❄ 🔒 🖥	1/1-31/12	130	15000	
HR ***		**Abeba** ◉ 🅖 🛏 ⊞ + $ 🔒 📺 I ✱ ❄ 🖥 🖥 🐕 Alcántara 63 ☎4011650 MARTIN ESTEBAN EMILIO ☎4027591		90	9350	
HR ***		**Alondras Sol,Las** ◉ 🛏 🔒 ⊞ + $ 🔒 📺 I ✱ ❄ 🖥 José Abascal 8 ☎4474000 ☎49454haln ⊟-V🐕 PALENCIA BARRADO INMACULADA ☎5938800	1/1-31/12	72	15690	
HR ***		**Anaco** ◉ 🛏 ⊞ + $ 🔒 ✱ ❄ 🖥 🖥 🖥 Tres Cruces 3 ☎5224604 RODRIGUEZ-DE-LA-CRUZ JOSE ANTONIO ☎5316484	1/1-31/12	39	7625	
HR ***		**Aramo** ◉ 🅖 ⊞ $ 🔒 📺 🔒 🔒 ✱ ❄ 🏠 🖥 🖥 🔒 Pº Sta.María Cabeza,73 ☎4739111 ☎45885hoare GONZALEZ VALDES JOSE FERNANDO ☎4739214	1/1-31/12	105	15000	
HR ***		**Aristos** ◉ 🛏 🔒 ⊞ I ✱ ❄ 🏠 🖥 🖥 🔒 ❄ Avda de Pío XII 34 ☎4570450 CASTELEIRO MACEIN ANGEL ☎4571023		25	10800	
M ***		**Avión** P 🛏 $ 🔒 📺 I ✱ ❄ 🖥 ❄ Ctra. De Barcelona Km. 14,200 ☎7476222 LOPEZ LORENTE JOSE AGUSTIN ☎7472736	1/1-31/12	64	10800	
HR ***		**Carlos V** ◉ 🅖 P 🛏 ⊞ + $ 🔒 📺 I ✱ ❄ 🖥 🖥 Maestro Vitoria,5 ☎5314100 ☎48547hcar GUTIERREZ HERRERA NICOLAS ☎5313761	1/1-31/12	67	11250	
HR ***		**Cáson del Tormes** ◉ 🅖 🛏 🔒 + $ 🔒 📺 I ✱ ✱ Río 7 ☎2419746 ZURBANO DIAZ-DE ILARRAZA M ROSARIO	1/1-31/12	61	8500	
HR ***		**Claridge** ◉ 🅖 ⊞ ✱ ✱ ☎ Plaza del Conde de Casal 6 ☎5519400 ☎44970 LOPEZ DELGADO LUIS ☎5010385	16/3-31/12 1/1-15/3	150	9500 8510	

1 ...... tienen aire acondicionado en las habitaciones.

2 ...... tienen transporte público cerca.

3 ...... tiene piscina.

4 ...... están en un sitio céntrico.

5 ...... tienen servicios de peluquería de señoras y de caballeros.

6 ...... tienen jardín o terraza.

7 ...... tienen calefacción central.

8 ...... tienen antena parabólica.

9 ...... tienen teléfonos en las habitaciones.

10 ...... tiene discoteca.

Y más . . .

Fíjate que también Julio dice que los sandwichs:

*. . . están **bastante** buenos.*

Aquí hay dos expresiones más:

*Hay **demasiada** gente.*

*Hay **bastante** sitio.*

Pon el adjetivo en la forma correcta.

Ejemplo.

Tengo ...... facturas que pagar. (*mucho*)

*Tengo **muchas** facturas que pagar.*

1 Tenemos ...... empleados. Tenemos que despedir a ...... personas. (*demasiado/alguno*)

2 Hoy en día en España hay ...... oportunidades para invertir. (*mucho*)

3 ...... nuestros modelos tienen una garantía de un año. (*todo*)

4 Es la misma historia ...... los días. Siempre llega tarde. (*todo*)

5 No tengo ...... interés en negociar un nuevo contrato. Todavía tengo ...... existencias. (*ninguno/bastante*)

6 No podemos pagar la nómina. Tenemos ......dinero. (*poco*)

Viceversa

Encuentra el contrario de las palabras en negrita. Los contrarios están debajo.

Ejemplo:

El gerente de **ventas** está de viaje esta semana. (*compras*)

largo • fácil • mal • menos
viejo • tarde • mala • débil
disminuimos • pequeña

1 Este sistema de fabricación es muy **nuevo**.

2 La subida de la bolsa ha sido muy **fuerte**.

3 El presupuesto está bastante **bien**.

4 El año pasado **ampliamos** nuestros canales de distribución.

5 El discurso del presidente fue muy **corto**.

6 La calidad de vida en España es **buena**.

7 La competencia entre las dos compañías es muy **grande**.

8 Este año vendimos **más** que el año pasado.

9 La presentación la haremos el viernes por la **mañana**.

10 Renovar este contrato va a ser **difícil**.

¿Quién lo dijo?

En esta sección has visto una reunión entre el gerente, Alan Cooke, y tres jefes de ventas, Marisé Rodríguez, Tracy Peck y Julio Hernanz. Aquí tienes algunas de las expresiones que utilizaron. Elige la correcta y di quién la dijo.

1 La semana pasada y esta semana serían { difíciles / fáciles / complicadas } este año.   Lo dijo . . .

2 Es muy { mal. / regular. / bien. }   Lo dijo . . .

3 Los departamentos más { fuertes. / débiles. / normales. }   Lo dijo . . .

4 Un stock muy { bueno. / malo. / indiferente. }   Lo dijo . . .

5 Es una camisa de poliéster, de manga { larga. / corta. / media. }   Lo dijo . . .

6 Un ciento uno por ciento, { menos / igual / más } que el año pasado.   Lo dijo . . .

7 Vamos a { reducir / ampliar / cambiar } para esta promoción la sección de caballeros.   Lo dijo . .

8 Estamos haciendo este cambio, que es bastante { necesario. / pequeño. / grande. }   Lo dijo . . .

9 Este jueves por la { mañana. / noche. / tarde. }   Lo dijo . . .

10 Estos son los sandwichs { nuevos. / viejos. / frescos. }   Lo dijo . . .

Sección 3

Un cambio de estrategia.

`08.45` Lee estas palabras y frases antes de ver el vídeo.

cheques = cheques	pago = payment	atendidos = served
cartelitos = signs	siempre = always	salvo = except
admitir = to accept/admit	impagados = unpaid	vendedores = sales persons
medio = means	pérdidas = losses	abordados = approached

Luego tengo también que hablar un poquito sobre . . .	Next I also have to say something about . . .
¿Qué respuesta tiene que darle?	What answer should he give her/him?
en el cartel pone . . .	on the sign it says . . .
no se admitirán cheques	cheques will not be accepted
se puede dirigir a una persona . . .	you can speak to someone . . .
si alguien pregunta . . .	if anyone asks . . .
la empresa no está dispuesta a tener estas pérdidas	the company is not prepared to put up with these losses
. . . que podemos cogerla sin ningún problema	. . . which we can accept without any problems.
. . . y una vez que ya piden consejo es cuando el vendedor actua	. . . and once they ask for advice is when the salesperson comes to help
Antes era precisamente todo lo contrario	Before it was quite the opposite

COMPRENSION

1 ¿De qué quiere hablar José Moreno?
2 ¿Dónde han bajado los cartelitos?
3 ¿Qué pone en los carteles?
4 ¿Qué indicará la persona si uno necesita más información?
5 ¿Durante cuánto tiempo han tenido problemas con los cheques?

6 ¿Cómo es el porcentaje de clientes que usan cheques?

7 ¿Qué tarjetas acepta Marks and Spencer según el gerente?

8 ¿A qué no está dispuesta la empresa?

9 ¿Cuándo atienden los vendedores directamente a los clientes?

10 ¿El sistema de ventas fue siempre así?

APLICACION

● E S A S I ●

G11 In this section we saw how to express possibilities in the future.

. . . **si necesita** información, se puede dirigir a una persona que le **indicará** otros medios de pago.

Si . . .

Relaciona las siguientes frases.

Ejemplo: **7b**
Si pagan con cheques, tendremos problemas.

1 Si Don Fernando está entrevistando, . . .

2 Como estás trabajando a comisión, si vendes mucho, . . .

3 Si hay huelga de autobuses, . . .

4 Si no tiene un billete de clase preferente, . . .

5 Si es la una de la tarde en Inglaterra, . . .

6 Si quieren dejar su puesto en esta compañía, . . .

7 Si pagan con cheques, . . .

a . . . tomaré un taxi.

b . . . tendremos problemas.

c . . . tendrán que dar un mes de preaviso.

d . . . conseguiré el puesto.

e . . . ganarás mucho.

f . . . no podrá cambiar el vuelo.

g . . . en España serán las dos.

● E S A S I ●

G21 Watch the video again and notice how José Moreno and Julio Hernanz use the following expressions:

. . . **últimamente** *no, siempre hemos tenido problemas . . .*
. . . *en cuestiones que ellos requieren* **personalmente**, . . .
Antes era **precisamente** *todo lo contario, . . .*

These expressions, adverbs, qualify the action of the verb.

Transforma

Transforma las frases como en el ejemplo:

Ejemplo:
. . . . los nuevos sandwichs llegarán mañana. (*seguro*)
Seguramente *los nuevos sandwichs llegarán mañana.*

1 . . . . llegaremos a un acuerdo. (*fácil*)

2 Expresa tus ideas . . . . (*claro*)

3 Salieron de la reunión . . . . (*urgente*)

4 Juan resolvió el problema . . . . (*hábil*)

5 En este asunto tendremos que actuar . . . . (*rápido*)

6 El tren llegó . . . . (*puntual*)

Completa

Coloca una sola de las palabras de abajo en cada uno de los espacios.

> LA PLANTILLA de la ...... tienda de M&S/Cortefiel ...... a disfrutar de una serie de ...... para su comodidad y esparcimiento.
> Se ha ...... una planta del edificio ...... los empleados, en la que se ...... roperos y aseos para señoras y para ...... provistos de duchas; ...... comedor renovado; nuevas ...... de formación y ...... ;
> máquina expendedora de bebidas ...... y gratuitas, y un horno ...... para quienes ...... hacerse ...... propias comidas a la ...... de comer.
> Todo el personal se beneficia de un ...... en las compras, entregándoseles un nuevo ...... de diseño especial en atractivos tonos ...... y melocotón.

> descuento • instalaciones • un • sus
> gris • nueva • para • incluyen
> va • uniforme • hora • caballeros •
> desean • salas • microondas • dedicado
> prácticas • calientes

¿En qué planta está?

Mira el directorio de esta tienda por departamentos y haz los ejercicios.

Sótano	supermercado • librería • instrumentos musicales • discos • acceso al aparcamiento
Planta baja	relojería • perfumería • juguetes • informática • papelería regalos
Primera planta	caballeros • zapatería • complementos • ropa interior • trajes de baño
Tercera planta	señoras • punto • complementos de moda • boutique de moda ropa de cama • lencería
Cuarta planta	muebles • electrodomésticos • muebles de cocina • jardinería ferretería • hogar menaje
Segunda planta	moda joven • oportunidades • deportes • niños y niñas • ropa de deporte

Según las pistas, di en qué planta y en qué departamento estás.

Ejemplo:
Buenas tardes. Necesito comprar una corbata.
Estoy en la primera planta. Estoy en el departamento de caballeros.

1 Por favor. ¿Tiene raquetas de squash?
Estoy . . .
2 Por favor. Quiero una calculadora de bolsillo.
Estoy . . .
3 Buenos días. Quería ver unos hornos microondas.
Estoy . . .
4 • ¡Oiga, por favor!
   ♦ ¿Sí?
   • Quisiera adquirir un conjunto de sábanas.
Estoy . . .
5 Hola, buenos días. Quería comprar un compact disc de Plácido Domingo.
Estoy . . .

De compras

A En la siguiente conversación, pon las frases de abajo en el orden correcto.
♦ Buenos días. Quería un par de zapatos.
• →
♦ El 42.
• →
♦ Prefiero mocasines.
• →
♦ Marrón, por favor.
• →
♦ Prefiero los otros. ¿Cuánto cuestan?
• →
♦ Está bien. Me los llevo.
• →

> Son 13.000 pesetas. • ¿Qué color quiere? • Gracias señor. • Sí señor. ¿Qué número calza? • Tenemos este estilo, o este otro que es más deportivo. • ¿Los quiere con cordones o prefiere mocasines?

B Las frases están mezcladas. Indica como progresa el diálogo, anotando el número que corresponde a cada frase. Las primeras dos están hechas.

- ☐ Muy bien. ¿Qué composición tiene?
- ☐ Azul, verde y blanco.
- ☐ Adiós. Buenos días.
- ☐ Sí señor. ¿La quiere de manga larga o de manga corta?
- ☐ Bueno. Llevaré una azul y otra verde de las de algodón.

- ☐ Ah, sí. Y ¿qué colores tiene?
- ☐ Y ¿cuánto cuestan?
- ☐ Muchas gracias. Aquí tiene 3.400 de vuelta. Gracias y buenos días.
- ☐ No me gusta el nailon. ¿No tiene de algodón?
- ☐ 1 Buenos días. ¿Le puedo ayudar en algo?
- ☐ Prefiero una camisa más casual. Las de manga larga me parecen muy formales.
- ☐ Las de nailon son 4.000 pesetas cada una y las de algodón cuestan 5.800 cada una.
- ☐ En efectivo. Aquí tiene, 15.000 pesetas.
- ☐ Sí. Tenemos éstas en algodón.
- ☐ 2 Hola, buenos días. Sí. Estoy buscando una camisa.
- ☐ Entonces quiere una camisa de manga corta. Aquí tiene.
- ☐ Muy bien. Son 11.600 pesetas. ¿Cómo lo va a abonar? ¿Con tarjeta o en efectivo?
- ☐ Es de nailon.

RECUERDA

In this unit you have studied:

- how to describe objects in more detail
  Es rectangular, tiene un código numérico y es plana.
  Es una tarjeta de crédito.
- how to express degrees of likes, dislikes and preferences
  ¿Qué te parece el nuevo modelo?
  Me gusta muchísimo.
  ¿Te gusta el pulpo?
  No está mal, pero prefiero *los calamares.*
  Es bonita la foto.
  No me gusta nada.
- the colours
  Blanco y **negro** *es una marca de whisky.*
- how to give advice
  Deberías *avisar a la policía.*
  Sería *una buena idea.*
  Yo no lo **recomendaría.**

- how to express quantities without using numbers
  Todo *el mundo tiene un ordenador en la oficina.*
  Algunos *empresarios no aprecian el impacto del '92.*
  No hay **ningún** *producto mejor que el nuestro.*
- the formation of adverbs
  Seguramente *estás cansado después del viaje.*
  Tengo que mandar el paquete **urgentemente**.
  Manipulaste la reunión muy **hábilmente**.
- how to purchase in a shop
  Quería un rollo de película de 35 mm.
  ¿Quiere blanco y negro o de color?
  Color, gracias. ¿Cuánto es?
  Son 535 pesetas.

Business Notes

THE RETAIL REVOLUTION

As is explained in the video sequence, one of the big challenges facing Marks and Spencer in Spain is educating the customer away from the expectation of a traditionally individual and personal service to acceptance of self-service. The concept of self-service in Spain is only thirty years old. The first large department store (*almacén*) opened in 1956, the first supermarket (*supermercado*) in 1960 and the first hypermarket (*hipermercado*) in Barcelona in 1973. Also, approximately three quarters of all supermarkets and self-service stores (*autoservicios*) have only opened in the last fifteen years. Since the 1980s, the retail revolution has spread very quickly as a result of a rise in consumer expenditure and foreign investment. Small traditional shops are still important but, with a lengthy chain of agents and an expensive distribution system, they are now in decline. At the turn of the decade, it was estimated that 95% of points of sale accounted for 54% of sales volume, while 5% (the self-service sector) accounted for 46%. Covered markets (*galerías de alimentación*) are also still used in Spain.

The rise of hypermarkets, often referred to as *los hiper*, is particularly noticeable. In 1992, they numbered about 150, with more planned, and they have changed the nature of routine shopping by shifting emphasis toward edge-of-town and out-of-town centres. Most stores belong to one of four companies which account for 75% of all hypermarket sales. In order of size, they are as follows:

Main hypermarkets in Spain

NAME	OWNERSHIP
Pryca	Carrefour and Grupo March (French)
Continente	Promodes and BBV (French
Alcampo	Auchamps (French)
Hipercor	El Corte Inglés (Spanish)

(Source: *Consumer Spain '91*)

New shopping centres have also arrived on the Spanish scene, with twelve built or planned since 1988, including three in Madrid. The largest of these, Parquesur in the capital city, covers 140,000 m² and has 320 shops, among them Alcampo, C&A and the department store Galerías Preciados (controlled by the British Mountleigh group), as well as 6,000 parking spaces.

According to a 1990 Nielsen Survey, the share of food sales from traditional small shops was only 25% compared with 75% in 1975. Many small shops have now adopted survival strategies such as specialisation and niche marketing, e.g. boutiques and delicatessens, and formation of associations for bulk purchasing. The leading Spanish retailers in terms of turnover are listed overleaf.

Leading Spanish retailers

NAME	TYPE	SALES TURNOVER IN 1988 (billion pesetas)
El Corte Inglés	department store	435
Pryca	hypermarket	213
Continente	hypermarket	147
Alcampo	hypermarket	122
Galerías Preciados	department store	81
Mercadona	self-service store	81
Simago	self-service store	55

(Source: *Consumer Spain '91*)

MARKS AND SPENCER–CORTEFIEL JOINT VENTURE

In early 1990, Marks and Spencer embarked upon a joint venture with Cortefiel in Madrid. Marks and Spencer España is 67% owned by Marks and Spencer and 33% by Cortefiel. There are plans for ten more stores across Spain to complement the Madrid store shown in the video. Cortefiel is a family-owned group of department stores selling clothes. It is much smaller than El Corte Inglés and Preciados, but its importance in the clothes market is best gauged by comparing Cortefiel with other specialist clothes stores.

Specialist clothes stores

NAME	SALES TURNOVER IN 1988 (billion pesetas)	EMPLOYEES	STORES
Cortefiel	28.0	2,500	70
Zara	44.0	–	95
C&A	6.0	450	6

(Source: *Consumer Spain '91*)

Cortefiel, which holds interests in several clothing manufacturers, has entered into the joint venture with Marks and Spencer in order to expand the operations of both companies in Spain. Marks and Spencer can bring to the partnership the experience of selling in Spain which the UK company acquired through a franchising arrangement with Galerías Preciados in their Madrid and Barcelona stores. This arrangement ended in December 1991, after Marks and Spencer had generated yearly sales of 80 million pesetas through franchises. Interestingly, Mothercare is currently engaged in a similar franchising agreement with Preciados in about thirty stores.

As is obvious from the video sequence, Marks and Spencer adopt their own individual approach to retailing abroad. The company believes in taking time to become established in a new country and maintains a low profile in the marketing world, with no marketing department. Marks and

Spencer first opened a store abroad in 1975, the Paris store on the Boulevard Haussmann, and now has 600 stores in nine countries, with an export business in twenty others. The St Michael brand name, classic British clothing and other goods constitute the flagship of their consumer appeal. Marks and Spencer have always been concerned to convey the same corporate message in a common corporate style in all the countries where they operate. This concern manifests itself both in the products sold and the promotional materials used by the company to market themselves overseas. Wherever possible, Marks and Spencer use products and promotional material generated in the UK as a starting point and apply a local 'stamp' to these if necessary.

A different approach to retailing

One of the most interesting aspects of the video sequence is the contrast that emerges between the Spanish consumers' expectation of how a retailer operates and Marks and Spencer's attempt to export a British approach to retailing. The wider range of products as well as the distinctive nature of some of the British items on sale are clearly appealing to most Spanish customers. Although there may be problems in convincing Spanish consumers to purchase gooseberry crumble, the advantages of being able to purchase ready-made sets of sheets or curtains, instead of the more usual Spanish practice of choosing material and having this made up, are immediately apparent. The need to educate the Spanish customer to exercise a free choice when examining products rather than expecting the traditional personal attention of a shop assistant is, however,

discussed in the video and is perceived to be a factor in the poor sales performance of the men's clothes section.

Methods of payment again are different to the UK, since cheques are not widely accepted in Spain, where payment in cash (*en efectivo*) or by credit card (*tarjeta*) is the norm. Education of the workforce to fit in with Marks and Spencer's corporate identity and employment traditions will also be a key factor in the company's future in Spain. Whether Marks and Spencer can repeat their French success story will be fascinating to watch, in a market where the main competitor, Zara, the leading textile group in Spain, is pioneering modern marketing methods introduced by Harvard-trained management.

A MEETING OF MINDS

━━━━━

Study plan

SEQUENCE SUMMARY

IN THIS SEQUENCE, WE TAKE UP THE THREAD OF SOME OF THE EARLIER SEQUENCES AND CONTINUE THE STORY. THE VIDEO SHOWS THREE MEETINGS, AS FOLLOWS:

- KAREN RAMAGE OF CURZON DIRECT TAKING ADVICE FROM DON MANUEL
- DAVID LANDRY OF ACTION COMPUTERS DISCUSSING HIS COMPANY'S FINANCIAL REQUIREMENTS WITH BANCO NATWEST
- WAYNE ROSEMIN OF ADDISON AND DAMIAN HERNANDEZ OF RENFE FINALISING DETAILS OF THE AVE LAUNCH

THIS VIDEO SEQUENCE FEATURES SOPHISTICATED AND COMPLEX SPANISH. AS SUCH, IT PLACES HIGH DEMANDS ON THE LEARNER. WATCH IT AS OFTEN AS YOU NEED TO AND CONSULT THE SECTIONS WHICH FOLLOW, THE TUTOR CASSETTE AND THE WORDLIST FOR HELP AND INFORMATION.

WHAT YOU WILL LEARN

Sección 1	*Sección 2*
• how to use words such as *con, de* and *en* after verbs	• how to give reasons for calling a meeting
	• how to say the same thing in different ways
• how to describe and complete a bill of exchange	• how to prepare to write a report

Sección 3	*Business Notes*
• how to make last-minute checks for a meeting	Understanding the business environment
• how to give some more instructions	Understanding the financial environment
• how to confirm details	Beyond 1993

LEARNING STRATEGY FOR EACH SECTION

Study the key words in the **Palabras y frases útiles** box and watch the video sequence, listening out for the key words. Make notes of what you have understood.

Then study the key phrases in the **Palabras y frases útiles** box and watch the video again.

Complete the **Comprensión** section that follows the **Palabras y frases útiles**.

Now you are ready to listen to the **Tutor cassette**. The cassette will take you through the exercises in this unit section by section.

When you have completed the language exercises in each section, study the **Business Notes** at the end of the unit for further information on business and industry in Spain.

8

A MEETING OF MINDS

Sección 1

Curzon Direct.

11.20 Lee estas palabras y frases antes de ver el vídeo.

pedido = order	requisitos = requirements	mediante = by means of
factura = invoice	emisor = issuer	seguridad = security
unidades = units	Hacienda = Treasury	letra = letter of credit
plazo = expiry date	al contado/en efectivo = in cash	vencimiento = maturity
entrega = delivery		

El pedido lo que detalla es el número de unidades . . .	What the order details is the number of units . . .
. . . y las condiciones de pago	. . . and the terms of payment
la factura es el documento fiscal y mercantil	the bill is the fiscal and commercial document
Que es un número que asigna a cada contribuyente el Ministerio de Hacienda	Which is a number the Ministry of Finance assigns to each taxpayer
la letra tiene un vencimiento de noventa días	the credit note matures in ninety days

COMPRENSION

1 ¿Cómo es la factura de este cliente?
2 ¿Qué ha preparado Karen?
3 ¿Qué detalla un pedido?

4 Después de que el cliente acepta la oferta de precio, ¿qué hace? Y ¿qué tendría que hacer el vendedor? (Karen y Andy, en este caso.)
5 ¿Qué tipo de documento es una factura?

6 Cita cuatro cosas que tienen que ir perfectamente identificadas en una factura.

7 ¿Cómo se llama el número que el Ministerio de Hacienda asigna a cada contribuyente?

8 ¿Qué quiere decir 'pago al contado'?

9 ¿Cuál es la norma habitual de pago?

10 ¿Qué dos fechas tienen que estar perfectamente detalladas en una letra?

APLICACION

• E S A S I •

G22 Watch the video again and notice how Karen and don Manuel use certain verbs.

*Bueno, quería **hablar de** varias cosas.*
. . . esa identificación fiscalmente en España
*. . . **consiste en** detallar. . .*

As in English, certain verbs in Spanish can be followed by a preposition. Here are some examples of these verbs and what they mean.

hablar de: expresar verbalmente algo referente a una persona o a un tema

hablar con: intercambio verbal

hablar por teléfono: comunicarse con alguien a través del teléfono

consistir en: querer decir, significar

tratar de: discutir, hablar; intentar

olvidarse de: no recordar

acordarse de: recordar

salir de: pasar de dentro afuera; marcharse, irse

entrar en: pasar de fuera adentro

quedar con: tener una cita

invitar a: una invitación

tardar en: emplear tiempo en hacer algo

Completa

Escribe la preposición adecuada en cada frase.

1 Ana y Rafael salieron ...... la oficina a las tres y media.

2 Jaime tiene muy buena memoria, siempre se acuerda ...... todo.

3 El señor Alvarez está hablando ...... teléfono.

4 Vamos, te invito ...... cenar.

5 Trataré ...... explicar las consecuencias de la compra de la compañía.

6 Hablaré ...... el jefe de personal esta tarde.

7 Pagar con una letra consiste ...... una forma de pago aplazada.

8 Me olvidé ...... llevar el pasaporte.

9 La directora de márketing entró ...... su despacho a las nueve de la mañana y todavía está allí.

10 El autobús tardó diez horas ...... llegar.

11 Hablaremos ...... ese problema en la próxima reunión.

12 Lo siento, no puedo ir a la conferencia porque quedé ...... Alberto a las siete.

¿Cuál es la correcta?

Mira la primera secuencia del vídeo otra vez y elige la respuesta adecuada.

1 En un pedido se detalla . . .

  a el número de unidades y las condiciones de pago.

  b el número de unidades, el plazo en que hay que servir el pedido y las condiciones de pago.

  c cuánto hay que pagar.

2 Una factura es . . .
  a un cheque.
  b un documento fiscal.
  c un documento fiscal y mercantil.
3 El emisor de una factura es . . .
  a el cliente.
  b el vendedor.
  c el banco.
4 El número de indentificación fiscal es . . .
  a el número dcl carnct de identidad del cliente.
  b el número de teléfono del Ministerio de Hacienda.
  c el número que el Ministerio de Hacienda asigna a cada contribuyente.
5 Un talón es lo mismo que . . .
  a una letra.
  b un giro.
  c un cheque.
6 Pagar al contado quiere decir . . .
  a pagar cuando se efectua la compra.
  b pagar dentro de quince días.
  c pagar a plazos.
7 Una letra es . . .
  a un documento de pago aplazado.
  b una carta.
  c una orden de compra.
8 Los talones . . .
  a dan muchísima seguridad.
  b no dan ninguna seguridad.
  c no dan absoluta seguridad.

Leer y entender

En esta sección don Manuel habla de las Letras de Cambio. Aquí hay una breve descripción sobre esta forma de pago.

Una letra de cambio es una forma de crédito muy corriente en España. Es un documento que emite un acreedor (el librador) que obliga al deudor (el librado) a pagar una cierta cantidad de dinero en una fecha determinada (el vencimiento) a una persona o entidad determinada. La letra es una forma de pago aplazada. Normalmente se paga a noventa días después de la emisión de la letra, pero puede haber letras de sesenta días, treinta días o menos. También se puede fraccionar el pago. Por ejemplo, se puede dividir una factura de noventa mil pesetas en tres pagos de treinta mil cada uno con diferentes fechas de vencimiento.

Una práctica muy generalizada es llevar la letra a un banco. Si una empresa o persona necesita dinero para pagar a un proveedor o para gastos corrientes, normalmente el banco puede anticipar el dinero sobre esa letra si considera que la garantía que ofrece el deudor es suficiente.

A Aquí tenemos unos términos que aparecen en una letra de cambio. Estudia las definiciones.

Lugar de libramiento: sitio donde se emite la letra

Importe: el valor de la letra

Fecha de libramiento: fecha en que se emite la letra

Vencimiento: día en que hay que pagar la letra

Por esta Letra de Cambio pagará usted al vencimiento expresado a . . . : aquí va el nombre de la persona o entidad, generalmente de un banco, que representa al librador

La cantidad de . . . : aquí el importe en letra

En el domicilio de pago siguiente: el banco del librado quien tiene que pagar al banco del librador

Cláusulas: generalmente se pone *sin gastos*

Nombre y domicilio del librado: persona o compañía que tiene que pagar la letra

Firma, nombre y domicilio del librador: firma, nombre y dirección de la persona que recibe el importe

B Mira esta letra de cambio y contesta las preguntas.

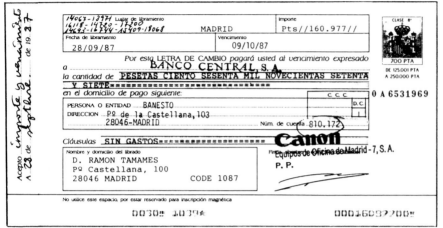

1 El librador es . . .
2 ¿En qué mes tiene que pagar?
3 La fecha de libramiento es el . . .
4 ¿Quién es Ramón Tamames?
5 ¿Dónde fue librada la letra?
6 ¿Cuál es el banco de Canon?
7 ¿Cuál es el banco de Ramón Tamames?

C Ahora lee la carta y rellena la letra de cambio según los datos.

Lugar de libramiento		Importe	
Fecha de libramiento		Vencimientos	

Por esta LETRA DE CAMBIO *pagará usted al vencimiento expresado*
a
la cantidad de

DE 0.000.000 PTA
A 00.000.000 PTA

en el domicilio de pago siguiente: C.C.C.   0 A 0000000

PERSONA O ENTIDAD...............   D.C.
DIRECCION.............................
......................Núm. de cuenta...............

Cláusulas

Nombre y domicilio del librado	Firma, nombre y domicilio del librador

EDITEX/CTEX07

No utilice este espacio, por estar reservado inscripción magnética

Acepto.
A. . . . de . . . . de 19 . . .

MM Megamarketing S.A.
C/Miguel Angel, 32 –4º
28013 Madrid

3/02/19...

Sr Don Arturo Fernández de Córdoba
C/ Rosalía de Castro, 37–8º
28003 Madrid

Estimado señor:

La presente es para comunicarle que hoy hemos enviado, para el pago de su pedido, Ref. A–3267, una letra por valor de 328.725 ptas.

La letra está domiciliada en el Banco Mediterráneo, donde tenemos nuestra cuenta corriente. La dirección es:
C/ Marqués de Valladares, 83
28013 Madrid

El vencimiento es a 90 días y cobraremos el importe a través de su banco:
Banco Gallego
C/ San Martín, 39
28013 Madrid
Aprovechamos esta oportunidad para saludarle.

Atentamente,

Juan Ramón Lojo Cividanes

Sección 2

NatWest y Action Computers.

16.25 Lee estas palabras y frases antes de ver el vidéo.

herramienta = tool	préstamo = loan	poliza = draft
impresoras = printers	conveniente = useful	desagradar = to displease
dirigir = to direct	maniobra = operation	sensato = sensible
facilidades = facilities	incremento = increase	cuenta = account
ampliación = extension	ingreso = income	dato = fact
crédito = credit		

quería presentarte una nueva iniciativa de márketing	I would like to show you a new marketing iniciative
Endorsa lo que es la política del catálogo	It backs up the policy of the catalogue
¿Y esto lo haces de forma conjunto con Hewlett-Packard?	And you do this jointly with Hewlett-Packard?
. . . tener un colchón de tesorería para financiar este proyecto	. . . to have the treasury back-up to finance this project
¿ . . . o quieres apartarlo y tenerlo en una cuenta?	. . . or do you want to set it aside in an account?
. . . este fondo de maniobra para poder . . .	. . . this operational fund to allow . . .
Te interesa más, supongo, un crédito que un préstamo . . .	I assume you are more interested in a credit facility than a loan . . .
. . . con un tipo de interés, si es posible, revisable al año, . . .	. . . with a rate of interest to be reviewed in a year, if it's possible, . . .
Yo creo que lo mejor que podemos hacer es	I think the best thing we can do is
para pedir permiso	to get the go ahead
cuando tengáis la información del cierre del año . . .	when you have the data for the end of the tax year . . .

COMPRENSION

1. ¿Para qué utiliza Action Computers los trípticos?
2. Despés del éxito del primer flyer, ¿con qué productos quiere Action Computers repetir el concepto?
3. ¿Cuál es el objetivo de la visita de David Landry y Francisco Tejera?
4. ¿Según Francisco Tejera, en qué plazo de tiempo pueden volver a lanzar el flyer?
5. ¿Cuál es la característica principal del flyer?
6. ¿Qué efecto va a tener el flyer cuando llega a manos del consumidor final?
7. ¿Qué le interesa más al señor Tejera, un crédito o un préstamo?
8. ¿Cuál es la ventaja de tener un crédito?
9. ¿Qué plazo de revisión del tipo de interés preferería Francisco Tejera?
10. ¿Para quién tiene que preparar una solicitud David Breden?

APLICACION

Una reunión de negocios

Francisco Tejera dice que el propósito de la reunión en el Banco NatWest era conseguir financiación para la nueva iniciativa de márketing. Hay muchas razones para convocar una reunión, dentro y fuera de la empresa. Mira la lista de razones para convocar una reunión y empareja cada una con una de las situaciones.

Ejemplo: **3a**

Razones para convocar una reunión

1. Oír, evaluar y aceptar informes.
2. Analizar y resolver un problema.
3. Obtener aprobación para una iniciativa nueva.
4. Reconciliar opiniones opuestas.
5. Reactivar un proyecto que ha quedado estancado.
6. Demostrar un producto o sistema.
7. Generar nuevas ideas.

Situaciones

a. Para atraer clientes a tu banco quieres un mes de promoción. Quieres ofrecer la posibilidad de ganar premios a cada cliente nuevo durante ese mes en una lotería. El primer premio sería un coche. Has hecho unos estudios de mercado y estás seguro de que la iniciativa tendrá éxito, pero tienes que convencer a los demás.

b. Hay diferencias de opinión sobre el desarrollo de un nuevo producto en tu empresa. El director técnico quiere más dinero para completar el proyecto antes de Navidad. El director financiero no está muy convencido de que el producto va a tener éxito y dice que no hay más dinero este año.

c. Hace tiempo propusiste clases de idiomas extranjeros para los ejecutivos, pero pocas personas estaban interesadas. Ahora, con el mercado único, tu compañía va a abrir agencias en todos los países europeos y crees que tu proyecto inicial ya tiene validez.

d. Las ventas de tus productos no ha aumentado durante el último año y quieres analizar la estrategia de márketing para ver si alguien tiene ideas innovadoras para incrementar las ventas.

e. El director de producción acaba de regresar de un viaje de investigación en los Estados Unidos y quieres que todo el mundo se entere de los resultados de su visita.

f. Hay un problema con la distribución de los productos desde el almacén al cliente.

No sabes donde está el fallo pero tienes que resolverlo antes de que empieces a perder clientes.

g La empresa acaba de poner en práctica un nuevo plan de jubilación para los empleados y quieres explicarlo a cada jefe de sección.

De otra manera

A ¿Cómo expresarías las siguientes palabras y frases de otra manera, pero sin cambiar el sentido? Empareja cada número con su letra correspondiente.

Ejemplo: **11b**
Fluctuación = Variación

1 No deseamos utilizar
2 Ampliación
3 Mejor dicho
4 Demasiado dinero
5 Entiendo
6 Sería conveniente
7 Tirar el dinero
8 Apartarlo
9 Efectivamente
10 Después del éxito que experimentamos
11 Fluctuación

a Mucho dinero
b Variación
c Con el buen resultado que tuvimos
d Incremento
e Claro, por supuesto
f No queremos usar
g Comprendo
h Gastar inútilmente
i Separarlo
j Es decir
k Sería una buena idea

B Completa el siguiente texto utilizando una frase o una palabra (de **a** a **k** arriba) en los espacios dados. Tienes que usarlas

todas pero solamente se pueden usar una vez. Tienes una.

El motivo de esta reunión es para explicar por qué .... la publicidad que utilizamos el año pasado para este producto. .... con esa campaña publicitaria muchos se preguntarán si no .... usarla otra vez.

...... sus dudas y por eso voy a tratar de que ustedes comprendan también mi posición. Con esa campaña gastamos .... y, aunque hubo un ...... en las ventas al principio, después este incremento se hizo negativo, ... , se mantuvo estático, no hubo .... Por lo tanto, creo que .... tanto dinero, otra vez, no es una buena idea.

Actualmente el presupuesto publicitario es global. Lo que yo quiero para este producto es ...... de ese presupuesto global y, así controlar más eficazmente los gastos. *Claro, por supuesto*, esto va a generar más trabajo en el departamento pero estoy segura de que es más sensato.

El informe

A Al final de la reunión, David Breden dice que antes de confirmar la concesión del crédito, tiene que preparar un informe para el comité de créditos.

¿Cómo se elabora un informe?

A continuación hay una serie de acciones a seguir y otra serie de preguntas. Estas acciones y preguntas tienen que estar emparejadas porque explican el proceso de elaboración de un informe. Las acciones a seguir están en orden, pero las preguntas no. ¿Qué preguntas te haces para ejecutar la acción correspondiente?

Ejemplo: **1e**

Establecer el fundamento.
¿Debo o no escribir un informe?

Acción a seguir

1 Establecer el fundamento.
2 Identificar al lector.
3 Determinar el propósito.
4 Identificar y organizar ideas y hechos. Investigar conclusiones.
5 Escribir el informe
6 Revisar el informe.

Preguntas

a ¿Quién tiene que leer y entender el informe?
b ¿Cómo redactar bien el informe?
c ¿Es un informe claro, eficaz y objetivo?
d ¿Cómo debo desarrollar el mensaje?
e ¿Debo o no escribir un informe?
f ¿Cuál es el objetivo?

B Y ahora, con tus propias palabras y usando las expresiones dadas para describir un proceso, en la primera sección de la secuencia 6, explica cómo se elabora un informe.

 Utiliza la forma pasiva del verbo.

Ejemplo:
En primer lugar se establece el fundamento del informe, seguidamente se pregunta si se debe o no escribir el informe. . . .

¿Eres flexible?

Durante la reunión David Breden pregunta a Francisco Tejera *si quería una línea de tipo fijo o algo más flexible.* En los negocios hay que saber adaptarse a situaciones nuevas. Con este test descubrirás si tu personalidad es flexible o no.

Test

¿Tiene usted una personalidad flexible?

PARA SABER hasta qué punto se adapta a las situaciones que se le presentan, le invitamos a responder a las siguientes preguntas.

PREGUNTAS

1 Acaban de crear un departamento en su empresa y buscan personal. ¿Le interesa apuntarse?

a Sí, se apunta. Le parece una buena oportunidad.
b Lo consulta con sus colegas para ver qué piensan.
c No. Es un trabajo del que no sabe nada.

2 En su empresa se baraja la idea de un cambio de sistema informático. Si le consultan, ¿qué opinaría?

a No le parece lógico adquirir un nuevo sistema cuando están acostumbrados a otro.
b Opina que el tiempo de adaptación al nuevo sistema se compensa con la facilidad de uso.
c No le parece una buena idea, pero si sus colegas están de acuerdo . . .

3 Su empresa se declara en bancarrota. Por tanto, le toca buscar un nuevo empleo. ¿Qué hace?

a Busca el mismo tipo de empleo y se pone en contacto con la competencia.
b Toma algunos días para estudiar el mercado laboral.
c Le gustaría intentar algo nuevo ahora que tiene la oportunidad, pero no se siente preparado.

4 La expendedora automática de su empresa siempre tenía su producto favorito. Un día encuentra qu lo reemplazan por otra marca. ¿Qué hace?

a Se queja porque ahora se verá obligado a salir fuera para comprarlo.
b Prueba el otro producto, pero no le gusta.
c Se conforma.

5 ¿Suele hacer sugerencias a su jefe sobre cómo mejorar la organización de la empresa?

a Cada vez que se le ocurre una manera más eficaz de hacer una tarea, lo dice.
b Le parece que todo marcha muy bien tal y como está.
c Hace sugerencias en lo que concierne sólo a su trabajo.

6 ¿Suele hablar con la misma facilidad con el portero que con un alto directivo?

a Se siente más cómodo con un alto cargo. No tiene nada que decirle al portero.
b Sí.
c Depende.

7 Está destinado en un país extranjero por razones laborales. ¿Cómo se comporta?

a Vive en un barrio donde están otros ejecutivos de la empresa y sale con ellos.
b Aprende el idioma del país y se hace amigo de gente nativa.
c Intenta entablar amistad con gente nativa pero le resulta muy difícil.

8 Fichan a su mayor enemigo para trabajar en su empresa. ¿Cómo reacciona?

a Hace un esfuerzo para llevarse bien con él.
b Intenta por todos los medios hacerle la vida imposible.
c Lo evita a toda costa.

9 Es una persona creativa y no le gusta verse obligada a vestirse de ejecutivo. Tiene que hacer una presentación y su jefe le pide que lleve traje. ¿Qué hace usted?

a Accede a ponerse el traje adecuado.
b No le hace caso y lleva la ropa de siempre.
c Lo discute con su jefe.

10 Un producto que habitualmente utiliza se retira del mercado. ¿Qué hace?

a Llama a la empresa que lo fabrica para ver dónde puede conseguirlo.
b Se resigna a comprar otra marca.
c Intenta encontrar otra marca que le gusta.

11 Ha estado trabajando duramente en un proyecto para un cliente. Repentinamente éste le llama e intenta cambiar todo el planteamiento del proyecto. ¿Qué hace?

a Vuelve a comenzar otra vez.
b Se niega a hacerlo de nuevo.
c Intenta convencerle de que mantenga su acuerdo.

Soluciones	
1 a5 b3 c1	**6** a1 b5 c3
2 a1 b5 c3	**7** a1 b5 c3
3 a1 b5 c3	**8** a5 b1 c3
4 a1 b3 c5	**9** a5 b1 c3
5 a5 b1 c3	**10** a1 b3 c5
	11 a5 b1 c3

De 40 a 55: flexible
De 25 a 39: razonable
De 11 a 24: tozudo

PERFIL PSICOLOGICO

Flexible

Usted es una persona con probada capacidad de adaptación. En el ámbito laboral, su versatilidad hace que sea un ganador nato. Se demuestra en su agilidad mental y su carácter tolerante y, sobre todo, abierto. Estas cualidades le otorgan el don de saber extraer lo mejor de cada situación.

Además, su flexibilidad facilita la convivencia laboral. No es una persona propicia a causar problemas o a rebelarse por cambios inesperados. Sus colegas seguramente saben que pueden contar con usted sin temer una reacción violenta.

Razonable

Su capacidad para adaptarse es esporádica. Por regla general, es una persona versátil y se encuentra capacitado para afrontar y resolver los obstáculos que se presentan. Sin embargo, cuando un cambio es extremadamente radical, deja de mostrarse tan flexible y surge una persona diferente.

No suele tener ningún problema en la vida diaria, pero en las cuestiones más insólitas su cabeza se vuelve rígida. Se siente más cómodo ocupándose de tareas más bien rutinarias que le garantizan que los cambios son menos abruptos. Intente hacer mayores esfuerzos para aceptar nuevas ideas y situaciones, de forma que no se vea sorprendido por los radicales cambios que en cualquier momento pueden presentarse.

Tozudo

Según demuestra su puntuación, es una persona muy poco flexible. Se obstina en mantener a cualquier precio sus ideas y no hay quien le haga cambiar de opinión. Aprenda a ser más abierto a los cambios que ocurren a su alrededor. Le costará un esfuerzo inicial, pero luego comprobará que las dificultades de lo novedoso no son tan insoportables como imaginaba.

Tenga mucho cuidado, porque en el ámbito profesional, la flexibilidad y capacidad de adaptación son aptitudes muy importantes. En una compañía, por ejemplo, todo un grupo de consultores puede dedicarse a la gestión de cambio. Nunca se puede estar seguro de que la situación actual perdurará durante mucho tiempo. Prepárase para que, cuando esto ocurra, no resulte traumático.

Sección 3

Wayne Rosemin y Damián Hernández repasan los últimos detalles del diseño del interior del AVE para asegurarse que la visita de la presidenta de RENFE será todo un éxito.

PALABRAS Y FRASES UTILES

19.12 Lee estas palabras y frases antes de ver el vídeo.

maqueta = model	moqueta = carpet	encargar = to order
diseño = design	pared = wall	cabezal = headrest
iluminación = lighting	frescura = freshness	billete = ticket
panel = panel	mesa = table	preocupación = worry
techo = ceiling	forma = shape	éxito = success
nivel = level		

comprobarlos cara a la visita	check them with a view to the visit
. . . máxime como ella es nueva	. . . especially as she is new
. . . y después este iluminación más ambiental	. . . and also this more general lighting
. . . hace el conjunto y el juego con el resto del salón	. . . forms a whole and blends in with the rest of the compartment
en España el sol y el calor contaban mucho, . . .	in Spain the sun and the heat count for a lot, . . .
. . . como si fuera a servicio	. . . as if it were in service
el día trece les hemos dado de plazo, . . .	we've given them until the thirteenth, . . .
. . . de manera que cuando vayan	. . . so that when they go to board the train . .
a subir al tren . . .	
Sería fenomenal si pudiéramos hacer esto	It would be great if we could do this
no deben tener ningún tipo de connection preocupación cara al . . .	they needn't have any worries in with . . .

COMPRENSION

1 ¿Qué tendrán que explicar a la presidenta?

2 ¿Cuántos niveles de iluminación hay en el tren?

3 Cita los tres tipos de iluminación que Wayne menciona.

4 ¿Cuáles son las diferencias entre la moqueta del AVE y la moqueta de TGV?

5 ¿Por qué son diferentes las moquetas del AVE y del TGV?

6 ¿Para cuándo está confirmada la visita?

7 ¿Qué están encargardas?

8 ¿Qué van a dar a la presidenta y al director general?

9 ¿Qué información va a contener el billete?

10 ¿Cuál es la fecha de inauguración del AVE y con qué otro acto coincide?

APLICACION

¡Ya está!

Damián y Wayne quieren estar seguros de que todo va a estar a punto para la inauguración del AVE. En cualquier reunión es importante que todo esté preparado, hasta el último detalle.

Rogelio y su secretaria de dirección, Juana, están repasando los últimos detalles de una importante reunión de directores que van a celebrar en un hotel local esta tarde.

Marca cada cosa en la lista con ✔ si Juana confirma la acción, con **x** si no ha hecho el trabajo, y con **?** si ella tiene dudas.

Rogelio Bueno, Juana. ¿Está todo en orden para la reunión?

Juana Casi todo. Hemos reservado el salón Atlántico en el Hotel Europa para las nueve de la mañana.

```
Reservar salón
Confirmar hora
Proporcionar papel y lápiz
Organizar agua, café, té y refrescos
Escribir tarjetas con el nombre de cada participante
Probar retroproyector
Conectar proyector de diapositivas
Conseguir vídeo VHS
Instalar enchufes suficientes
Pedir repuestos
Copiar orden del día para cada participante
Poner ceniceros
Verificar interruptores de las luces
```

Rogelio ¿Has confirmado la reserva?

Juana Sí. Y el hotel proporcionará bebidas frías y calientes y he pedido un retroproyector, un proyector de diapositivas y una pantalla grande.

Rogelio Bien, pero creo que uno de los participantes quería usar un vídeo.

Juana Pues no sabía. Tendré que hablar con el hotel. ¿Quiere VHS o Beta.?

Rogelio No sé. Habrá que llamarle. Cada persona va a tener una copia del orden del día, ¿verdad?

Juana Sí. Acabo de hacer varias copias.

Rogelio Vale. Además cada uno va a necesitar papel y lápiz y una tarjeta con su nombre.

Juana Creo que el hotel va a proporcionar papel y lápiz. Los nombres no están hechos.

Rogelio ¿Sabes si hay suficientes enchufes para el equipo técnico? Y para estar seguros necesitaremos tener unos repuestos para el equipo técnico. Y otra cosa, los interruptores de la luz también tienen que estar cerca de la persona que va a hablar.

Juana La verdad es que no estoy segura de cuántos enchufes hay, pero me imagino que habrá suficientes. No había pensado en tener repuestos. Ya me encargaré de eso. Respecto a las luces, creo que se pueden encender y apagar desde el podio, pero no estoy segura.

Rogelio	¿Hay ceniceros?
Juana	Pensé que no íbamos a dejar fumar durante las presentaciones, así que no puse ceniceros.
Rogelio	Bueno, pero como fuma casi todo el mundo creo que sería mejor ponerlos.
Juana	Vale, de acuerdo.

¿Qué tengo que hacer?

Unos meses después Rogelio y Juana tienen que organizar otra reunión, pero esta vez Juana ha anticipado todo. Mira la lista otra vez, da instrucciones y responde como en el ejemplo. Para hacer el ejercicio repasa los párrafos 13 y 16 de la sección Gramática.

Ejemplo:
Reservar salón.

Rogelio   *Reserva un salón.*
Juana   *El salón ya está reservado.*

Completa

Rellena los espacios en blanco con la forma y el tiempo adecuados de los verbos entre paréntesis.

1 El director de mantenimiento .... todos los días a la misma hora. (*llegar*)

2 La reunión de ayer .... a las ocho de la tarde. (*terminar*)

3 En la compañía donde .... antes sólo había treinta empleados. (*él/trabajar*)

4 Mañana .... el informe. (*yo/redactar*)

5 Creo que .... mejor poner la mesa al lado de la ventana. (*ser*)

6 Luis .... en esta empresa toda su vida. (*haber/trabajar*)

7 El director no puede atenderle porque es este momento .... por teléfono. (*estar/hablar*)

8 Antes Rodrigo .... al trabajo en autobús. (*venir*)

9 Yo .... en 1953. (*nacer*)

10 Nosotros todavía no .... el contrato. (*haber/firmar*)

11 En España los bancos .... el sábado por la tarde. (*estar/cerrar*)

12 El mes que viene Félix y María .... a Méjico. (*ir/ir*)

13 Federico está en el hospital porque la semana pasada .... un accidente. (*tener*)

14 La directora de recursos humanos siempre .... a todas las reuniones. (*asistir*)

15 Ellos no .... que yo tenía un cargo nuevo. (*saber*)

16 Nosotros, frecuentemente, ... en ese restaurante. (*comer*)

17 Si Luisa no viene en cinco minutos, ... a su casa. (*llamar*)

18 En caso de robo, ... a la policía. (*avisar*)

19 Antes de ayer, el presidente y el director general .... la nueva planta embotelladora. (*visitar*)

20 Si no le importa .... pagar con tarjeta. (*preferir*)

Crucigrama

Horizontales

2 preposición
4 pronombre impersonal
8 el contrario de 'oferta'
9 terminación verbal
10 'leo' en el pasado
11 el Ministerio que controla tus impuestos
12 del verbo 'atar', sinónimo de enlazo
13 material que cubre el suelo de los vagones del AVE
16 un metal precioso
18 el contrario de 'no'
19 igual que en 9
20 el día en que se celebran elecciones generales en Gran Bretaña
24 afirmación
25 David Landry y Francisco Tejera van a una reunión para conseguir uno
26 siglas del número que identifica a un contribuyente
29 percibe con los ojos
30 'Hoover' es una ...... registrada.
32 persona o entidad que produce una factura
34 'va' en el futuro
35 forma de pago habitual en España
36 persona que compra un producto o un servicio

Verticales

1 pago que se efectua en el momento de la compra
2 pago que no se efectua en el momento de la compra
3 fecha límite para pagar una letra
4 yo sé, tú sabes, usted ......
5 preposición
6 habitación
7 triunfo
11 ni ayer ni mañana
14 un sinónimo de cheques
15 terminación verbal
17 lo contrario de 8
18 posesivo de él, de ella o de usted
21 está en las dos primeras letras de 'estar'
22 afirmación
23 noticia que se da de un negocio o persona
26 'digo' en el pasado
28 bebida muy popular en el Reino Unido – en España, Marks and Spencer lo tiene ahora en bolsitas individuales
29 'yo veo' en el pasado
31 la misma terminación verbal que en las otras pistas
33 artículo: cuando es pronombre lleva acento

RECUERDA

In this unit you have:

- studied the use of certain prepositions
  *Estuve hablando **con** Manuel y me dijo que . . .*
  *Voy a tratar **de** arreglar la situación.*
  *No tardará **en** llegar.*
- studied the language of bills of exchange
  *La fecha de **vencimiento** es el 12 de octubre.*
  *El **importe** es el valor de la letra.*
  *El **librado** soy yo.*
- looked at reasons for calling meetings
  Para obtener aprobación para una nueva iniciativa.
  Analizar y resolver un problema.
  Generar nuevas ideas.

- revised how to explain more difficult processes
  *En **primer lugar** se establece el fundamento del informe.*
  ***Después** se pregunta si se debe o no escribir el informe.*
  ***Finalmente** se revisa el informe.*
- made last-minute checks
  Ya está reservado el salón.
  El retroproyector está echufado.
  No había pensado en eso.
- revised a range of vocabulary, verbs and important gramatical structures.

Business Notes

UNDERSTANDING THE BUSINESS ENVIRONMENT

The final video sequence, by refocusing on three different business meetings, underlines the emphasis throughout this course on understanding the business environment in Spain. This is clearly a matter of developing communication skills, as evidenced by the language competence of the British business people shown. It is just as important to spend time and effort in discovering how the business environment functions.

In the UK in 1991, there were twenty-six seminars on trading in Spain held under various auspices, in addition to trade missions from all parts of the country. The Department of Trade and Industry alone ran twenty-two presentations as part of their Spotlight on Spain campaign in late 1991 and 1992. Media coverage of Spain has never been as high, and advice and assistance on penetrating the Spanish market never so readily available. The video sequence reiterates a number of important lessons to transform interest and information into success.

• Some knowledge of the language is desirable, especially when it must not be assumed that all, or even most, Spaniards can do business in English. In trade missions to Spain, the language barrier has been seen as the biggest anxiety among potential venturers into the Spanish market. It is wise to have trade leaflets, brochures and other forms of promotional material available in Spanish from the outset. In the absence of language competence, local people who speak Spanish should be employed.

• Spanish accounting and financial systems are different and require a British company to engage local financial and legal advice, preferably from Spaniards who understand something of British business practice.

• Time, patience and a strong constitution will be necessary in dealing with what, to the British business person, may seem like needless bureaucracy or unnecessary procrastination. Paperwork may be heavy but, once in a queue, it is better to persist until the problem is solved. Letters may be ignored, and telephone calls should be used where personal contact is not possible. Spaniards will take time in forging a personal business relationship, often in social situations, and although tough negotiators, they will nonetheless remain friends.

• Although massive changes have taken place in the business environment in recent years, a certain insularity (a hangover from the Franco era) may be encountered in some business sectors. Prospective partners are unlikely to be hostile to foreign intervention but are more likely to be somewhat apprehensive of the implications.

UNDERSTANDING THE FINANCIAL ENVIRONMENT

Two of the three situations in the video sequence show business meetings which revolve around seeking financial backing or advice. Action Computers are successful in securing additional credit on a flexible basis from Banco NatWest partly because the bank has full information on the operation of Action Computers in the UK, a point made in the video sequence.

Curzon Direct, a small family concern, is anxious to obtain the best financial advice from someone who understands the system. In the video sequence, Karen Ramage consults a financial adviser about the best means of negotiating payment terms with clients. Throughout Spain, businesses, large and small, as well as private individuals, rely very heavily on a local agent or 'fixer', known as a *gestor*, who can conduct business with government departments and both advise on and complete paperwork on behalf of a client. Thus the agent's office, or *gestoría*, is a focal point for financial and also legal advice. Curzon Direct are advised that a tax code (*código de identificación fiscal*) is necessary for any taxpayer (*contribuyente*), whether individual or corporate, before orders (*pedidos*) and invoices (*facturas*) can be processed. It is explained that methods of payment in Spain do not traditionally include cheques (*talones* or *cheques*), which do not carry the security they do in other countries. The most usual method of payment between businesses is a bill of exchange (*pago mediante letra* (*de cambio*)), and especially where this involves payment in instalments (*pagos aplazados*). Obviously, with smaller sums involved, cash payment is possible (*pago al contado*). With bills of exchange there is usually a ninety-day, sixty-day or thirty-day agreement between the date of invoice (*fecha de factura*) and the date of delivery (*fecha de entrega*). Curzon Direct are also advised to consult

with their bank about the credit worthiness of a potential client and to verify what information is required.

The lesson for any company seeking to establish itself in the Spanish market on a sound financial footing is to have full information and documentation available to satisfy both trading partners and the financial institutions.

BEYOND 1993

The UK companies and business people shown in this and the other video sequences have been successful in meeting Spanish business culture halfway. The events of 1992 in Spain have provided a springboard for other British companies interested in the Spanish market. Britain's approach to Expo '92 was described by the UK government in these terms in 1990: 'Expo '92 in Seville will provide an important opportunity to promote the resurgence of British business, technology and services'. 1492 and the discovery of America heralded the beginning of Seville's – and Spain's – golden age, with the southern Spanish city the trade capital of the new world. Beyond 1993, the grandiose project of Cartuja '93 is intended to map out a high-tech future for Seville and Spain. Despite problems – an unemployment rate which is still the highest in the EC, and sporadic ETA terrorism – a spirit of innovation pervades the Spanish business scene. The opportunity is there for a new discovery, the discovery of Spain by many more members of the British business community.

GRAMMAR SECTION

This grammar summary is only a brief guide to the basics of Spanish grammar. For additional explanations and a comprehensive list of irregular verbs, it is well worth investing in a good Spanish grammar book.

G1 **Genders**
• Generally speaking, nouns ending in **-o** are masculine, and those ending in **-a** are feminine.
el consejo   la manera
There are, however, some exceptions.
el día   la mano

• Nouns ending in **-dad**, **-tad**, **-tud**, **-ción**, **-sión** are feminine.
*la ciudad   la mitad   una solicitud   la nación
una inversión*

• Nouns ending in **-ma** are masculine.
el clima   el tema   el problema   el telegrama

• Nouns ending in **-e** are usually masculine, although there are a few exceptions.
*el coche   el viaje   el aceite   el café   el nombre
la calle   la noche   la tarde   la gente*

Plurals
• Nouns ending in a vowel form the plural simply by adding **-s**.
los teléfonos   las maneras   los coches

• Nouns ending in a consonant form the plural by adding **-es**.
las ciudades   los papeles

Definite/indefinite articles
• The definite articles (*the*) are as follows:

	Singular	Plural
masculine	**el**	**los**
feminine	**la**	**las**

• The indefinite articles (*a/an*) are as follows:

	Singular	Plural
masculine	**un**	**unos**
feminine	**una**	**unas**

• Note that **a** + **el** becomes **al** and **de** + **el** becomes **del**.

G2 **Ser/estar**
• In Spanish there are two verbs which mean *to be*. These two verbs have different uses and are not interchangeable.

• **Ser** is used:
1 to establish the identity and the profession of the subject:
*Ella **es** Maribel. (She is Maribel.)*
*Manolo **es** el jefe de calidad de servicios. (Manolo is head of customer services.)*

2 with adjectives which express a permanent quality or characteristic, e.g. nationality, colour, size, shape:
*Lord Alexander **es** inglés. (Lord Alexander is English.)*
*El tamaño **es** A4. (The size is A4.)*

3 with the preposition **de** to show origin, material or possession:
*Manolo **es** de Madrid. (Manolo is from Madrid.)*

4 to express time and dates:
*La inauguración **es** por la noche. (The inauguration is in the evening.)*
***Son** las nueve de la noche. (It's nine o'clock at night.)*

• **Estar** is used:
1 to express location:
*La nueva sede del Banco NatWest **está** en Madrid. (The new headquarters of Banco NatWest is in Madrid.)*
*Lord Alexander **está** en el cóctel. (Lord Alexander is at the party.)*

2 to indicate a temporary or variable state or condition:
*Hoy Maribel **está** contenta. (Maribel is happy today.)*
*El café **está** frío. (The coffee is cold.)*

3 to form the present continuous:
*Ellos **están** comprando el catálogo. (They are buying the catalogue.)*
*Lord Alexander **está** hablando con los invitados. (Lord Alexander is talking to the guests.)*

4 with the past participle to show the result of an action:
*El banco **está** cerrado. (The bank is closed.)*
*Los catálogos **están** dirigidos a las empresas privadas. (The catalogues are aimed at private companies.)*

Regular -ar verbs
• To form the present tense of **-ar** verbs, the infinitive ending **-ar** is dropped and the following endings are added for each person:
-o -as -a -amos -áis -an

Example:
HABLAR

yo	habl**o**	nosotros	habl**amos**
tú	habl**as**	vosotros	habl**áis**
él		ellos	
ella	} habl**a**	ellas	} habl**an**
usted		ustedes	

• Because the ending changes according to the person, the subject pronouns (*yo, tú, él, ella, usted, nosotros/as, vosotros/as, ellos, ellas, ustedes*) are generally omitted:
Trabajo mucho. (I work a lot.)
Exportan naranjas. (They export oranges.)
Gana poco. (He/she/you doesn't earn very much.)

• You can usually tell from the context whether verbs ending in **-a** refer to 'he', 'she' or 'you' and whether verbs ending in **-an** refer to 'they' or 'you'. If there is any ambiguity, the pronouns *él, ella, usted; ellos, ellas, ustedes* can be added.

• Note that you use the **tú** (singular) and **vosostros/as** (plural) forms when talking to people you know well and the **usted** (singular) and **ustedes** (plural) forms when talking to people you don't know or when showing respect.

Regular -er and -ir verbs
• As with **-ar** verbs, the **-er** and **-ir** are dropped from the infinitive and the following endings are added:
-er verbs: -o -es -e -emos -éis -en
-ir verbs: -o -es -e -imos -ís -en
Examples:
COMER

yo	com**o**	nosotros	com**emos**
tú	com**es**	vosotros	com**éis**
él		ellos	
ella	} com**e**	ellas	} com**en**
usted		ustedes	

SUBIR

yo	sub**o**	nosotros	sub**imos**
tú	sub**es**	vosotros	sub**ís**
él		ellos	
ella	} sub**e**	ellas	} sub**en**
usted		ustedes	

Irregular verbs: present tense
A Verbs in which the main part changes:
1 from **e** to **ie**

empezar empi**e**zo empi**e**zas empi**e**za empezamos empezáis empi**e**zan
atender ati**e**ndo ati**e**ndes ati**e**nde atendemos atendéis ati**e**nden
preferir prefi**e**ro prefi**e**res prefi**e**re preferimos preferís prefi**e**ren

• Some other verbs which follow the same rule are:
pensar cerrar comenzar despertarse sentarse querer perder entender invertir sugerir sentir

2 from **o** to **ue**
probar pr**ue**bo pr**ue**bas pr**ue**ba probamos probáis pr**ue**ban
volver v**ue**lvo v**ue**lves v**ue**lve volvemos volvéis v**ue**lven
dormir d**ue**rmo d**ue**rmes d**ue**rme dormimos dormís d**ue**rmen

• Some other verbs which follow the same rule are:
contar costar acordar recordar

3 from **e** to **i**
• This change only occurs in **-ir** verbs.
medir m**i**do m**i**des m**i**de medimos medís m**i**den

• Some other verbs which follow the same rule are:
pedir impedir despedir repetir

• Note that the above changes do not affect the *nosotros* or *vosotros* parts of the verb.

B Verbs which are irregular in the first person singular:
conocer cono**zc**o conoces conoce, etc
conducir condu**zc**o conduces conduce, etc.
producir produ**zc**o produces produce, etc.
traducir tradu**zc**o traduces traduce, etc.
hacer ha**g**o haces hace, etc.
poner pon**g**o pones pone, etc.
salir sal**g**o sales sale, etc.
dar d**oy** das da, etc.
saber s**é** sabes sabe, etc.
traer trai**g**o traes trae, etc.
ver v**e**o ves ve, etc.
• These are the most common verbs of this type.

C Verbs which are irregular in the first person singular and which change their stem (i.e. A+B):
decir d**ig**o d**i**ces d**i**ce decimos decís d**i**cen
tener ten**g**o ti**e**nes ti**e**ne tenemos tenéis ti**e**nen
venir ven**g**o vi**e**nes vi**e**ne venimos venís vi**e**nen

D Verbs ending in **-uir**:
• These verbs take a **y** in all forms of the present tense, except *nosotros* and *vosotros*.
atribuir atribu**y**o atribu**y**es atribu**y**e atribuimos atribuís atribu**y**en

• Other verbs in this category include:
construir contribuir destituir disminuir distribuir

G6 The future intentional

• The construction **ir** + **a** + infinitive is used to express a future intention, and corresponds to the English *to be* + *going to* + infinitive.

Examples:
Voy a visitar *la Expo esta tarde. (I am going to visit Expo this afternoon.)*
*¿**Vas a ver** a Luis? (Are you going to see Luis?)*
Va a llegar *en el tren de las cinco. (He/she is going to arrive on the five o'clock train.)*
Vamos a subir *a la torre después. (We're going to go up the tower afterwards.)*
*¿No **vais a ingresar** el dinero? (Aren't you going to pay in the money?)*
Van a comprar *una impresora Rapidacta. (They're going to buy a Rapidacta printer.)*

G7 Adjectives

A Agreement between nouns and adjectives
• Adjectives must agree with the noun they modify in gender and number.

• Adjectives which end in -o in the masculine form change their ending to -a in the feminine singular. The plural is formed by adding -s to the singular form.
El plato *es pequeño.* ***Los platos*** *son pequeños.*
La máquina *es pequeña.* ***Las máquinas*** *son pequeñas.*

• Adjectives which end in -e are the same for both masculine and feminine singular nouns. For the plural, simply add an -s.
*Es **un producto** excelente.*
*Son **unos productos** excelentes.*
*Es **una máquina** excelente.*
*Son **unas máquinas** excelentes.*

• Adjectives which end in a consonant are the same for both masculine and feminine nouns in the singular, and add -es in the plural.
*Es **un hombre** muy popular.*
*Son **unos hombres** muy populares.*
*Es **una marca** muy popular.*
*Son **unas marcas** muy populares.*

• Most adjectives follow the noun, but there are some exceptions to this rule, e.g. *mucho, otro*. See also the following section on shortened adjectives.

B Shortened adjectives
• Several adjectives have a shortened (or apocopated) form in the masculine singular when they go before the noun:
bueno *Es un **buen** director.*
malo *Da muy **mal** ejemplo.*
primero *Los servicios están en el **primer** piso.*
tercero *Mi oficina está en el **tercer** piso.*
alguno *¿Sabes si tiene **algún** interés?*
ninguno *No, no tiene **ningún** interés.*
ciento *En la planta trabajan **cien** obreros.*

C Demonstrative adjectives
• Demonstrative adjectives (*this, that, these, those*) also come before the noun, and agree in gender and number.

	Singular *(this)*	Plural *(these)*
masculine	este	estos
feminine	esta	estas
	(that)	*(those)*
masculine	ese	esos
feminine	esa	csas
	(that over there)	*(those over there)*
masculine	aquel	aquellos
feminine	aquella	aquellas

Esta *tarde damos la clase en un bar. (This evening we're having the class in a bar.)*
*Van a subir por **esos** andenes. (They're going to go up those ramps.)*
Aquellos *tubos de allí arriba son los tubos del aire acondicionado. (Those pipes up there are the air conditioning pipes.)*
Aquella *construcción es el monasterio. (That building over there is the monastery.)*

• **Ese** refers to something close to the person being spoken to, while **aquel** refers to something at a distance from both the speaker and the person being spoken to.

G8 Indirect and direct object pronouns

• The indirect object pronouns are used with 'impersonal' verbs such as **gustar**. The pronouns are:
me te le nos os les

• Other verbs which also require these pronouns include:
parecer doler sorprender encantar
These verbs are conjugated in the same way as **gustar**.
Me *duele la cabeza. (My head hurts.)*
Me *duelen las piernas. (My legs hurt.)*
*A María **le** encanta la ópera. (María loves the opera.)*
*A María **le** encantan las fiestas. (María loves parties.)*

• The direct object pronouns are:
me te lo/la nos os los/las

• *¿Quién construye el pabellón británico? (Who built the British Pavilion?)*
♦ *Trafalgar House **lo** construye. (Trafalgar House built it.)*
• *¿Dónde está mi maleta? (Where is my suitcase?)*
♦ *Aquí **la** tienes. (Here it is.)*

• In most cases, these pronouns go before the verb. However, when the verb is in the infinitive or when it is an affirmative imperative, the object pronouns come after and are attached to the end of the verb.
Sácame una copia. (Get me a copy.)
Sácanos unas copias. (Get us some copies.)
¿Puedes llevarme en tu coche? (Can you give me a lift?)
¿Puedes llevanos en tu coche? (Can you give us a lift?)

 Reflexive pronouns and verbs
• Reflexive verbs are those where the action is both executed and received by the subject. Reflexive verbs are formed in the same way as other verbs, but they need a reflexive pronoun before the verb. The reflexive pronouns in Spanish correspond to the English pronouns *myself, yourself, himself, ourselves,* etc. Here is an example of a common reflexive verb with the corresponding pronouns.

LLAMARSE

yo	**me** llamo	nosotros	**nos** llamamos
tú	**te** llamas	vosotros	**os** llamáis
él		ellos	
ella	**se** llama	ellas	**se** llaman
usted		ustedes	

• Other common reflexive verbs are:
marcharse acordarse olvidarse sentarse lavarse equivocarse prepararse dedicarse

• *Normalmente ¿a qué hora **te acuestas**? (What time do you normally go to bed?)*
♦ *Me acuesto a las doce de la noche. (I go to bed at midnight.)*

 Passive 'se'
• The reflexive **se** is also a way to express the passive. The passive is used when the action is more important than the person who is carrying it out. **Se** is used with the third person singular or plural of the verb.

• In the following example, the emphasis is on Casanueva:
Casanueva vende apartamentos en Torremolinos. (Casanueva sells apartments in Torremolinos.)
To change the emphasis to the apartments, use the passive **se**:
Se venden apartamentos en Torremolinos. (There are apartments for sale in Torremolinos.)
Note that the verb now agrees with **apartamentos**.

The future tense
• The future tense of all regular verbs is formed simply by adding the following endings to the infinitive of the verb:
-é -ás -á -emos -éis -án

Examples:
HABLAR

yo	hablar**é**	nosotros	hablar**emos**
tú	hablar**ás**	vosotros	hablar**éis**
él		ellos	
ella	hablar**á**	ellas	hablar**án**
usted		ustedes	

COMER

yo	comer**é**	nosotros	comer**emos**
tú	comer**ás**	vosotros	comer**éis**
él		ellos	
ella	comer**á**	ellas	comer**án**
usted		ustedes	

SUBIR

yo	subir**é**	nosotros	subir**emos**
tú	subir**ás**	vosotros	subir**éis**
él		ellos	
ella	subir**á**	ellas	subir**án**
usted		ustedes	

• There are some verbs which are irregular in the future; this irregularity occurs in the main part of the verb, not in the ending.
poner pon**dré** pon**drás** pon**drá**, etc.
salir sal**dré** sal**drás** sal**drá**, etc.
valer val**dré** val**drás** val**drá**, etc.
venir ven**dré** ven**drás** ven**drá**, etc.
poder po**dré** po**drás** po**drá**, etc.
decir di**ré** di**rás** di**rá**, etc.
hacer ha**ré** ha**rás** ha**rá**, etc.
tener ten**dré** ten**drás** ten**drá**, etc.
saber sa**bré** sa**brás** sa**brá**, etc.
querer que**rré** que**rrás** que**rrá**, etc

The past participle
• The verb **estar** is used in conjunction with the past participle to describe the result of a previous action. The past participle is formed by adding **-ado** to the stem of **-ar** verbs and **-ido** to the stem of **-er** and **-ir** verbs.

• The past participle agrees in number and gender with the noun it describes, so from the verb **cerrar** come **cerrado, cerrada, cerrados** and **cerradas**
La tienda está cerrada. (The shop is closed.)
Los bancos están cerrados. (The banks are closed.)

• Some past participles are irregular.
abrir abierto
cubrir cubierto

decir dicho
descubrir descubierto
devolver devuelto
envolver envuelto
escribir escrito
freir frito
hacer hecho
imponer impuesto
morir muerto
poner puesto
proponer propuesto
romper roto
ver visto
volver vuelto

Hecho en España. (Made in Spain.)
patatas fritas (chips, literally: fried potatoes)

The imperative

● There are two forms of the imperative: the formal (*usted/ustedes*) and the informal (*tú/vosotros*).

● The formal imperative is formed in the singular by taking the stem of the *yo* form of the present tense and adding **-e** for **-ar** verbs and **-a** for **-er** and **-ir** verbs.
hable lea conduzca

● The plural of the formal imperative is formed adding **-n** to the singular form.
hablen lean conduzcan

● The informal imperative is formed in the singular using the third person singular of the present tense.
habla lee conduce

● The plural of the informal imperative is formed by replacing the final **r** of the infinitive with a **d.**
hablad leed conducid

● There are some verbs which are irregular in the informal imperative in the singular.
tener ten
venir ven
ir ve
decir di
hacer haz
salir sal
poner pon
ser sé

● To express a negative command in the *informal* imperative singular, add an **s** to the affirmative form of the *formal* imperative and put **no** before the verb.
*hable **no** hables*
*lea **no** leas*
*conduzca **no** conduzcas*

● To express a negative command in the informal imperative plural, add **-éis** to the *yo* form of **-ar** verbs and **-áis** to the *yo* form of **-er** and **-ir** verbs, and add

no in front of the verb.
*hablar **no** habléis*
*leer **no** leáis*
*conducir **no** conduzcáis*

● For a negative formal command in both singular and plural forms, just put **no** before the affirmative formal command.
*hable **no** hable   hablen **no** hablen*
*lea **no** lea   lean **no** lean*
*conduzca **no** conduzca*
*conduzcan **no** conduzcan*

Comparatives and superlatives

A Comparison of superiority

● To form the comparative of adjectives, use: **más** + adjective + **que**. (Remember that the adjectives must agree in number and gender with the noun.)
*Ahora la compañía es **más** competitiva **que** antes. (Now the company is more competitive than before.)*
*Estos edificios son **más** altos **que** los otros. (These buildings are higher than the others.)*

● There are some common adjectives which are irregular and do not use **más.**
bueno   mejor
malo   peor
grande   mayor
pequeño   menor
*El hotel Central es **mejor que** el hotel Marcos. (Hotel Central is better than Hotel Marcos.)*

B Superlatives

● To form the superlative of adjectives, use: definite article (+ noun) **+ más** + adjective + **de.**
*Esta compañía es **la más** importante **de** España. (This company is the most important in Spain.)*
*Es el coche **más** caro **del** mercado. (It's the most expensive car on the market.)*

Expressing obligation

● **Tener que** + infinitive expresses a personal obligation.
Tengo que llamar a Inglaterra. (I must/I've got to call England.)

● **Hay que** + infinitive expresses an impersonal obligation.
Hay que aumentar la producción. (You/we must increase production.)

● **Deber** indicates what should be done.
Debes hablar con el director. (You should talk to the director.)

The present perfect tense

● The present perfect in Spanish is formed with the present tense of the verb **haber** + the

past participle of another verb.
haber he has ha hemos habéis han

• This tense is used to express an action which has recently been done, without reference to a particular time.
He estado en Madrid. *(I've been/I was in Madrid.)*
Ha estudiado medicina. *(He/she studied/has studied medicine.)*

G17 The past tense (preterite)
• This tense describes an action completed in the past at a particular time. It is often used in conjunction with certain adverbial phrases of time, such as **ayer, la semana pasada, antes de ayer, hace una hora**.

• Regular **-ar** verbs are formed by adding the following endings to the main part of the verb:
-é -aste -ó -amos -asteis -aron

Example:
HABLAR

yo	hablé	nosotros	hablamos
tú	hablaste	vosotros	hablasteis
él		ellos	
ella	habló	ellas	hablaron
usted		ustedes	

• Regular **-er** and **-ir** verbs form the preterite by adding the following endings to the main part of the verb:
-í -iste -ió -imos -isteis -ieron

Examples:
VENDER

yo	vendí	nosotros	vendimos
tú	vendiste	vosotros	vendisteis
él		ellos	
ella	vendió	ellas	vendieron
usted		ustedes	

SUBIR

yo	subí	nosotros	subimos
tú	subiste	vosotros	subisteis
él		ellos	
ella	subió	ellas	subieron
usted		ustedes	

• Two points to watch out for:

1 the *nosotros* form is the same in the present and preterite tenses. The context will tell you which is meant;

2 the **-o** ending characteristic of the *yo* form in the present tense transfers to the *él/ella/usted* form in the preterite.
hablo *(I speak)* **habló** *(he/she spoke)*

• There are several irregular verbs. Here are some of the more common.
estar estuve estuviste estuvo estuvimos estuvisteis estuvieron
ir fui fuiste fue fuimos fuisteis fueron
dar di diste dio dimos disteis dieron
hacer hice hiciste hizo hicimos hicisteis hicieron
tener tuve tuviste tuvo tuvimos tuvisteis tuvieron
saber supe supiste supo supimos supisteis supieron
ser fui fuiste fue fuimos fuisteis fueron
poder pude pudiste pudo pudimos pudisteis pudieron

• Note that **ser** and **ir** are the same in the preterite tense. You can usually tell which is meant by the context.
*El verano pasado **fui** a Sevilla. (Last summer I went to Seville.)*
Fui *director de SEAT durante dos años. (I was the director of SEAT for two years.)*

G18 The imperfect tense
• This tense is more common in Spanish than in English. It refers to an action which is not completed in the past. It can be translated in English by both *was/were doing* or *used to do*.

• Regular **-ar** verbs add the following endings to the main part of the verb:
-aba -abas -aba -ábamos -abais -aban

Example:
HABLAR

yo	hablaba	nosotros	hablábamos
tú	hablabas	vosotros	hablabais
él		ellos	
ella	hablaba	ellas	hablaban
usted		ustedes	

• Regular **-er** and **-ir** verbs add the following endings to the main part of the verb:
-ía -ías -ía -íamos -íais -ían

Examples:
VENDER

yo	vendía	nosotros	vendíamos
tú	vendías	vosotros	vendíais
él		ellos	
ella	vendía	ellas	vendían
usted		ustedes	

SUBIR

yo	sub**ía**	nosotros	sub**íamos**
tú	sub**ías**	vosotros	sub**íais**
él		ellos	
ella }	sub**ía**	ellas }	sub**ían**
usted		ustedes	

- Note that the *yo* form and the *él/ella/usted* form are the same in the imperfect. The context will tell you which is meant.

- The majority of the verbs are regular in this tense. The most common irregular ones are shown below.
dar daba dabas daba dábamos dabais daban
ser era eras era éramos érais eran
ir iba ibas iba íbamos ibais iban
ver veía veías veía veíamos veías veían

G19 The present and past continuous

- The present and the past continuous are formed using the present and the imperfect tenses of the verb **estar** + present participle. The present participle is formed by adding **-ando** to the stem of **-ar** verbs, and **-iendo** to **-er** and **-ir** verbs.
*habl**ando** vend**iendo** sub**iendo***
***Estaba hablando** con Maribel. (He/she was talking to Maribel.)*
***Estaban vendiendo** naranjas. (They were selling oranges.)*

- There are some verbs with irregular present participles:
ir yendo
leer leyendo
oír oyendo
caer cayendo
construir construyendo
distribuir distribuyendo
sentir sintiendo
pedir pidiendo
decir diciendo
venir viniendo

G20 The conditional tense

- The conditional is formed by adding the following endings to the infinitive of the verb:
-ía -ías -ía -íamos -íais -ían

Examples:
HABLAR

yo	hablar**ía**	nosotros	hablar**íamos**
tú	hablar**ías**	vosotros	hablar**íais**
él		ellos	
ella }	hablar**ía**	ellas }	hablar**ían**
usted		ustedes	

VENDER

yo	vender**ía**	nosotros	vender**íamos**
tú	vender**ías**	vosotros	vender**íais**
él		ellos	
ella }	vender**ía**	ellas }	vender**ían**
usted		ustedes	

SUBIR

yo	subir**ía**	nosotros	subir**íamos**
tú	subir**ías**	vosotros	subir**íais**
él		ellos	
ella }	subir**ía**	ellas }	subir**ían**
usted		ustedes	

- It is used to give advice and to make suggestions and to express the English *would do*.

*Yo **vendería** la fábrica. (I would sell the factory.)*
- Verbs which are irregular in the future are irregular in the conditional.
ir irá → iría
poder podremos → podríamos

G20 Adverbs

- Adverbs are formed by adding **-mente** to the feminine singular form of the adjective.

Adjective	Adverb
último	últimamente
preciso	precisamente
fuerte	fuertemente
inteligente	inteligentemente
difícil	difícilmente
popular	popularmente

- Note that accents on the adjective remain in the same place for the corresponding adverb.

G20 Prepositions

The most frequent prepositions, with their principal uses, are:
a

- place
*El teléfono está **a** la derecha. (The telephone is on the right.)*

- motion
*Susana va **a** Sevilla. (Susana is going to Seville.)*

- **a** is also used to show that the object of the verb is a person
*Vi **a** la directora ayer. (I saw the director yesterday.)*

con

- togetherness
*Café solo **con** azúcar. (Black coffee with sugar.)*

- the means of way of doing something
*Escribo **con** un ordenador. (I'm writing using a computer.)*

de

- possession
*La agenda es **de** Roberto. (It's Roberto's diary.)*

- material
*La camisa es **de** algodón. (It's a cotton shirt.)*

- origin
*Lord Alexander es **de** Inglaterra. (Lord Alexander is from England.)*

en

- means
*Van **en** avión. (They are going by plane.)*

- place
*Cartuja está **en** Sevilla. (Cartuja is in Seville.)*

- time taken to do something
*Terminaré los informes **en** dos horas. (I'll finish the reports in two hours.)*

para

- destination
*Ese es el tren **para** Barcelona. (That's the train for Barcelona.)*

- purpose
*Necesito un taxi **para** ir a la oficina. (I need a taxi to go to the office.)*

- suitability
*Estas camisas no son **para** señoras. (These shirts aren't for ladies.)*

por

- reason
*Estoy muy cansada, **por** eso necesito descansar. (I'm very tired, so I need to rest.)*

- exchange
*Tengo que cambiar los cheques de viajero **por** dinero. (I've got to exchange the traveller's cheques for money.)*

- percentage
*Conseguí un descuento del cinco **por** cien. (I got a 5% discount.)*

- time expressions
*El avión llega **por** la tarde. (The plane arrives in the afternoon.)*

* Stress and pronunciation

- Spanish has very regular rules for pronouncing words. You will soon get used to the sounds of Spanish by watching the video and listening to the audiocassettes. A summary of the rules for stress (i.e. where the emphasis is placed on a word) is given below to help you with new words.

1 In words ending in a vowel, **n** or **s**, the stress normally falls on the penultimate syllable.
*co**c**he ma**ne**ra Eu**ro**pa **ha**blan pa**pel**es*

2 In words ending in a consonant apart from **n** or **s**, the stress falls on the last syllable.
*nacionali**dad** re**loj** ha**blar***

3 If the stress differs from the above two rules, an accent (´) is used to show the stressed syllable.
má**quina **có**digo in**glés** na**ción

If, however, the accent falls on the final syllable of a word ending in a consonant, the accent disappears in the plural.
inglés ingleses nación naciones

- Note that the accent in Spanish is used purely as a stress marker and does not indicate a change in the sound as in French.

WORDLIST

- This Wordlist contains the main items of vocabulary that appear in this book; it does not list all the words that you will hear in the video. You should ensure that you also have access to a good bilingual dictionary.

- Note that Spanish has three 'letters' which do not exist in English: ch, ll and ñ. They are considered as separate letters and follow c, l and n respectively in dictionaries, etc.

- The following abbreviations are used in this Wordlist:
nm = masculine noun
nf = feminine noun
nm/f = noun that can be either masculine or feminine
nmp = masculine plural noun
nfp = feminine plural noun
adv = adverb
adj = adjective
interr = interrogative pronoun
rel = relative pronoun
conj = conjunction

A

a to
abonar to pay (for)
abrir to open
aburrido boring
acceso (nm) entry, admittance
acción (nf) action; share
aclarar to clarify, to resolve
aconsejar to advise
acrílico acrylic
acuerdo (nm) agreement
agente (nm/f) agent
agradecer to thank
agua (nf) water
ahora now
ahorro (nm) saving
aire (nm) air
   aire acondicionado (nm) air conditioning
ajedrez (nm) chess
alcanzar to reach
alemán German
Alemania Germany

algo something
algodón (nm) cotton
almacén (nm) warehouse; store
almidón (nm) starch
almuerzo (nm) lunch
alquilar to rent
alquiler (nm) rent, rental
alto high, tall
altura (nf) height
amargor (nm) bitterness
ambiente (nm) environment, atmosphere
americano American
amplio wide, spacious
ancho wide
andén (nm) platform; ramp
anotar to note down, to annotate
atena (nf) aerial, atenna
anterior preceding, previous
anteriormente previously, before
antes before, previously
anuncio (nm) advertisement
anual annual
añadir to add
año (nm) year
aparcamiento (nm) parking place, car park
aplazar to postpone, to put off
aportar to contribute
aprender to learn
aprobación (nf) approval, consent
aprobado approved
aquel that
árbol (nm) tree
área (nf) area
arista (nf) edge
arriba above, upstairs
asegurar to assure, to affirm
asesor (nm) advisor, consultant
asunto (nm) topic, subject
atender to attend to, to pay attention to
aumento (nm) increase
aún still, yet
automóvil (nm) car, automobile
autónomo autonomous
autopista (nm) motorway
avance (nm) advance
avión (nf) aeroplane

ayudar to help, to aid
azúcar (nm) sugar

B

bajo low, short
balasto (nm) sleeper
banco (nm) bank; bench
bandera (nf) flag
baño (nm) bathing, bath
barco (nm) boat
barril (nm) barrel, keg
barrio (nm) district, quarter, suburb
basar to base
bastante enough, sufficient
beber to drink
beneficio (nm) benefit, profit, gain
bienes (nmp) goods, possessions
billete (nm) ticket
bolsillo (nm) pocket
boquerón (nm) anchovy
bueno good, fine
británico British

C

cada each
café (nm) coffee
caja (nf) box, safe
cajón (nm) box, drawer
calamar (nm) squid
cálculo (nm) calculation
calefacción (nf) heating
calendario (nm) calendar
calidad (nf) quality
calle (nf) street
cama (nf) bed
camarero (nm) waiter
camión (nm) lorry, truck
camisa (nf) shirt
campaña (nf) campaign
campo (nm) country, countryside; field
Canadá Canada
canadiense Canadian
cancelar to cancel
cantidad (nf) amount, quantity
caña (de cerveza) (nf) glass of beer
capacidad (nf) capacity
capital (nf) capital (money)

capital (nm) capital (city)
cara (nf) face
característica (nf) characteristic
cargo (nm) post, job, office
carnero (nm) sheep, ram
carnet (de identidad) (nm) identity card
caro expensive
carretera (nf) road
carril (nm) rail
carta (nf) letter
cartel (nm) poster
cartilla (de seguro) (nf) social security card
cartón (nm) cardboard
casa (nf) house
casi nearly
castellano (nm/adj) Castilian; Spanish
catálogo (nm) catalogue
categoría (nf) category, class
cebada (nf) barley
celebrar to celebrate, to hold
cenicero (nm) ashtray
centro centre
cerámica (nf) ceramics, pottery
cerca near
cerveza (nf) beer
cielo (nm) sky
científico scientific
cinturón (nm) belt
circulación (nf) circulation
cita (nf) appointment
ciudad (nf) city
claro clear
clase (nf) class, kind, sort
cliente (nm/f) client, customer
cobro (nm) collection, payment
cocción (nf) cooking
cóctel (nm) cocktail
código (nm) code
colectivo collective
coloquio (nm) conference
color (nm) colour
comenzar to start
comercial commercial, business
comercio (nm) commerce, trade, business
comida (nf) meal, food
comisión (nf) committee, commission
como (adv) as, like
cómo (interr) how?, why?
comodidad (nf) comfort
cómodo comfortable
compañía (nf) company
competidor (nm) competitor, rival

complementos (nmp) accessories
completo complete
componer to compose, to make up
compra (nf) purchase
común common
comunidad (nf) community
con with
conceder to concede, to admit
concepto (nm) concept, notion
conducir to drive, to direct
conducto (nm) conduit, tube, pipe
confederación (nf) confederation, league
confirmar to confirm
conjunto joint, united
conmemorar to commemorate
conocer to know, to know about
consejero (nm) board member
considerar to consider, to think about
construcción (nf) building, construction
consulado (nm) consulate
consumidor (nm) consumer
contabilidad (nf) accounting, book-keeping
contenido (nm) content(s)
contento satisfied, content
contestar to answer
contrario opposite
contrato (nm) contract
contribuyente (nm/f) taxpayer, contributor
copia (nf) copy
cordón (nm) shoelace, cord
cortina (nf) curtain
corto short
correcto right, correct
correo (nm) post, mail
correos (nmp) post office
cosa (nf) thing
coche (nm) car
crear to create
crecer to grow
crecimiento (nm) growth, increase, rise
crédito (nm) credit
creer to believe
cristal (nm) glass, a pane of glass
cuadrado square
cual (rel) which
cúal (interr) which (one)?
cuando (adv/conj) when
cuándo (interr) when?

cubierto covered
cúbico cubic
cuello (nm) neck
cuero (nm) leather
cumbre (nf) summit, top

D

dar to give
dato(s) (nm) datum (data)
de of, from
debajo under, underneath
decir to say
dejar to leave
demanda (nf) demand
demasiado too (much), excessive(ly)
dentro inside, in
deportivo sports car; sporting
depósito (nm) deposit
derecha (nf) right
desarrollo (nm) development
descapotable convertible
describir to describe
descuento (nm) discount
desde from
desear to want
designar to designate, to appoint, to name
despacho (nm) office
despedir to fire, to sack
despegar to take off
después after, afterwards
detalle (nm) detail
determinar to determine
detrás behind
devaluar to devalue
día (nm) day
diapositiva (nf) slide, transparency
diario daily
dibujo (nm) drawing
diccionario (nm) dictionary
dimitir to resign, to relinquish
dinero (nm) money
dirigir to direct, to manage
disco (nm) record, disc
discoteca (nf) disco
diseñar to design
diseño (nm) design
disponer to arrange, to have at one's disposal
disuelto dissolved
diverso diverse; several
documento (nm) document
donde (conj) where
dónde (interr) where?
duda (nf) doubt
durante during

E

economía (nf) economy
económico economic, economical
edificio (nm) building
efectivo (nm) cash
eficaz efficient
eficiente efficient; effective
ejecución (nf) execution, performance
ejecutivo (nm) executive
ejemplo (nm) example
ejercicio (nm) fiscal year; exercise
el the
él he
elección (nf) election, choice
electrodoméstico (nm) home appliance
elemento (nm) element
ella she
ellos them
embotellar to bottle
embotellador (nm) bottler
embotelladora (nf)
emparejar to pair, to match
empezar to start
empleado (nm) employee
empleo (nm) employment; job
empresa (nf) company, firm
en in, into, on
encantado delighted, charmed
encargado (nm) agent, representative, person in charge
encima above, over
encuesta (nf) survey
enchufe (nm) plug, socket
enfoque (nm) focus; grasp
enfriar to cool
ensalada (nf) salad
entender to understand
entidad (nf) entity
entonces then, at that time
entrada (nf) entrance
entrar to enter
entre between
entrega (nf) delivery
entregar to deliver
entrevista (nf) interview, meeting
envase (nm) package, wrapping, container
enviar to send
envidia (nf) envy, jealousy
envio (nm) consignment, lot
enzima (nf) enzyme

época (nf) period, time
equipaje (nm) luggage
equipo (nm) equipment; team
escalera (nf) stair, stairway
escuchar to listen
ese that
espacio (nm) space
España Spain
español Spanish, Spaniard
esposa (nf) wife
esta this
establecer to establish
estación (nf) station
Estados Unidos United States of America
estampado printed (cloth)
estancar to stagnate, to block, to hold back
estándar standard
estar to be
estatal state
estático static
este this
este (nm) east
estilo (nm) style
estrato (nm) layer
estructura (nf) structure
estupendo stupendous, wonderful
etapa (nf) stage
excesivo excessive, too much
exceso (nm) excess, surplus
existencias (nfp) stock, goods
éxito (nm) success
expansión (nf) expansion
expediente (nm) file, records
exportación (nf) export, exportation
extensión (nf) extension, extent, size
extranjero foreign

F

factura (nf) bill, invoice
fallo (nm) shortcoming, failure
farmacia (nf) chemist's
fecha (nf) date
ferial (nm) fair, fairground
fertilidad (nf) fertility, richness
fibra (nf) fibre
fijar to fix
fijarse to notice
fin (nm) end, ending
    fin de semana weekend
final (nm) end
finalmente finally
financiado financed
firmar to sign

fiscal fiscal, financial
fiscalidad (nf) taxation
físico physical
folleto (nm) pamphlet, leaflet
fondo (nm) fund
formar to form
fracaso (nm) failure
francés French
Francia France
frente (nm) front
    en frente in front, opposite
frequentamente frequently
frito fried
fronterizo frontier
fuente (nf) source, origin; fountain
fuera outside
fuerte strong
fuerza (nf) strength
fumar to smoke
fusión (nf) fusion, joining
futuro (nm) future

G

ganado (nm) cattle
garaje (nm) garage
garantía (nf) guarantee
gasolina (nf) petrol
gastar to spend
generar to generate
giro (nm) draft, bill of exchange
gracias (nfp) thank you
gramo (nm) gramme
grande big
gratis free
guerra (nf) war
gustar to like

H

habitual habitual, customary, usual
hablar to talk
hacer to make; to do
hasta until; even
hecho (nm) fact; deed
herencia (nf) inheritance
hidrocarburo (nm) hydrocarbon
historia (nf) history
histórico historical
hoja (nf) leaf; page
hombre (nm) man
horario (nm) timetable; working hours
horno (nm) oven
hoy today
huelga (nf) strike, stoppage

I

identificación (nf) identification
identificar to identify
idioma (nm) language
iglesia (nf) church
igual equal, the same
imagen (nf) image, picture
importante important
importar to import
impresión (nf) impression, issue
impresora (nf) printer
impuesto (nm) tax
inauguración (nf) opening, inauguration
incrementar to increase
incremento (nm) increment, increase
indicar to indicate
industria (nf) industy
infantil infantile
informática (nf) computer science
ingeniero (nm) engineer
Inglaterra England
inglés English
ingresar to deposit, to pay in
ingreso (nm) income, revenue
inicial initial
inicio (nm) start, beginning
inmejorable unsurpassable
innovación (nf) innovation
instituto (nm) institute
instrumento (nm) instrument
intercambio (nm) interchange, exchange
interés (nm) interest
interesante interesting
interruptor (nm) switch
invertir to invest
investigar to investigate
invierno (nm) winter
invitación (nf) invitation
invitado (nm/f) guest
isla (nf) island
Italia Italy
italiano Italian
izquierdo left

J

jamón (nm) ham
Japón Japan
japonés Japanese
jardín (nm) garden
jefe (nm/f) boss
jornada (nf) working day
joven young
juguete (nm) toy

junta (nf) board, council, committee
junto together
jubilación (nf) retirement

L

la the
lámpara (nf) lamp, light, bulb
lana (nf) wool
lanzar to launch, to promote
lápiz (nm) pencil
largo long
láser (nm) laser
lavar to wash
lector (nm) reader
leer to read
lencería (nf) lingerie
lengua (nf) language; tongue
lento slow
letra (nf) letter, bill, draft
levadura (nf) yeast
librería (nf) bookshop
libro (nm) book
líquido (nm) liquid
liso plain, unadorned; flat
localización (nf) location, setting
lotería (nf) lottery
luego then, next
lugar (nm) place
lujo (nm) luxury
lúpulo (nm) hop
luz (nf) light

LL

llamar to call
llave (nf) key
lleno full

M

madera (nf) wood
mañana (nf) morning; tomorrow
malta (nf) malt
mandar to send, to order
manera (nf) way, manner, fashion
manga (nf) sleeve
mano (nf) hand
mantenimiento (nm) maintenance
maquinaria (nf) machinery
marca (nf) make, brand
marcar to mark, to show
marisco (nm) shellfish, seafood
más more
mástil (nm) mast, pole, support
material (nm) material
matriz (nf) mould, die
    casa matriz head office

mecánico mechanical
medio (nm) means
mejicano Mexican
Méjico Mexico
memoria (nf) note, report; memory
mensaje (nm) message
mercado (nm) market
mercancia (nf) goods, merchandise
mercantil mercantile
mes (nm) month
mesa (nf) table
meta (nf) goal, aim, objective
metro (nm) metre
mezcla (nf) mixture
miembro (nm) member
mínimo minimum
mocasín (nm) moccasin
moda (nf) fashion
modelo (nm) model
modernizar to modernize
moderno modern
monarquía (nf) monarchy
moneda (nf) coin; currency
monumento (nm) monument
morro (nm) nose, snout
motivo (nm) motive, reason
mucho a lot of, much
mueble (nm) piece of furniture
mujer (nf) woman
multa (nf) fine
mundo (nm) world
muy very

N

nación (nf) nation
nacional national
nacionalidad (nf) nationality
nada nothing
Navidad (nf) Christmas
necesitar to need
negociación (nf) negotiation, deal
negocio (nm) business
nieve (nf) snow
ninguno none
noche (nf) night
nombre (nm) name
nómina (nf) payroll
normalmente normally
normativa (nf) rules, guidelines
norte (nm) north
noruego Norwegian
nosotros we
nuevo new
número (nm) number
nunca never

O

objetivo objective
objeto (nm) object, thing
obra (nf) work, piece of work
obrero (nm) worker
ocupado busy
oeste (nm) west
oferta (nf) offer
oficina (nf) oficina
oír to hear
ojo (nm) eye
oleoducto (nm) (oil) pipeline
onza (nf) ounce
opuesto opposite, contrary
orden (nm) order
   orden del día agenda
ordenador (nm) computer
organizador (nm/f) organizer
otoño (nm) autumn

P

pabellón (nm) pavilion
pagar to pay
país (nm) country
palabra (nf) word
panorámico panoramic
pantalla (nf) screen
papel (nm) paper
papelería (nf) stationery,
   stationer's
paquete (nm) packet, parcel
par (nm) pair
para for, towards, in order to
parcial partial
párrafo (nm) paragraph
participar to participate
partido (nm) party (political);
   game
pasaporte (nm) passport
pasivo passive
patata (nf) potato
pedido (nm) order, request
pedir to request, to ask for
película (nf) film
peligro (nm) danger
peligroso dangerous
peluquería (nf) hairdresser's
pendiente pending, outstanding
pequeño small
perder to lose
perfumería (nf) perfumery
periódico (adj) periodic
periódico (nm) newspaper
persona (nf) person
personalmente personally
pirata pirate
piscina (nf) swimming pool

piso (nm) floor; apartment
pista (nf) clue
plancha (nf) grill; iron
   a la plancha grilled
planchar to iron
plano flat, level
planta (nf) plant
plato (nm) plate, dish
plazo (nm) time, period, term
plomo (nm) lead
pobre poor
poco little, not much
poder to be able, can
podio (nm) podium
polaco Polish
policía (nf) police force
policía (nm) policeman
por for, by, in
   por favor please
   por qué why?
porcelana (nf) porcelain
porcentaje (nm) percentage
porque because
portátil portable
posición (nf) position, status
positivo positive
potente powerful
práctico practical
precio (nm) price
precioso precious, valuable
preferir to prefer
premio (nm) prize
presentar to present
préstamo (nm) loan
presupuesto (nm) budget,
   estimate
previamente previously
primavera spring
primero first
principal principal, main
príncipe (nm) prince
procesión (nf) procession
proceso (nm) process
producción (nf) production
producir to produce
producto (nm) product
profesor (nm) teacher
profundidad (nf) depth
prohibición (nf) prohibition,
   ban
prolongado long, lengthy
propio own, of one's own
propósito (nm) purpose, aim
propuesta (nf) proposal
provincia (nf) province
proximidad (nf) nearness,
   proximity
próximo near, close, next

proyectar to project
proyecto (nm) project
proyector (nm) projector
prudente prudent
público (nm) public
puente (nm) bridge
punta (nf) tip, point

Q

que (conj) who, that, which
qué (interr) what?, which?
queso (nm) cheese
quien who
químico (nm) chemical
quinielas (nfp) football pools
quiebra (nf) bankruptcy
quizá(s) perhaps, maybe

R

rampa (nf) ramp, incline
rápido quick, fast
raqueta (nf) racquet
raya (nf) line, stripe
razón (nf) reason
   tener razón to be right
recado (nm) message, errand
recepción (nf) reception
recinto (nm) precinct, area
recuadro (nm) inset
recursos (nmp) resources,
   means
redactar to write, to draw up
refinería (nf) refinery
refresco (nm) soft drink
regalo (nm) gift, present
región (nf) region, district
registrado registered
regresar to return
Reino Unido (nm) United
   Kingdom
religioso religious
relojería (nf) watchmaker's
renta (nf) income; interest,
   return
rentable profitable
repartir to distribute, to share
repetir to repeat
representante (nm/f)
representative
representar to represent, to act
for
repuesto (nm) spare,
   replacement
resbalar to slip
reserva (nf) reservation, reserve
resolver to resolve, to solve
respuesta (nf) answer

resultado (nm) result
resumen (nm) summary, résumé
retraso (nm) delay
retroproyector (nm) overhead
  projector
reunión (nf) meeting
revisar to check, to revise
revolución (nf) revolution
riqueza (nf) wealth, riches
robo (nm) robbery
rodante rolling
  material rodante rolling stock
rojo red
ropa (nf) clothes, clothing

S
saber to know
salida (nf) exit, way out
salto (nm) jump
saludo (nm) greeting
sardina (nf) sardine, pilchard
secretaria (nf) secretary
seda (nf) silk
sede (nf) headquarters, central
  office
seguidamente immediately after,
  next
seguir to follow
según according to
segundo second
seguridad (nf) safety, security
seguro safe, secure
semana (nf) week
sensato sensible
señor Mr, sir, gentleman
señora Mrs, madam, lady
ser to be
serio serious, grave
servicio (nm) service
servicios (nmp) toilets
sigla (nf) abbreviation, acronym
siglo (nm) century
significado significance, meaning
siguiente following, next
simultaneamente
  simultaneously
sin without
sindical (adj) union
sindicato (nm) trade union
singularidad (nf) singularity,
  peculiarity
sinónimo (nm) synonym
sobre on, upon, on top of
sociedad (nf) society, company,
  partnership
socio (nm) associate, member
solamente only
solicitud (nf) request, petition

sólido solid
solo single, sole; alone
subir to raise, to lift up
submarino (nm) submarine
sucursal (nf) branch, branch
  office
sueldo (nm) salary, pay
suelo (nm) ground, floor
Suiza Switzerland
suizo Swiss
supermercado (nm)
  supermarket
sur (nm) south
suscripción (nf) subscription

T
tamaño (nm) size
tarifa (nf) tariff, rate, fare
tabla (nf) table, list, chart
tapa (nf) lid, top
tapas (nfp) bar snacks
tarde (adv) late
tarde (nf) afternoon
tarjeta (nf) card
taza (nf) cup
técnico technical
teatro (nm) theatre
técnica (nf) technique
teléfono (nm) telephone
temprano early
terminar to end
terraplén (nm) embankment
terraza (nf) terrace, balcony
tesoro (nm) treasure
textil textile
texto (nm) text
tiempo (nm) time
tienda (nf) shop, store
tinto (nm) red wine
típico typical, characteristic
tipo (nm) type; rate (exchange,
  interest etc)
todavía still, yet
todo all, whole, entire
tonelada (nf) ton
torre (nf) tower
tortilla (nf) omelette
trabajador (nm) worker
trabajar to work
trabajo (nm) work
traer to bring, to carry
traje (nm) dress, costume, suit
tratar to try to; to deal with
traviesa (nf) sleeper
tren (nm) train
tríptico (nm) three-part
  document
triunfo (nm) triumph

trono (nm) throne
tú you (informal singular form)
túnel (nm) tunnel

U
ubicación (nf) whereabouts,
place, position
último last
unidad (nf) unit
urgente urgent
usted/Vd. you (polite singular
form)
ustedes/Vds. you (polite plural
form)
utilizar to use

V
vacación (nf) holiday, vacation
vacuno bovine
vagón (nm) coach, carriage
validez (nf) validity
valor (nm) value
valorar to value, to price
varios several, some, a number
of
vehículo (nm) vehicle
velocidad (nf) speed
vendedor (nm) salesman
ventaja (nf) advantage
ventana (nf) window
ventas (nfp) sale, selling
ver to see
verano (nm) summer
vez (nf) time, occasion, instance
  una vez once
  otra vez again
viajar to travel
viaje (nm) trip, journey
vidrio (nm) glass
viejo old
vino (nm) wine
visita (nf) visit
visitar to visit
vista (nf) view
vosotros you (informal plural
form)
vuelo (nm) flight
vuelta (nf) turn, return

Y
y and
ya already
yo I

Z
zapatería (nf) shoeshop
zapato (nm) shoe

ANSWER KEY

For some exercises in this book there is more than one correct answer. This answer key gives the most likely/fullest version.

1 BANKING ON ACTION

Sección 1

Comprensión

1 por la noche. 2 Lord Alexander.
3 en España. 4 el jefe de calidad de servicios del Banco NatWest. 5 Hola, ¿Cómo estás Maribel? 6 Fernando.
7 ¿Qué hay? Encantado. 8 bien.
9 un cliente. 10 mal.

¿El, la, los o las?

1 la 2 el 3 el 4 las 5 los 6 el 7 las
8 la 9 el 10 el 11 la 12 el

Completa

El • del • las • los • al • la • las • los • la • la • la • del

Completa

1 Qué 2 Cómo 3 Qué 4 Hola
5 Muy 6 Buenas

Relaciona

1 f 2 d 3 e 4 b 5 a 6 c

Completa

1 soy 2 está 3 es 4 están 5 son
6 es 7 está 8 es 9 sois 10 soy

Completa

1 Qué 2 Dónde 3 Quién 4 Dónde
5 Cuál/Qué 6 Cuándo

Repasa

1 • Hola, buenos días.
   ♦ Hola, ¿qué tal?
2 • Te presento a Maribel.
   ♦ Hola, ¿cómo estás?
   • Encantada.
3 • ¿Qué tal, Mariano?
   ♦ ¿Qué tal, Manolo? ¿Cómo estás?
   • Bastante bien.

Contesta

1 Lord Alexander quiere dirigir unas palabras a las señoras y los señores del cóctel.
2 El motivo del cóctel es la inauguración de la nueva sede del Banco NatWest en España.
3 Manolo es jefe de calidad de servicios del Banco NatWest.
4 Hola, ¿cómo estás, Maribel?
5 El nombre de la segunda persona que le presentan es Fernando.
6 ¿Qué hay? Encantado.
7 ¿Qué tal, Mariano?
8 ¿Qué tal, Manolo, ¿cómo estás?
9 Hablan de un cliente.
10 Bastante mal.

Sección 2

Comprensión

1 último tríptico promocional.
2 un éxito tremendo. 3 el catálogo principal. 4 catorce. 5 treinta mil ejemplares del flyer. 6 por la tarde.
7 de Action Computers. 8 con leche con azúcar.

Completa

1 considero 2 llama 3 deseáis
4 utilizan 5 lanzan 6 represento
7 indica 8 hablo 9 copian
10 compramos

¿Verdadero o falso?

1 verdadero 2 verdadero 3 falso
4 verdadero 5 falso 6 verdadero
7 falso 8 falso 9 verdadero 10 falso

Números

1 ocho mil setecientos cincuenta y nueve
2 903
3 catorce mil setecientos quince
4 701
5 cinco millones setecientos seis mil veinticuatro

6 6.384
7 ciento cincuenta mil catorce.
8 168
9 siete mil setecientos setenta y siete
10 90.990.009

Escribe el número

1 cuatro 2 doscientos cincuenta
3 treinta 4 diez 5 tres 6 cincuenta

Repasa

1 es • el • una
2 La • la • está • un/el
3 es • una
4 son
5 El • unos
6 Las • son
7 están • un/el
8 son • unas

¿Dígame?

1 0130 80 0034 2 Colombia 3 0800 89 0034 4 Irlanda 5 El segundo tono

Completa

1 repetimos 2 trae 3 sabe
4 conoces 5 dice • concede
6 preferís 7 cree • es 8 suben
9 reparte 10 reciben

Apunta

2
Nombre: Ana Márquez
Cargo: Directora comercial
Empresa: Ibertel SA
Dirección: Calle Raimundo Fernández Villaverde, 37
Cód. Postal: 20172
Provincia: Madrid
Nº Teléfono: 321 45 39
Nº Fax: 321 45 45
Nº de empleados: 350
¿Es usted responsable de compras?
Sí No x

Contesta

1 El propósito de la reunión es considerar el último tríptico promocional.
2 Normalmente llaman al tríptico el flyer.
3 Experimentan un éxito tremendo con el flyer anterior.
4 El fin del flyer que desean lanzar ahora es dirigir atención al catálogo principal.
5 El número del catálogo en circulación es el catorce.
6 El mensaje dice que es fácil de copiar, es rápido pero también es ilegal.
7 Francisco Javier Tejera y David Landry tienen una entrevista con David Breden.
8 El agente de seguridad quiere ver la documentación.
9 David Breden quiere el expediente de Action Computers.
10 Francisco toma el café con leche con azúcar.

2 LAYING FOUNDATIONS

Sección 1

Comprensión

1 Falso 2 Verdadero 3 Verdadero
4 Verdadero 5 Verdadero 6 Falso
7 Falso 8 Falso 9 Verdadero
10 Falso

Completa

1 Tiene 2 tiene 3 Tiene 4 tenéis
5 tenemos 6 Tiene

¿Cómo es?

1 ¿Cuánto pesa la lata de sardinas? Pesa 111 gramos (peso neto) y 65 gramos (peso escurrido).
2 ¿Cuánto mide la furgoneta? La furgoneta mide 2 metros de alto, 2 metros de ancho y 5 metros de largo.
3 ¿Qué profundidad tiene la mina? La mina tiene una profundidad de 700 metros.
4 ¿Cuánto miden las oficinas? Tienen una extensión de 300 metros cuadrados.

¿Sabías que . . .?

1 c 2 b 3 c 4 a 5 b 6 a

¿Puedes . . .?

a Puede/3 b puede/2 c Puedes/7
d Puedo/1 e podemos/4
f Pueden/podéis/5 g puedo/6

Comprensión

1 José Carlos llega al pabellón británico.
2 Quiere hechar un vistazo al pabellón.
3 No, pero la mayor parte son del Reino Unido.
4 El material de construcción viene del Reino Unido.
5 Es la cortina de agua más grande en el mundo.
6 El ingeniero jefe del pabellón británico se llama Pedro Arozamena.
7 Las dos estructuras son de metal y de hormigón.
8 El pabellón tiene setenta metros de largo.
9 Tiene cuarenta metros de ancho.
10 Hay sesenta trabajadores.

Sección 2

Comprensión

1 el área de recepción.
2 por ese puente.
3 unos vídeos sobre el Reino Unido.
4 cinco minutos.
5 una película sobre el Reino Unido.
6 en la parte central.
7 cuatro partes.
8 los cuatro elementos.
9 el aire acondicionado.
10 cuatro

Completa

va a recibir • va a entrar • va a entrar • van a ver • van a subir • van a ver

Responde

1 Va a escribir una carta.
2 Va a enviar una carta.
3 Van a firmar un contrato.
4 Va a depositar dinero.
5 Van a vender una fábrica.

¿Para qué sirve?

A
El número uno es un teléfono.
El número dos es una impresora.
El número tres es un ordenador.
El número cuatro es un televisor y vídeo.
El número cinco es una fotocopiadora.
El número seis es un fax.

B
1 Es un ordenador y sirve para hacer cálculos y escribir informes.
2 Es un busca y sirve para avisar a una persona.
3 Es un teléfono y sirve para hablar con otra persona.
4 Es una fotocopiadora y sirve para hacer copias de documentos.
5 Es un fax y sirve para enviar planos, documentos, etc.
6 Es una impresora y sirve para imprimir los documentos del ordenador.

Comprensión

1 El público va a entrar por un puente.
2 El público puede ver unos vídeos sobre el Reino Unido.
3 Pueden ver una película sobre el Reino Unido.
4 Hay dos teatros.
5 Los cuatro elementos que menciona el señor Arozamena son la tierra, el aire, el agua y el fuego.
6 Las dos exhibiciones están en la parte central.
7 Los conductos sirven para distribuir el aire acondicionado.
8 Los conductos son elípticos.
9 Las torres que suben el aire acondicionado están aquí atrás y en la parte norte.

Sección 3

Comprensión

1 derecha. 2 acabada.
3 internacionales. 4 Alemania.
5 Siemens. 6 Noruega. 7 Europa.
8 España. 9 avenida. 10 visita.

¿Qué nacionalidad?

1 La ropa Benetton es italiana. Es de Italia.
2 Los coches BMW son alemanes. Son de Alemania.

3 El queso Camembert es francés. Es de Francia.

4 Las hamburguesas McDonald's son americanas/estadounidenses. Son de los Estados Unidos.

5 Las videocámaras Sony son japoneses. Son de Japón.

6 El chocolate Cadbury's es inglés. Es de Inglaterra.

7 La cerveza Guinness es irlandesa. Es de Irlanda.

8 El vino de Rioja es español. Es de España.

9 El reloj Swatch es suizo. Es de Suiza.

10 La tequila El Cuervo es mejicana. Es de Méjico.

Así se dice

1 • ¿Es Pérez de Cuellar mejicano?
   ♦ No, es peruano.
2 • ¿Son Esther y Alicia Koplovitz polacas?
   ♦ No, son españolas.
3 • ¿Es Jacques Delors portugués?
   ♦ No, es francés.
4 • ¿Son el rey Juan Carlos y Doña Sofia italianos?
   ♦ No, son españoles.
5 • ¿Es George Bush canadiense?
   ♦ No, es americano/estadounidense.
6 • Es Anita Roddick americana?
   ♦ No, es inglesa.

¿Dónde está?
B
1 servicios
2 Archivosa
3 Electrónica Edison
4 Química Curie
5 Márketing y Publicidad-Marcomás
6 información
C
4 El Hotel Príncipe de Asturias.
1 El pabellón de España.
6 El pabellón de Méjico.
D Aparcamiento
2 El pabellón de Andalucía.
8 Avenida de las Palmeras.

Contesta

1 La estación del tren de alta velocidad está a la derecha.
2 No. Está casi acabada.
3 El primer tren va a llegar en febrero.

4 El mástil del pabellón de Alemania va a tener una cubierta.
5 La cubierta sirve para dar sombra a la plaza.
6 El pabellón de España está al final de la Avenida de Europa.
7 Todos los pabellones de la Comunidad Europea están a ambos lados de la avenida.
8 Siemens es una empresa privada alemana.

3 TAPAS AND TECHNOLOGY

Sección 1

Comprensión

1 Van a dar la clase en un bar.
2 Para hacer algo diferente.
3 Dices 'oiga' para llamar a un camarero en España.
4 'Tapas' son pequeños platos con comida.
5 Robin llama al camarero.
6 Calamares son pequeños pulpos con tentáculos.
7 Prefieren beber cerveza.
8 Piden cuatro cervezas.
9 Falta el queso.
10 Los boquerones son pequeños.

¿Qué adjetivo?

1 rápido. 2 ancha. 3 bajos. 4 buenas.
5 cortas. 6 tremendo. 7 nueva.
8 prácticas. 9 estupendo. 10 lentos.

¿Qué van a tomar?

Tú: ¡Oiga, por favor!
Tú: ¿Qué tapas hay hoy?
Tú: ¿Te gusta los calamares?
Tú: ¿Te gusta el vino blanco?
Tú: ¿Te gusta algo?
Tú: ¿Te gustan las sardinas?
Tú: ¿Te gusta el jamón?
Tú: ¿Te gusta el vino/una caña/la cerveza?
Tú: ¡Oiga, por favor!
Tú: Para la señora de tapa, jamón, y para beber un vaso de agua.
Para el señor de tapa, tortilla de patatas, y para beber una caña.
Y para mí de tapa, queso, y para beber un vaso de vino tinto.

Calcula

Son 920 pesetas.

Una encuesta

Respuestas:
1 No, no me gustan.
2 Porque consumen mucha gasolina.
3 Me gustan los Volvos.
4 Porque son fiables.
5 No, no me gusta conducir.
6 Sí, me gustar viajar, pero no me gusta conducir.

Informe:
A Isabel Ferrer no le gustan los coches deportivos porque consumen mucha gasolina. Le gustan los coches Volvo porque son fiables. No le gusta conducir pero le gusta viajar en coche.

Completa

1 Se 2 te 3 Se 4 nos 5 me 6 se 7 os
8 se 9 Nos 10 Os

Sección 2

Comprensión

1 Cartuja '93 es un proyecto de la creación de un medio de innovación tecnológica.
2 Instituciones públicas y empresas privadas participan en este proyecto.
3 Va a aportar un desarrollo a la comunidad española.
4 Cartuja se localiza en Andalucía por su localización geográfica y por su riqueza.
5 El CESIC es un organismo nacional y público que se encarga de la investigación a alto nivel en el territorio nacional.
6 El CESIC instalará seis institutos de investigación.
7 No puede aclarar sus programas de investigación.
8 Los institutos de investigación aportarán un número importante de investigadores nacionales.
9 Ana menciona Telefónica de España, IBM, Rank Xerox y Phillips.
10 La diferencia que existe entre Cartuja '93 y el Centro de Innovación Tecnológica es que allí se puede fabricar y en Cartuja está prohibido la producción.

11 El Centro de Innovación Tecnológica está en Málaga.

12 Los proyectos están financiados por la Junta de Andalucía.

¿Dónde se pone?

1 Se cierra los sábados.

2 Se habla inglés.

3 Se cierra a las dos.

4 Se prohibe fumar.

5 ¿Cómo se dice 'credit card' en español?

6 ¿Dónde se celebra el Expo?

7 ¿Cuándo se abre el Expo?

8 Se venden oficinas.

Relaciona

1 c 2 e 3 f 4 a 5 b 6 g 7 d

Completa

la • la • la • un • las • la • el • Una • la • la • La • la • una • el • la • la • la

Completa

1 crecerá 2 ayudará 3 mandaremos 4 establecerán 5 será 6 invertirán 7 estaré 8 gastará 9 formarán 10 estarán

¿Cuándo?

1 En febrero en Colombia.

2 Los ministros de la OPEP en noviembre.

3 Portugal.

4 En el seno de la ONU en marzo.

5 En octubre.

6 Gran Bretaña.

7 En septiembre.

8 En junio.

9 El Fondo Monetario Internacional y el Banco Mundial.

10 El Forum sobre la Economía Mundial en febrero.

11 En diciembre.

12 En Barcelona.

13 A Helsinki.

14 En noviembre.

15 En Japón

Un banco nuevo

está abierto • está creada • está dispuesto • está valorado • está compuesto • está basada • estar... atendidos • están diseñadas

4 STARTING UP IN SPAIN

Sección 1

Comprensión

1 Andy va a llegar un poco tarde porque un pedido acaba de llegar al almacén.

2 Dice que va a llegar a las cuatro.

3 El horario de trabajo por la tarde es de cinco a ocho.

4 Andy va a llegar a las cinco.

5 Andy va a llevar el boceto del nuevo anuncio.

6 Andy quiere hablar con Carlos.

7 Andy quiere la palabra 'gratis' mucho mayor porque a la gente le gusta ver esta palabra.

8 Quiere la foto más ancha.

9 El cupón es muy importante.

10 El cupón es muy importante porque tiene que poner muchos datos.

¿Que hora es?

1 Son las diez y media.

2 Son las cinco y cuarto de la tarde.

3 Son las dos menos cuarto de la mañana.

4 Son las tres y diez de la tarde.

5 Son las nueve menos veinticinco de la tarde.

6 Son las dos menos diez de la mañana.

¿A qué hora . . . ?

1 A las nueve y media.

2 A las once y cuarto.

3 No, es a las doce y media.

4 Es a la una.

5 A las dos y media.

6 A las seis.

7 A las siete.

Responde

1 Acaba de llegar.

2 Acaban de salir.

3 acabo de empezar.

4 acaba de entrar.

5 acaba de despegar.

6 acaba de enviar un fax.

7 Acabo de hablar con él.

8 Acabamos de recibir un aumento de sueldo.

9 Acaban de ingresar un cheque.

10 Acabamos de firmar el contrato.

¿Qué hago?

Envia una carta al Hotel Charlton para reservar una habitación.

Compra un regalo para la esposa de George.

Cambia dinero para tener algo en efectivo.

Habla con el señor Cabezas para cancelar la cita.

Escribe el informe para llevar una copia a Inglaterra.

Haz fotocopias para entregar en la próxima reunión.

Alquila un coche para visitar clientes allí.

Reserva el billete para asegurar el vuelo.

Avisa a George Hall que voy a estar libre para jugar golf el sábado por la tarde.

Compara

El tren es más cómodo que el avión.

El avión es más rápido que el tren.

El tren es más frequente que el avión.

El tren está más cerca del centro de la ciudad que el avión.

El servicio es mejor en el tren que en el avión.

El tren es más puntual que el avión.

El tren tiene más variedad de categorias que el avión.

Transforma

1 Su secretaria es muy eficiente.

2 Tus diseños son estupendos.

3 Nuestra fábrica es muy moderna.

4 Vuestro horario de trabajo es muy flexible.

5 Sus productos son muy baratos.

6 Vuestras oficinas son muy céntricas.

Sección 2

Comprensión

1 Quiere pedir una cita porque tiene unos temas pendientes.

2 Manuel estará fuera todo el día mañana.

3 Karen va a tener la cita el viernes.

4 A las siete.

5 El calendario fiscal es de octubre.

6 Pone lo del IVA en el circular del nuevo impuesto sobre actividades económicas.

7 Don Manuel tendrá que explicar el circular sobre sociedades anónimas.

8 Karen está incluida en la cartilla de la seguridad social.

9 Karen tiene que esperar un momentito porque don Manuel va a terminar una llamada telefónica.

Eschucha

jueves • viernes • octubre

¿Cuándo?

El doce de octubre de mil cuatrocientos noventa y dos Colón llega a América.

El dos de mayo de mil ochocientos ocho empieza la Guerra de Independencia en España.

El dieciocho de julio de mil novecientos treinta y seis empieza la Guerra Civil española.

El veintidós de noviembre de mil novecientos setenta y cinco el rey don Juan Carlos I sube al trono.

El primero de enero de mil novecientos ochenta y seis España entra como miembro del Mercado Común.

El primero de abril de mil novecientos noventa y dos se abre la Expo '92 en Sevilla.

Crucigrama

							¹E		
²M			³D	O	M	I	N	G	O
A			I				E		
Y		⁴O	C	T	U	B	R	E	
O			I				O		⁵M
	⁶J	U	E	V	E	S			A
			M						R
	⁷F	E	B	R	E	R	O		T
			R						E
	⁸M	I	E	R	C	O	L	E	S

¿Dígame?

Tú: Buenas tardes.

Tú: Quiero hablar con el señor Cameselle.

Tú: Prefiero hablar con él personalmente.

Tú: Entonces voy a llamar a las ocho. ¿Está bien?

Tú: Bueno. ¿Puedo llamar a las siete?

Tú: Bueno. Quedamos en eso. Muchas gracias.

¿Hoy o mañana?

1 Entonces, hasta luego.

2 El año que viene.

3 Bueno, llamaré después.

4 Entonces, hasta pasado mañana.

5 Entonces tendremos el ingreso en el banco dentro de un mes.

6 Bueno, comeremos mas tarde.

¿El IVA?

IRPF = Impuesto sobre la Renta de las Personas Físicas

INI = Instituto Nacional de Industria

PSOE = Partido Socialista Obrero Español

SEAT = Sociedad Española de Automóbiles de Turismo

CEOE = Confederación Española de Organizaciones Empresariales

INH = Instituto Nacional de Hidrocarburos

UGT = Unión General de Trabajadores

CCOO = Comisiones Obreras

NIF = Número de Identificación Fiscal

Responde

1 Tiene que llamar para confirmar la cita con el señor Forsyth.

2 Tiene que comprar un regalo.

3 Tiene que enviar una carta al Hotel Charlton para reservar una habitación.

4 Tiene que alquilar un coche para visitar clientes.

5 Tiene que llevar una copia del informe a Inglaterra.

Deberes

1 tenemos que 2 hay que 3 debes
4 tiene que 5 hay que 6 hay que
7 tengo que 8 deben

Completa

1 la 2 lo 3 lo 4 lo 5 las 6 lo

5 ON THE FAST TRACK

Sección 1

Comprensión

1 La línea del AVE entre Madrid y Sevilla tiene cuatrocientos setenta y un kilómetros.

2 Se han construido treinta y un viaductos.

3 Se han utilizado las técnicas más importantes y más modernas.

4 El viaje entre Madrid y Sevilla durará dos horas cincuenta en la primera etapa.

5 Addison se ha encargado del diseño exterior y interior.

6 La compañía que colaboró con Addison es de Cataluña.

7 La diferencia fundamental que tiene el AVE con el TGV Atlantique es el morro.

8 El morro del TGV Atlantique es agresivo según las encuestas realizadas por los franceses.

9 Pensaron que debían suavizarlo.

10 El morro del AVE parece el morro de un Boeing.

¿Ahora o antes?

1 ha trabajado mucho.

2 han trabajado en el departamento de contabilidad.

3 ha estado de viaje por Galicia.

4 hemos leido las cartas de presentación de los nuevos representantes.

5 habéis venido al trabajo en taxi.

6 han aumentado las ventas.

Forma frases

1e Sí, el dólar ya se ha devaluado

2f No, ellos aún/todavía no han terminado el diseño del tren.

3d No, nosotros aún/todavía no hemos comprado acciones de Repsol.

4a Sí, Rodrigo ya ha leído el anuncio.

5b No, el gobierno aún/todavía no ha dicho nada sobre los nuevos impuestos.

6g Sí, Aurora y Julio ya han resuelto el problema.

7c Sí, yo ya he reparado el coche.

Nunca mejor

1 El ejercicio de 1989 ha sido un ejercicio de importante expansión.

2 Han alcanzado metas fijadas para un tiempo más lejano.

3 Sus ingresos consolidados han experimentado un crecimiento del 58%.

4 Los beneficios por accion han ascendido a 1.452 pesetas.

5 El grupo ha invertido 1.425 millones de pesetas durante el año.
6 Su división de distribución de maquinaria para la construcción, obras públicas y limpieza vial ha consolidado su posición como la segunda fuerza del país.
7 Se ha optado por separar la actividad de fabricación de elementos de interiorismo de la de instalación y servicios.
8 Se ha dado un nuevo enfoque a Cador Centro SA.
9 El indudable éxito les ha animado a extender esta iniciativa.
10 Todo ello confirma que su grupo nunca ha estado en mejor forma.

¿Verdadero o falso?
1 Falso. Hay treinta y un viaductos.
2 Verdadero
3 Verdadero
4 Verdadero
5 Falso. Existen diecisiete túneles.
6 Falso. El carril tiene un peso de ciento trece mil diez toneladas.
7 Falso. Hay treinta y cinco mil quinientas cuarenta y tres metros cúbicos de terraplenes.
8 Verdadero
9 Falso. La longitud total de los túneles es de quince mil ochocientos diecinueve metros.
10 Verdadero

¿Qué tal el viaje?
volé • visité • hiciste • Estuve • llevó • construyeron • dijiste • estuvieron • viste • se marchó • hablé • firmamos • dimos • pude • Estuviste • fui • empezamos • pagaron • escribí • tuve • fue

Fechas que hacen historia
El 30 de abril de mil novecientos ochenta y siete se aprobó el Plan de Transporte Ferroviario.

El 5 de octubre de mil novecientos ochenta y siete comenzaron las obras del tramo Brazatortas–Córdoba.

El 21 de octubre de mil novecientos ochenta y ocho el Consejo de Ministros encargó a RENFE un informe sobre la posibilidad de introducir el ancho de vía internacional.

El 11 de julio de mil novecientos ochenta y nueve se adjudicaron las obras de señalización y electrificación de los tramos Madrid–Getafe y Córdoba–Sevilla.

En agosto de mil novecientos ochenta y nueve se adjudicaron las obras del tramo Madrid–Getafe.

El 2 de octubre de mil novecientos ochenta y nueve los Reyes de España asistieron al montaje del primer tramo de vía, en ancho internacional, de la nueva línea.

El 2 de abril de mil novecientos noventa se adjudicaron las obras de electrificación y señalización de tramo Getafe–Córdoba.

En la primavera de mil novecientos noventa y uno se entregaron las primeras unidades AVE y comenzaron las pruebas de línea.

En abril de mil novecientos noventa y dos se puso en servicio comercial el tren de Alta Velocidad Madrid–Sevilla.

Todo a su tiempo
1 adquirir: adquirió
2 distribuir: ha distribuido
3 construir: construimos
4 vender: han vendido
5 organizar: ha organizado
6 fabricar: fabricó
7 embalar: habéis embalado
8 dividir: dividieron
9 progresar: ha progresado
10 crecer: creció

Sección 2

Comprensión
1 La reunión fue ayer.
2 La reunión ayer fue bastante bien.
3 Hablaron del tema de la sala club.
4 Llegaron a acuerdos con el gerente.
5 Dieron una vuelta por la estación.
6 Las señales faltan fuerza.
7 Puede ser un error poner más rótulos.
8 Van a seguir la conversación en la maqueta.
9 La otra cosa que quiere aclarar Wayne Rosemin es el tema de la visita.
10 Uno de los primeros puntos que quieren revisar es la inclusión del logotipo del RENFE.

11 Wayne Rosemin piensa que deben colocar el nombre de RENFE en la franja azul al lado de la puerta.
12 No, sólo pondrán el logo en las locomotoras.

¿Qué opinas tú?
A 1 c 2 b 3 e 4 f 5 j 6 i 7 a 8 d 9 h 10 g
B 1 c 2 d 3 a 4 f 5 e 6 b

Completa
1 Porque tiene calor.
2 Tiene dolor de cabeza.
3 Porque tienen sed.
4 Porque tengo frío.
5 Tienes razón.
6 Tienen suerte.
7 Porque tengo prisa.
8 No, y tengo sueño.
9 Porque tengo miedo.
10 Porque no tengo hambre.

Completa
1 tuvieron
2 sale
3 han terminado
4 ingresamos
5 visitaré
6 ha trabajado
7 va a hablar
8 envié
9 hemos recibido
10 fue

6 CHANGE IS BREWING

Sección 1

Comprensión
1 Sí, son la misma cosa.
2 Se muele y se mezcla la malta con agua caliente.
3 Aproximadamente el setenta y cinco por ciento del contenido de la malta se verá disuelta.
4 Pueden usar otras fuentes de almidón por consideraciones económicas y por razones fisioquímicas.
5 El proceso siguiente al de la mezcla es la filtración.
6 Se separa el estrato soluble de la parte insoluble.
7 Después de enfriar el mosto se oxigena y se siembra con levadura de cultivo.

8 En La Cruz del Campo hay tres grupos de producción.

9 La Cruz del Campo produce un millón de litros de cerveza al día.

10 No. La producción anual coloca a La Cruz del Campo como la segunda productora de cerveza en España.

¿Cómo se hace?

A En primer lugar • previamente • anteriormente • En segundo lugar • posteriormente • A continuación • En la última etapa •

B 2 • 1 • 6 • 3 • 5 • 7 • 4

Conecta

1c veintiocho coma treinta y cinco gramos de oro

2e medio litro de cerveza

3a medio metro de ancho

4f tres cuartos de kilo de cebada

5g setenta y cinco centímetros cúbicos de capacidad

6b el ocho por cien(to) de interés

7d un cuarto de la población

Organiza y escribe

1 La distancia aproximada por carretera entre Madrid y Vigo es de 650 km.

2 El 68% de las exportaciones españolas van a países de la CE.

3 En el centro de Madrid se vende un local de 240m².

4 En 1993, el grupo Zannier–Poro, líderes de la ropa infantil en Francia, facturará 3.000 millones de pesetas en el mercado español.

5 La capacidad del depósito de gasolina de un Honda Civic LSi es de 45 l.

6 El tren español AVE va a alcanzar una velocidad de más de 300km/h.

7 Una onza equivale a 28,35 gr.

Completa

1 de 2 con 3 en 4 por 5 sin
6 para 7 a 8 desde 9 hasta 10 entre

Sección 2

Comprension

1 Don Eduardo Osborne es vicepresidente de la compañía y subdirector general de asuntos corporativos.

2 La Cruz del Campo era una compañía eminentemente familiar.

3 La fórmula que La Cruz del Campo eligió para entrar en el mercado común era asociarse con una gran compañía europea.

4 Javier Personaga es subdirector de márketing del grupo Cruz Campo.

5 Las funciones de un departamento de márketing son estudiar y analizar las necesidades del consumidor, comprobar la capacidad de la compañía para producir esos productos y controlar si se puede hacer de una forma rentable.

6 Cinco compañías formaban parte de Cruz Campo antes de la fusión con Guinness.

7 Se está tratando de establecer un nuevo sistema de comunicación en la empresa.

8 Tienen que pensar en un mercado nacional y en un mercado europeo.

9 Desde la fusión con Guinness La Cruz del Campo sigue funcionando como una sociedad anónima.

10 La casa matriz de Guinness está en Irlanda.

Antes

A

1 Trabajaba en una fábrica textil.

2 Era muy serio.

3 Salíamos a las ocho de la tarde.

4 Había una fábrica de cerámica.

5 Teníamos diez.

B

1 Antes eran pobres.

2 Antes no trabajabas nada.

3 Antes eran muy lentos.

4 Antes no íbamos nunca.

5 Antes eran muy baratos.

Un pasado historico

venía • conmemoraba • celebraba • salía • terminaba • comenzaba • producía • mantenía

¿Puedo hablar con . . . ?

A

1 Es el director de construcción y se llama Manuel Pérez-Beato de Cos.

2 Es el director de recursos humanos y se llama Tomás García Ally.

3 Es el director de asimilación tecnológica y se llama Antonio Mansilla Prieto.

4 Es el director comercial y se llama Emilio Arsuaga Navasqües.

5 Es el director general adjunto Alta Velocidad y se llama Leopoldo Iglesia Lachica.

B

1 Es el Director Financiero-Administrativo de Bodegas y Bebidas.

2 Es Francisco Rubio Sebastián.

3 De Bodegas Capel.

4 Director de Comunicación.

5 Director General y Director Comercial.

Estamos trabajando

1 Está hablando con José Pérez.

2 Están comprando un coche.

3 Estamos reorganizando la compañía.

4 Están construyendo una fábrica nueva.

5 Está esperando para ver al director.

6 Estoy redactando el informe.

Antes . . . pero ahora . . .

1 estaba trabajando/estoy dirigiendo

2 estábamos pagando/estamos efectuando

3 estaban intentando/están tratando

4 estaba tratando/está adaptando

5 estábamos construyendo/estamos haciendo

6 estaba tomando/estoy esforzando

El más grande del mundo

1 el más importante

2 la más rica

3 el peor

4 las más competitivas

5 la mayor

6 los más bajos

7 la más interesante

8 los mejores

9 el más eficiente

10 el más caro

7 Retail in Spain

Sección 1

Comprensión

1 La señora quiere comprar un conjunto de sábanas.

2 Quiere las sábanas para una cama de uno treinta y cinco.

3 El conjunto de sábanas consiste en la sábana de arriba, la sábana bajera y el cubrecanapé.

4 Es cincuenta poliéster y cincuenta algodón.

5 No, es fácil de planchar y lavar en la lavadora.

6 Hay azul claro, rosa y estampado con rayas.

7 No tienen algodón cien por cien.

8 La señora prefiere el otro estampado.

9 Va a abonar en efectivo.

10 Tiene que pagar dieciséis mil novecientas pesetas.

¿Qué es?

1 Es una tarjeta de crédito.
2 Es una tetra brik™.
3 Es un retroproyector.
4 Es un lápiz.
5 Es una corbata.
6 Es una agenda.

Organiza

1 e 2 g 3 d 4 a 5 f 6 c 7 b

Reacciona

1 Es horrible
2 Me encantan
3 No me gustan nada
4 No estuvo mal
5 No me gusta mucho
6 Está bien

¿Cuál te gusta más?

1 Prefiero el modelo con motor gasolina porque no me gusta el diesel.

2 Prefiero cerveza sin alcohol porque tengo que conducir.

3 Prefiero paquetes de 100 unidades porque 1.000 unidades son excesivas.

4 Prefiero viajar en tren porque no me gusta volar.

5 Prefiero llevar dinero en cheques de viajero porque dan más seguridad.

6 Prefiero invertir en pagarés del INI porque son más rentables.

¿Qué color?

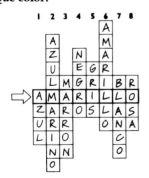

Sección 2

Comprensión

1 Alan Cooke cita el departamento de ventas.

2 La semana pasada y ésta.

3 Tuvieron un incremento de un 33% más que el año pasado.

4 El número que tiene la sección de abrigos y chaquetones es el 49.

5 El stock sesenta y ocho cero cero hace un 14% de todas las camisas.

6 Es una camisa de poliéster de manga corta.

7 El número de stock que corresponde al blazer azul marino es el 8006.

8 Van a ampliar la sección de caballeros. Las seis prendas que van a tener son: trajes, americanas, pantalones, abrigos, ropa interior y pijamas.

9 El cambio lo van a hacer este jueves por la noche.

10 Los días de la semana que son para clientes de M&S son el lunes, el martes y el miércoles.

Completa

aconsejarías • podrías • agradecería • deberías • sería • hablaría

¿Qué hago?

1 hablaría 2 Deberías 3 Tendrías
4 haría/Mandaría 5 sería

Completa

1 Todos 2 Algunos 3 Ninguno
4 Casi todos 5 Pocos 6 Casi ninguno 7 Muchos 8 Algunos
9 Todos 10 Ninguno

Y más . . .

1 demasiados • algunas
2 muchas
3 Todos
4 todos
5 ningún • bastantes
6 poco

Viceversa

1 viejo 2 débil 3 mal 4 disminuimos
5 largo 6 mala 7 pequeña 8 menos
9 tarde 10 fácil

¿Quién lo dijo?

1 difíciles *Lo dijo Alan Cooke.*
2 bien *Lo dijo Alan Cooke.*
3 fuertes *Lo dijo Marisé Rodríguez.*
4 bueno *Lo dijo Marisé Rodríguez.*
5 corta *Lo dijo Marisé Rodríguez.*
6 más *Lo dijo Marisé Rodríguez.*
7 ampliar *Lo dijo Tracy Peck.*
8 grande *Lo dijo Tracy Peck.*
9 noche *Lo dijo Tracy Peck.*
10 nuevos *Lo dijo Julio Hernanz.*

Sección 3

Comprensión

1 José Moreno quiere hablar de los cheques.

2 Han bajado los cartelitos en todas las plantas.

3 En el cartel pone que a partir del día treinta no se admitirán cheques.

4 Si uno necesita más información una persona indicará otro medio de pago.

5 Siempre han tenido problemas con los cheques.

6 El porcentaje de clientes que usan cheques no es muy grande.

7 Marks and Spencer accepta las tarjetas de Visa, Caja Madrid y la de Marks and Spencer.

8 La empresa no está dispuesta a tener pérdidas con este medio de pago.

9 Los clientes son atendidos una vez que ya piden consejo.

10 No. Antes era precisamente el contrario.

Si . . .

1 d 2 e 3 a 4 f 5 g 6 c 7 b

Transforma

1 fácilmente
2 claramente
3 urgentemente
4 hábilmente
5 rápidamente
6 puntualmente

Completa

nueva • va • instalaciones • dedicado • para • incluyen • caballeros • un • salas • prácticas • calientes • microondas • desean • sus • hora • descuento • uniforme • gris

¿En qué planta está?

1 Estoy en la cuarta planta. Estoy en el departamento de deportes.
2 Estoy en la planta baja. Estoy en el departamento de informática.
3 Estoy en la tercera planta. Estoy en el departamento de electrodomésticos.
4 Estoy en la segunda planta. Estoy en el departamento de ropa de cama.
5 Estoy en el sótano. Estoy en el departamento de discos.

De compras

A Sí señor. ¿Qué número calza? • ¿Los quiere con cordones o prefiere mocasines? • ¿Qué color quiere? • Tenemos este estilo o este otro que es más deportivo. • Son 13.000 pesetas. • Gracias señor.
B 6 • 11 • 18 • 3 • 14 • 10 • 12 • 17 • 8 • 1 • 4 • 13 • 16 • 9 • 2 • 5 • 15 • 7

• Buenos días. ¿Le puede ayudar en algo?
♦ Hola, buenos días. Sí. Estoy buscando una camisa.
• Sí señor. ¿La quiere de manga larga o de manga corta?
♦ Prefiero una camisa más casual. Las de manga larga me parecen muy formales.
• Entonces quiere una camisa de manga corta. Aquí tiene.
♦ Muy bien. ¿Qué composición tiene?
• Es de nailon.
♦ No me gusta el nailon. ¿No tiene de algodón?
• Sí. Tenemos estas en algodón.
♦ Ah, sí. Y ¿qué colores tiene?
• Azul, verde y blanco.
♦ Y ¿cuánto cuestan?
• Las de nailon son 4.000 pesetas cada una y las de algodón cuestan 5.800 cada una.
♦ Bueno. Llevaré una azul y otra verde de las de algodón.
• Muy bien. Son 11.600 pesetas. ¿Cómo quiere abonar? ¿Con tarjeta o en efectivo?
♦ En efectivo. Aquí tiene, 15.000 pesetas.
• Muchas gracias. Aquí tiene 3.400 de vuelta. Gracias y buenos días.
♦ Adiós. Buenos días.

8 A Meeting of Minds

Sección 1

Comprensión

1 La factura de este cliente es bastante grande.
2 Karen ha preparado una oferta de precio.
3 Un pedido detalla: el número de unidades, el plazo que hay que servir el pedido al cliente y las condiciones de pago.
4 Después de que el cliente acepta la oferta de precio, confirma el pedido. El vendedor tendría que confeccionar una factura.
5 La factura es un documento fiscal y mercantil.
6 En una factura tienen que ir perfectamente identificados: el emisor, el cliente, la cantidad y cómo se va a pagar.
7 El número que el Ministerio de Hacienda asigna a cada contribuyente se llama Código de Identificación Fiscal (CIF).
8 Pago 'al contado' quiere decir, pago en efectivo o mediante un talón o cheque.
9 La norma habitual de pago es mediante letra.
10 Las dos fechas que tienen que estar perfectamente detalladas en una letra son: la fecha de entrega y la fecha de factura.

Completa

1 de 2 de 3 por 4 a 5 de 6 con 7 en 8 de 9 en 10 en 11 de 12 con

¿Cuál es la correcta?

1 b 2 c 3 b 4 c 5 c 6 a 7 a 8 c

Leer y entender
B
1 Canon
2 En octubre
3 El 28 de septiembre, 1987
4 El librado
5 En Madrid
6 Banco Central SA.
7 Banesto

C
Lugar de libramiento: Madrid
Importe: Pts 328.725
Fecha de libramiento: 03/02/19 . . .
Vencimiento: 03/05/19 . . .
Por esta Letra . . . a: Banco Mediterráneo, Calle Marqués de Valladares, 83, 28013 Madrid
la cantidad de: trescientos veintiocho mil setecientos veinticinco
en el domicilio . . . : Banco Gallego, Calle San Martín, 39, 28013 Madrid
Cláusulas: sin gastos
Nombre y domicilio del librado: Megamarketing SA, Calle Miguel Angel, 31–4º, 28013 Madrid
Firma, nombre y domicilio del librador: Sr Don Arturo Fernández de Córdoba, Calle Rosalía de Castro, 37–8º, 28003 Madrid

Sección 2

Comprensión

1 Action Computers utiliza los trípticos para dirigir gente al catálogo.
2 Action Computers quiere repetir el concepto con productos de software.
3 El objetivo de la visita de David Landry y Francisco Tejera es requerir las facilidades del banco para financiar este proyecto.
4 Según Francisco Tejera pueden volver a lanzar el flyer en tres o seis meses.
5 La característica principal del flyer es que es autofinanciable.
6 El efecto que va a tener el flyer cuando llega a manos del consumidor va a ser producir un incremento en la demanda de sus productos.
7 Al señor Tejera le interesa más un crédito.
8 La ventaja de tener un crédito es que tiene la facilidad de pagar sólo lo que usa.
9 El plazo de revisión del tipo de interés que preferiría Francisco Tejera sería de un año.
10 David Breden tiene que preparar una solicitud para su comité de créditos.

Una reunión de negocios

1 e 2 f 3 a 4 b 5 c 6 g 7 d

De otra manera

A

1 f 2 d 3 j 4 a 5 g 6 k 7 h 8 i
9 e 10 c 11 b

B no queremos usar • Con el buen resultado que tuvimos • sería una buena idea • Comprendo • mucho dinero • incremento • es decir • variación • gastar inútilmente • separarlo

El informe

A 1 e 2 a 3 f 4 d 5 b 6 c

Sección 3

Comprensión

1 A la presidenta tendrán que explicarle todos los cambios que han habido.
2 En el tren hay tres niveles de iluminación
3 Los tres tipos de iluminación que Wayne menciona son: la iluminación del techo, la iluminación puntual de los leedores y la ilumiación más ambiental.
4 Las diferencias son que la moqueta del AVE es más ligera y que no tiene moqueta en las paredes.
5 Las moquetas del AVE y del TGV son diferentes por el calor y el sol de España, para dar la sensación psicológica de frescura.
6 La visita está confirmada para el día diez.
7 Están encargadas las cabezales.
8 A la presidenta y al director general les van a dar un billete.
9 El billete va a contener sus nombres y la fecha.
10 La fecha de inauguración del AVE es el 19 de abril de 1992 y coincide con la inauguración de la Expo.

¡Ya está!

Reservar salón
Confirmar hora
Proporcionar papel y lápiz **?**
Organizar agua, café, té y refrescos
Escribir tarjetas con el nombre de cada participante **x**
Probar retroproyector
Conectar proyector de diapositivas
Conseguir vídeo VHS **?**
Instalar enchufes suficientes **?**
Pedir repuestos **x**
Copiar orden del día para cada participante
Poner ceniceros **x**
Verificar interruptores de las luces **?**

¿Qué tengo que hacer?

Rogelio: Confirma la hora.
Juana: Ya está confirmada.

Rogelio: Proporciona papel y lápiz.
Juana: Ya están proporcionados.

Rogelio: Organiza agua, café, té y refrescos.
Juana: Ya están organizados.

Rogelio: Escribe tarjetas con el nombre de cada participante.
Juana: Ya están escritas.

Rogelio: Prueba el retroproyector.
Juana: Ya está probado.

Rogelio: Conecta el proyector de diapositivas.
Juana: Ya está conectado.

Rogelio: Consigue un vídeo VHS.
Juana: Ya está conseguido.

Rogelio: Instala enchufes suficientes.
Juana: Ya están instalados.

Rogelio: Pide repuestos.
Juana: Ya están pedidos.

Rogelio: Copia el orden del día para cada participante.
Juana: Ya están copiados.

Rogelio: Pon ceniceros.
Juana: Ya están puestos.

Rogelio: Verifica los interruptores de las luces.
Juana: Ya están verificados.

Completa

1 llega 2 terminó 3 trabajaba
4 redactaré 5 sería 6 ha trabajado
7 está hablando 8 venía 9 nací
10 hemos firmado 11 están cerrados
12 van a ir 13 tuvo 14 asiste
15 sabían 16 comemos 17 llamaré
18 avise 19 visitaron 20 preferiría

Crucigrama